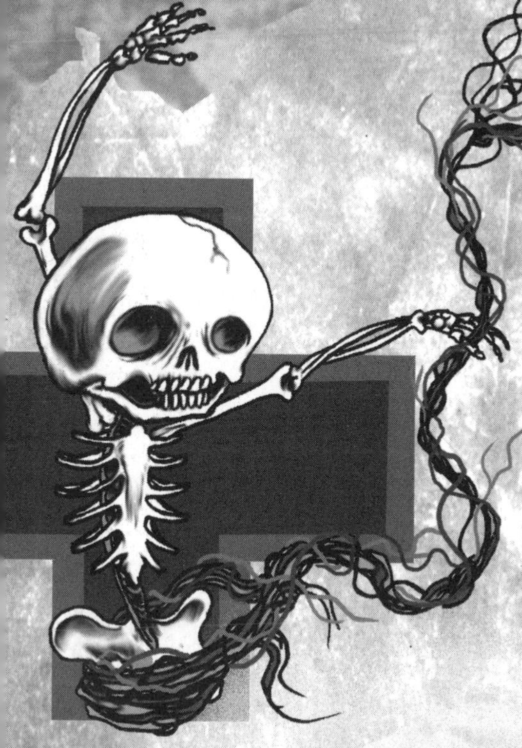

Roman Dirge's

LENORE

The Cute Little Dead Girl

Cooties

Collecting "Lenore" issues 9-12

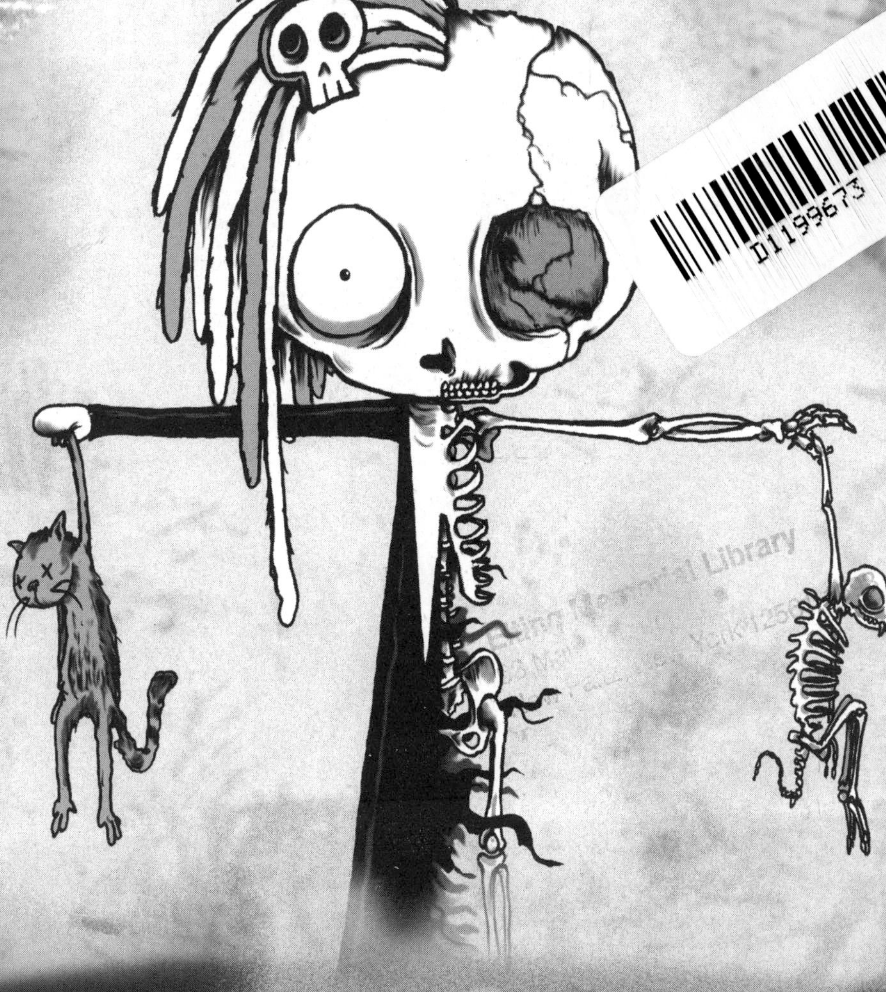

Written and illustrated by

Roman Dirge

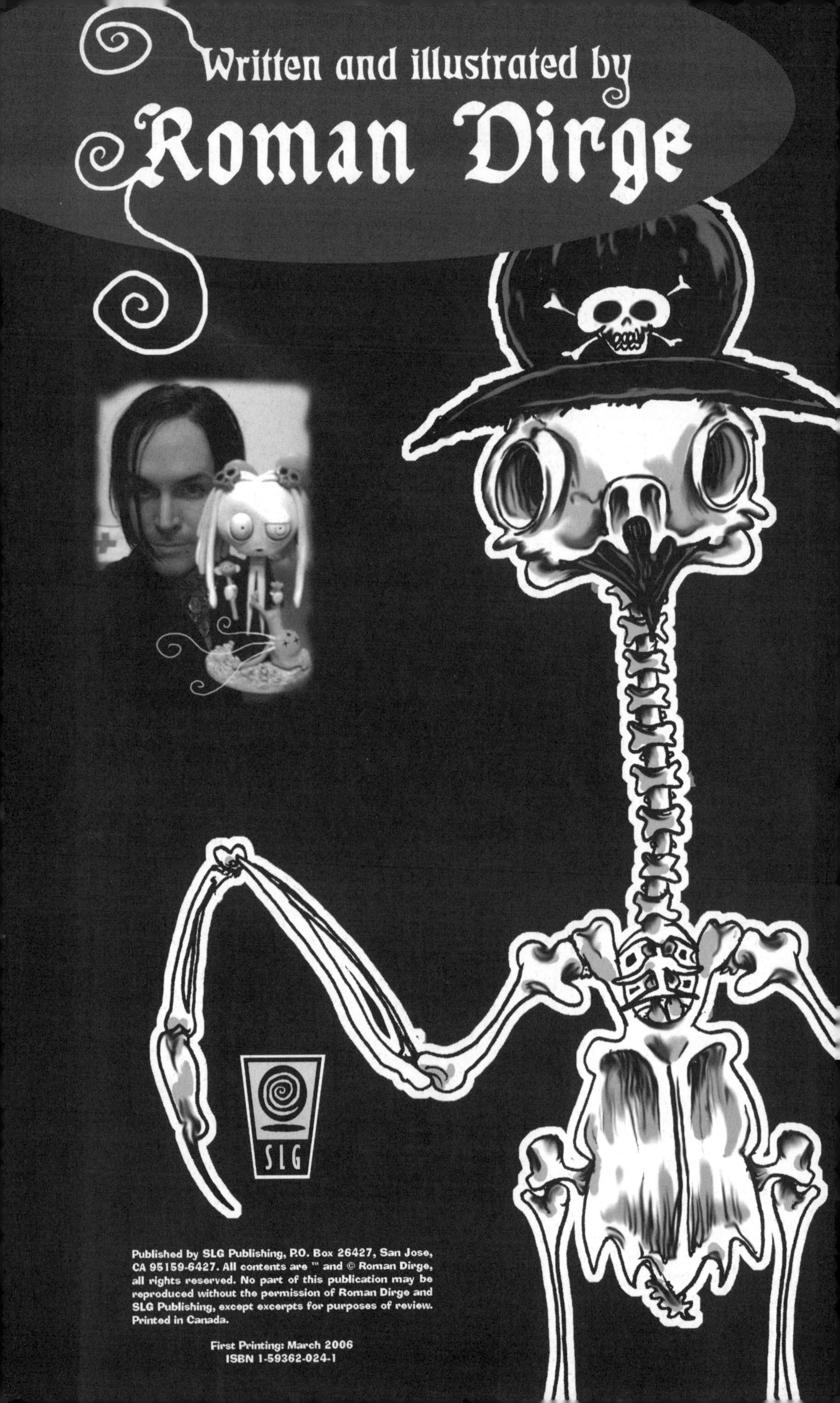

Published by SLG Publishing, P.O. Box 26427, San Jose, CA 95159-6427. Printed in Canada.

First Printing: March 2006
ISBN 1-59362-024-1

Contents

of — Stuff

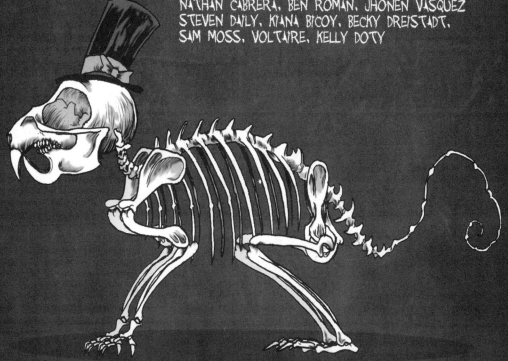

HELLO THERE...

h,

what a loooong gooey road this whole journey has been. When I published my first Lenore comic in 1992, there was no such entity-thing as "goth comics". No special section for my work to be exiled to in comic book stores. It was and still is just doing what I've always done and loved, penning the continuing adventures of a cute little dead girl who has the brain capacity about that of an old retarded squirrel. It's strange. Lenore has evolved into an almost real being to me. When I sit down to write each issue, it really writes itself. I can hear her voice in my head telling me what she'd say in every situation. Apart from the obvious indications that I may have some sort of mental disorder, what with voices in my head, this otherwise bodes well for me. It's like I can just sit back, drink beer, quest with my level 60 Warlock, and Lenore writes her own books. If she'd just learn to draw herself now, I'd be home free. I could retire and return to the exciting world of close up magic, whereas I'd once again be able to utter such phrases, to people trying to eat, as "Behold, the coin was in this hand but now it is gone.... And is in this OTHER hand now!" and then they'd go "Yeah, that's…that's great. Can you tell our waiter we need more napkins?" And then I'd look at them, a magical gleam in my eye, and I'd say "Yeah, ok."

What's my point in all this? I have no idea. All I know is that whatever else I do with my life, I will forever be remembered for birthing a stinky little zombie child with worms and I'm totally ok with that, especially since my chances of becoming an underwear model seem to be becoming more and more slim.

This compilation of the last four issues is special to me. Noogies, the first trade paperback, has a special place in my dark heart because it was the beginning of the adventure. Most of the tales within were reprints of the original Lenore comics from 1992. They're funny and short, BUT I really couldn't draw that well back then and I also didn't have any direction as to where it was all headed. I was all pimples and just out of high school. It's an odd feeling to have your old work being reprinted over and over and people will see it for the first time now and that is their original impression of you. I guess what I'm saying is that I'm a little embarrassed of the crappy art from back then but I stand by "the funny" of it. Wedgies, the second compilation book, showcases longer stories. I had the need to tell longer tales and the characters became more developed.

Now we stand at Cooties. Heh…Cooties. This book was going to be titled "Wet Willies", but I found out that can mean something entirely different and somewhat lurid in the UK. I love this book. For me, this one feels like everything just came together. It is the first time I chose to go the route of a continuing story line and that left me the room to go all out, rabid monkey style, which really lets Lenore shine. So, enough with the goblety gook. I hope you enjoy Lenore's adventures as much as I enjoyed making them. If not, too bad cause we all know it'll be like 4 more years before the next one comes out.

-Dirge

Issue #9

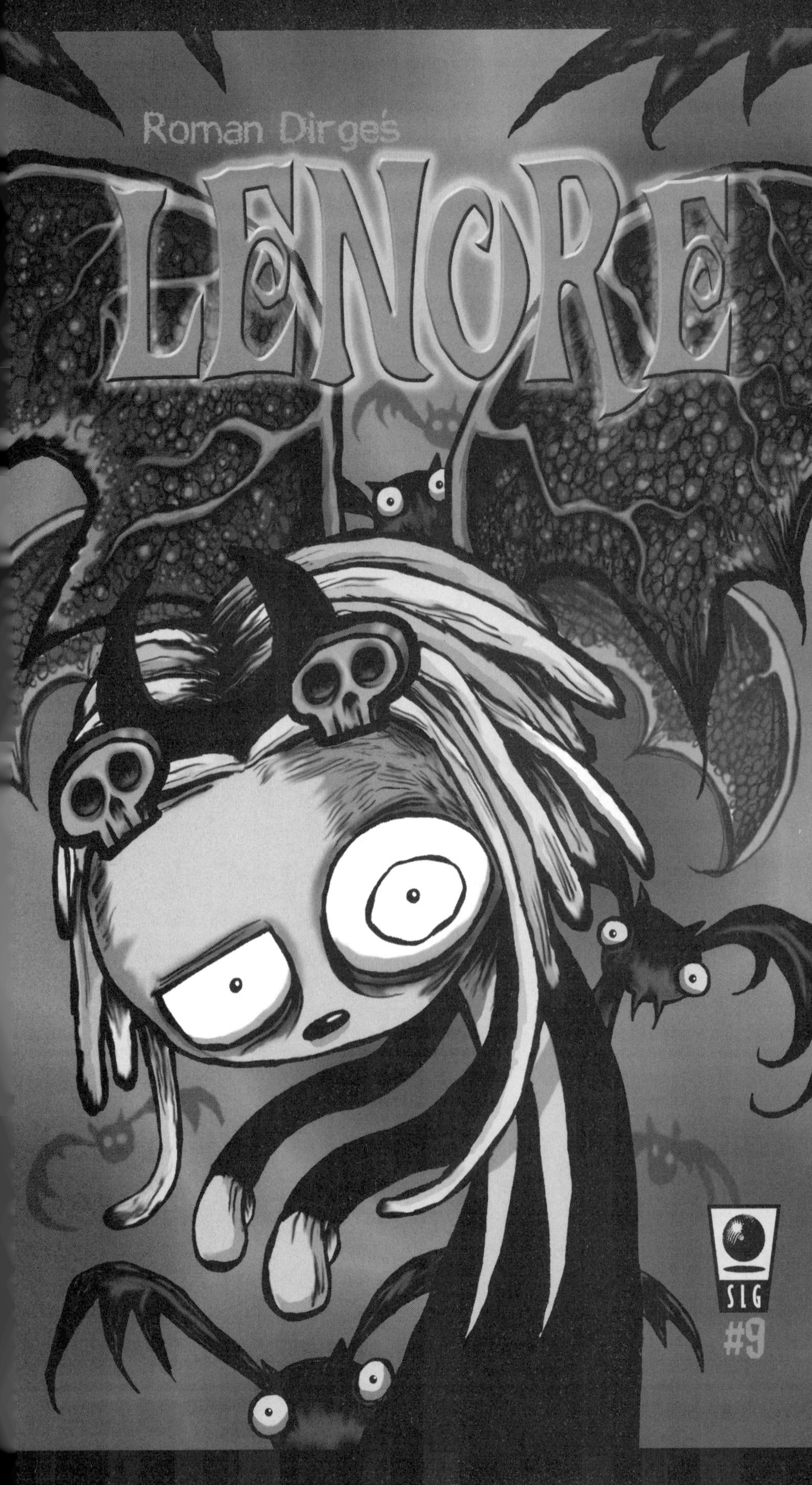
Roman Dirge's
LENORE
SLG
#9

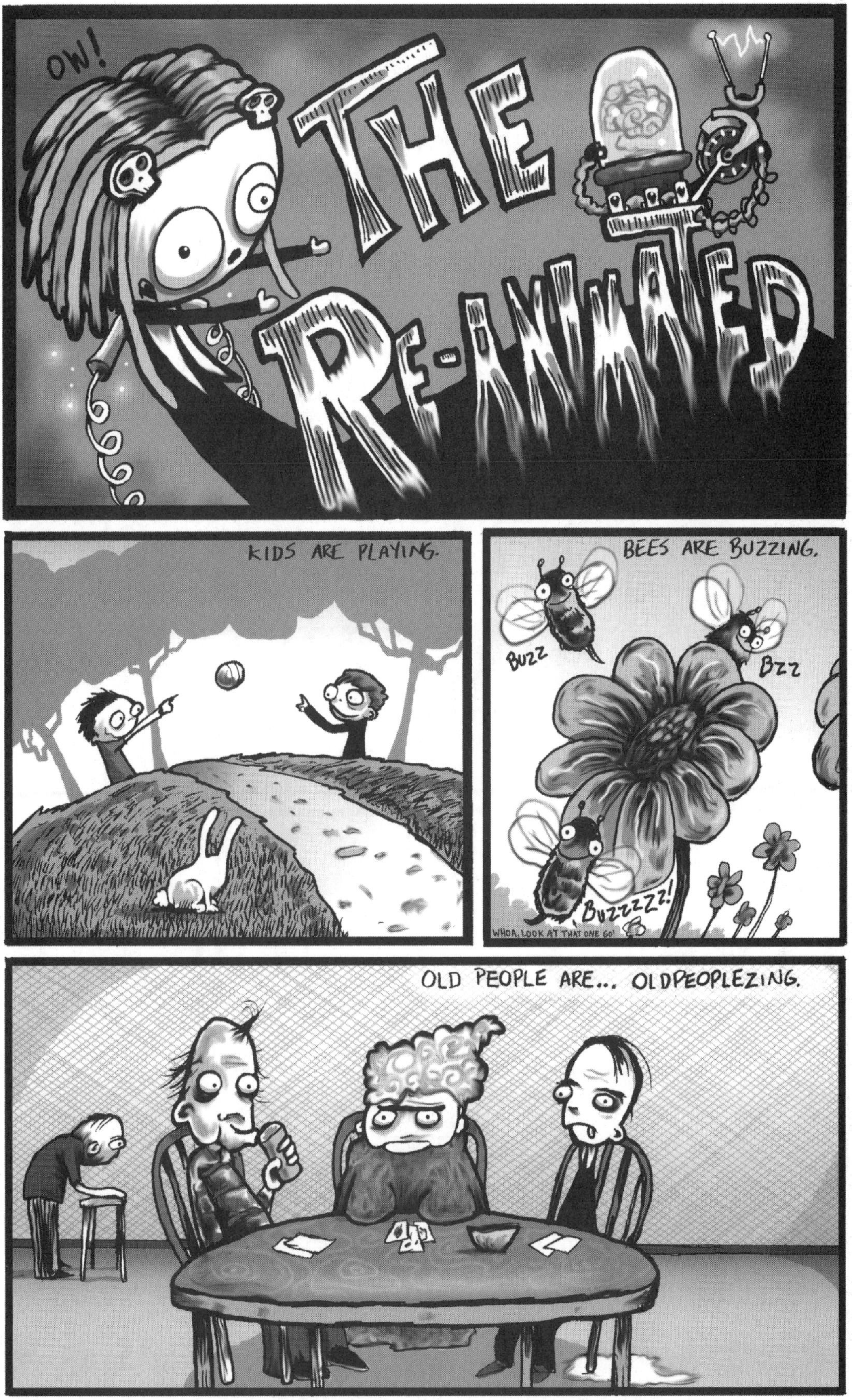
OW!
THE RE-ANIMATED
KIDS ARE PLAYING.
BEES ARE BUZZING.
Buzz
Bzz
Buzzzzz!
WHOA, LOOK AT THAT ONE GO!
OLD PEOPLE ARE... OLDPEOPLEZING.

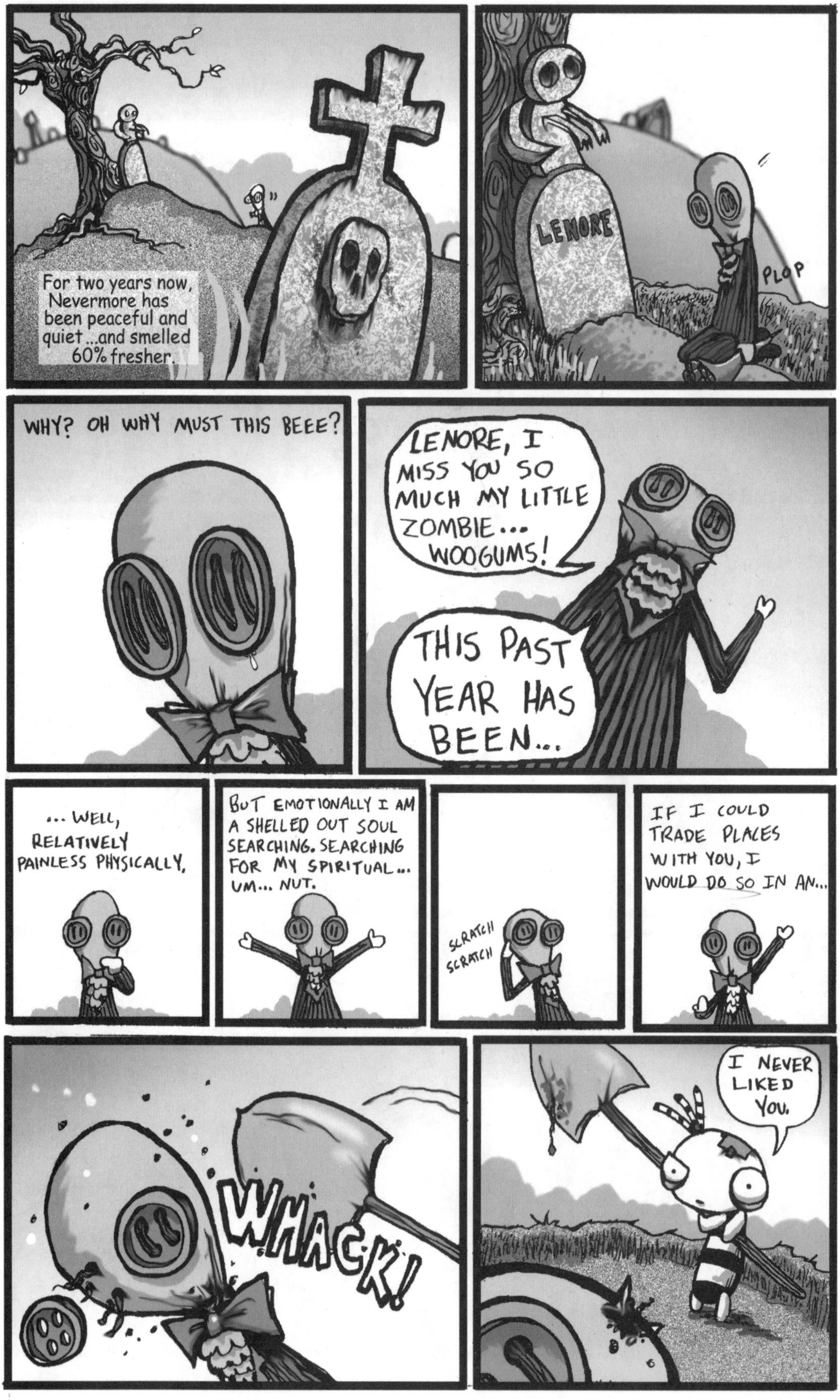

For two years now, Nevermore has been peaceful and quiet ...and smelled 60% fresher.
LENORE
PLOP
WHY? OH WHY MUST THIS BEEE?
LENORE, I MISS YOU SO MUCH MY LITTLE ZOMBIE... WOOGUMS!
THIS PAST YEAR HAS BEEN...
... WELL, RELATIVELY PAINLESS PHYSICALLY,
BUT EMOTIONALLY I AM A SHELLED OUT SOUL SEARCHING. SEARCHING FOR MY SPIRITUAL... UM... NUT.
SCRATCH SCRATCH
IF I COULD TRADE PLACES WITH YOU, I WOULD DO SO IN AN...
WHACK!
I NEVER LIKED YOU.

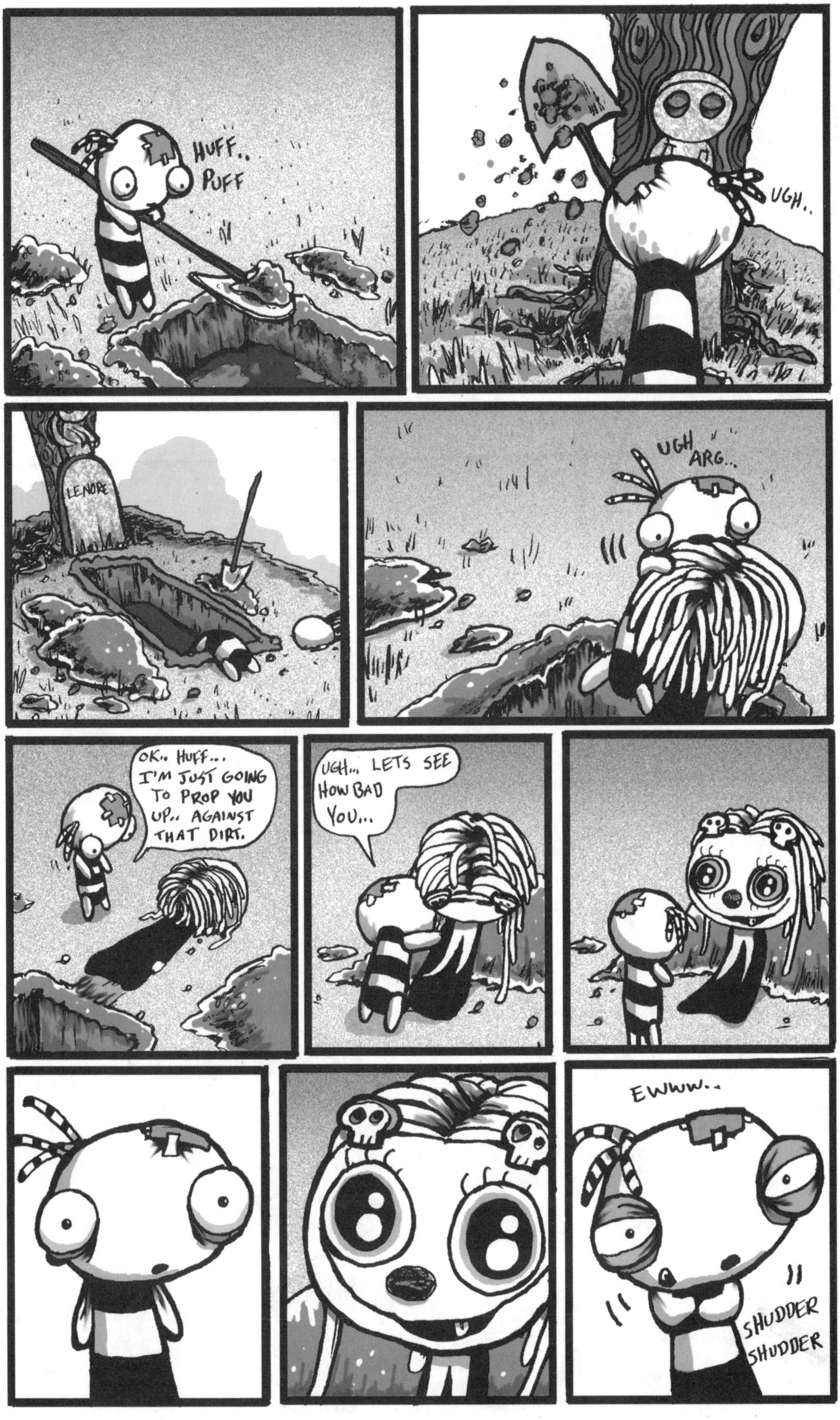

HUFF.. PUFF
UGH..
LENORE
UGH ARG...
OK.. HUFF... I'M JUST GOING TO PROP YOU UP.. AGAINST THAT DIRT.
UGH.. LETS SEE HOW BAD YOU...
EWWW..
SHUDDER SHUDDER

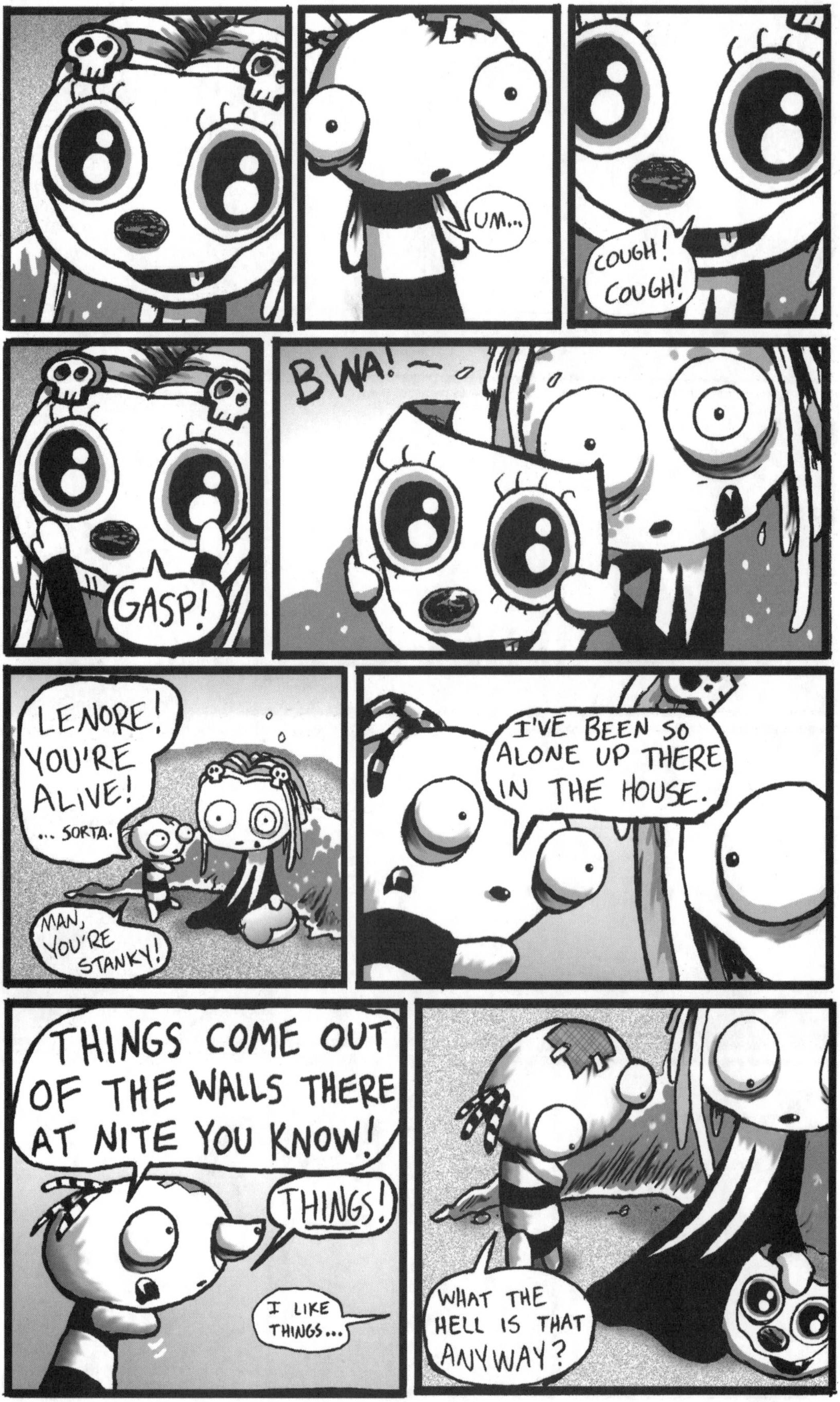
UM...
COUGH! COUGH!
GASP!
BWA!
LENORE! YOU'RE ALIVE! ... SORTA.
MAN, YOU'RE STANKY!
I'VE BEEN SO ALONE UP THERE IN THE HOUSE.
THINGS COME OUT OF THE WALLS THERE AT NITE YOU KNOW!
THINGS!
I LIKE THINGS...
WHAT THE HELL IS THAT ANYWAY?

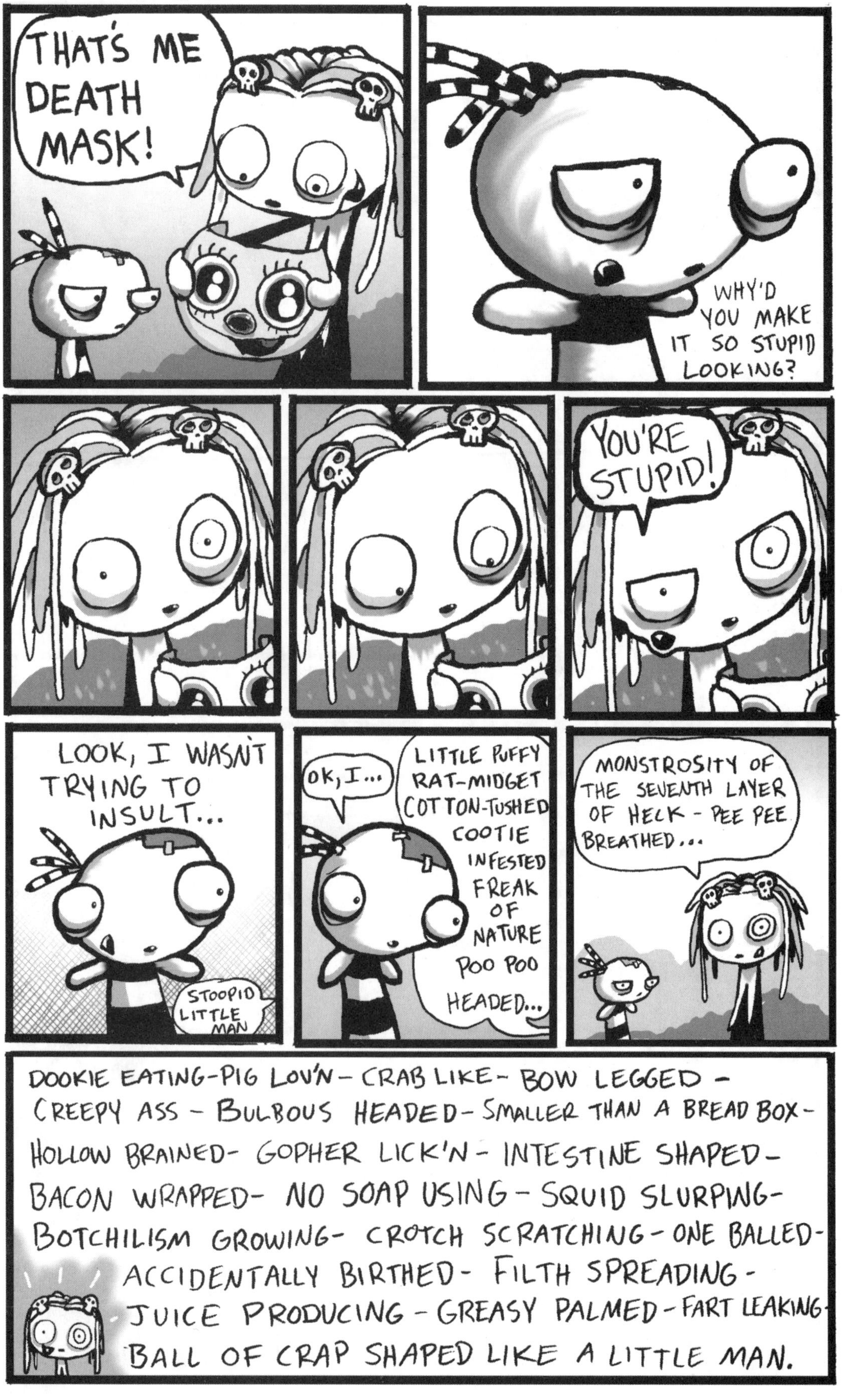
THAT'S ME DEATH MASK!
WHY'D YOU MAKE IT SO STUPID LOOKING?
YOU'RE STUPID!
LOOK, I WASN'T TRYING TO INSULT...
STOOPID LITTLE MAN
OK, I...
LITTLE PUFFY RAT-MIDGET COTTON-TUSHED COOTIE INFESTED FREAK OF NATURE POO POO HEADED...
MONSTROSITY OF THE SEVENTH LAYER OF HECK - PEE PEE BREATHED...
DOOKIE EATING-PIG LOV'N - CRAB LIKE - BOW LEGGED - CREEPY ASS - BULBOUS HEADED - SMALLER THAN A BREAD BOX - HOLLOW BRAINED - GOPHER LICK'N - INTESTINE SHAPED - BACON WRAPPED - NO SOAP USING - SQUID SLURPING - BOTCHILISM GROWING - CROTCH SCRATCHING - ONE BALLED - ACCIDENTALLY BIRTHED - FILTH SPREADING - JUICE PRODUCING - GREASY PALMED - FART LEAKING - BALL OF CRAP SHAPED LIKE A LITTLE MAN.

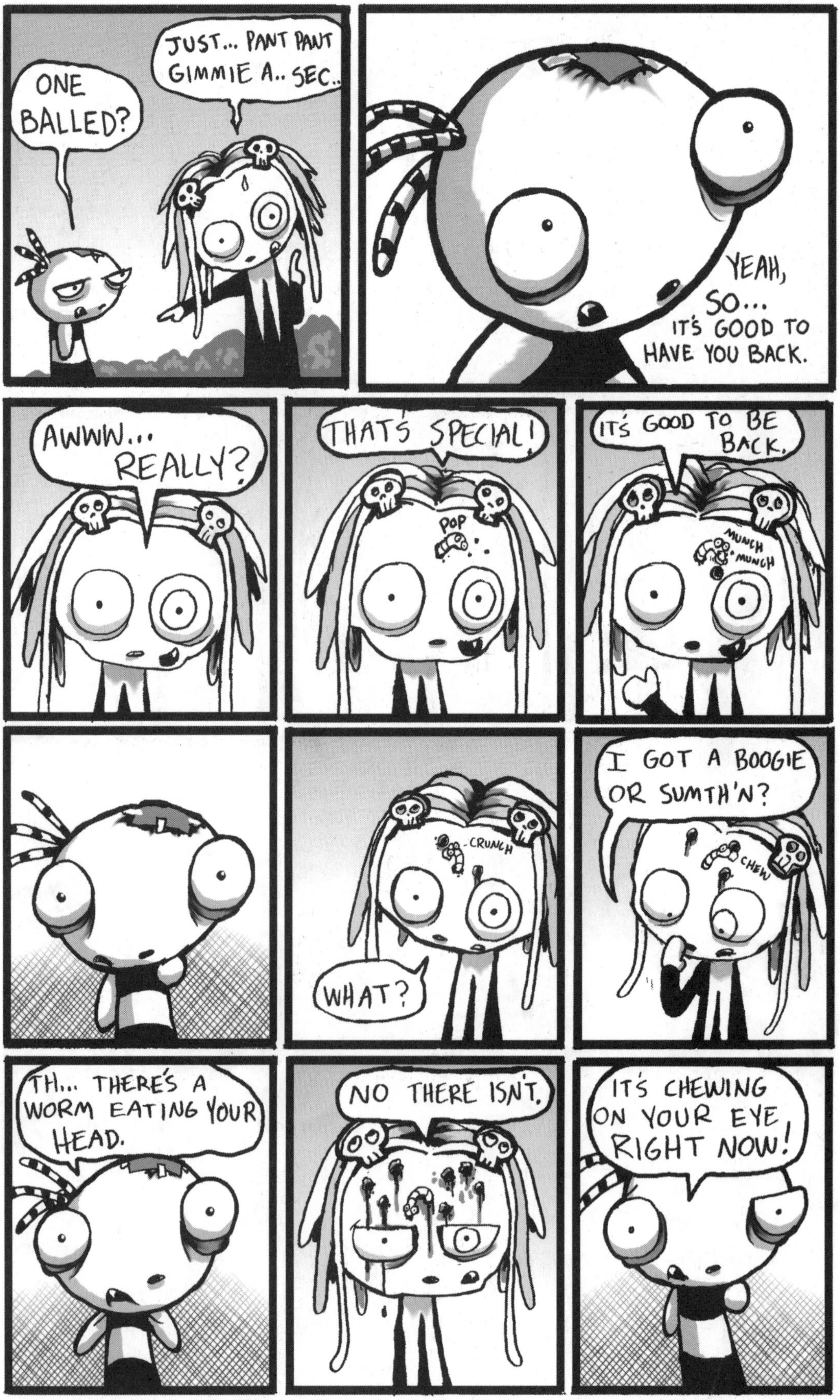
ONE BALLED?
JUST... PANT PANT GIMMIE A.. SEC..
YEAH, SO... IT'S GOOD TO HAVE YOU BACK.
AWWW... REALLY?
THAT'S SPECIAL!
POP
IT'S GOOD TO BE BACK.
MUNCH MUNCH
CRUNCH
WHAT?
I GOT A BOOGIE OR SUMTH'N?
CHEW
TH... THERE'S A WORM EATING YOUR HEAD.
NO THERE ISN'T.
IT'S CHEWING ON YOUR EYE RIGHT NOW!

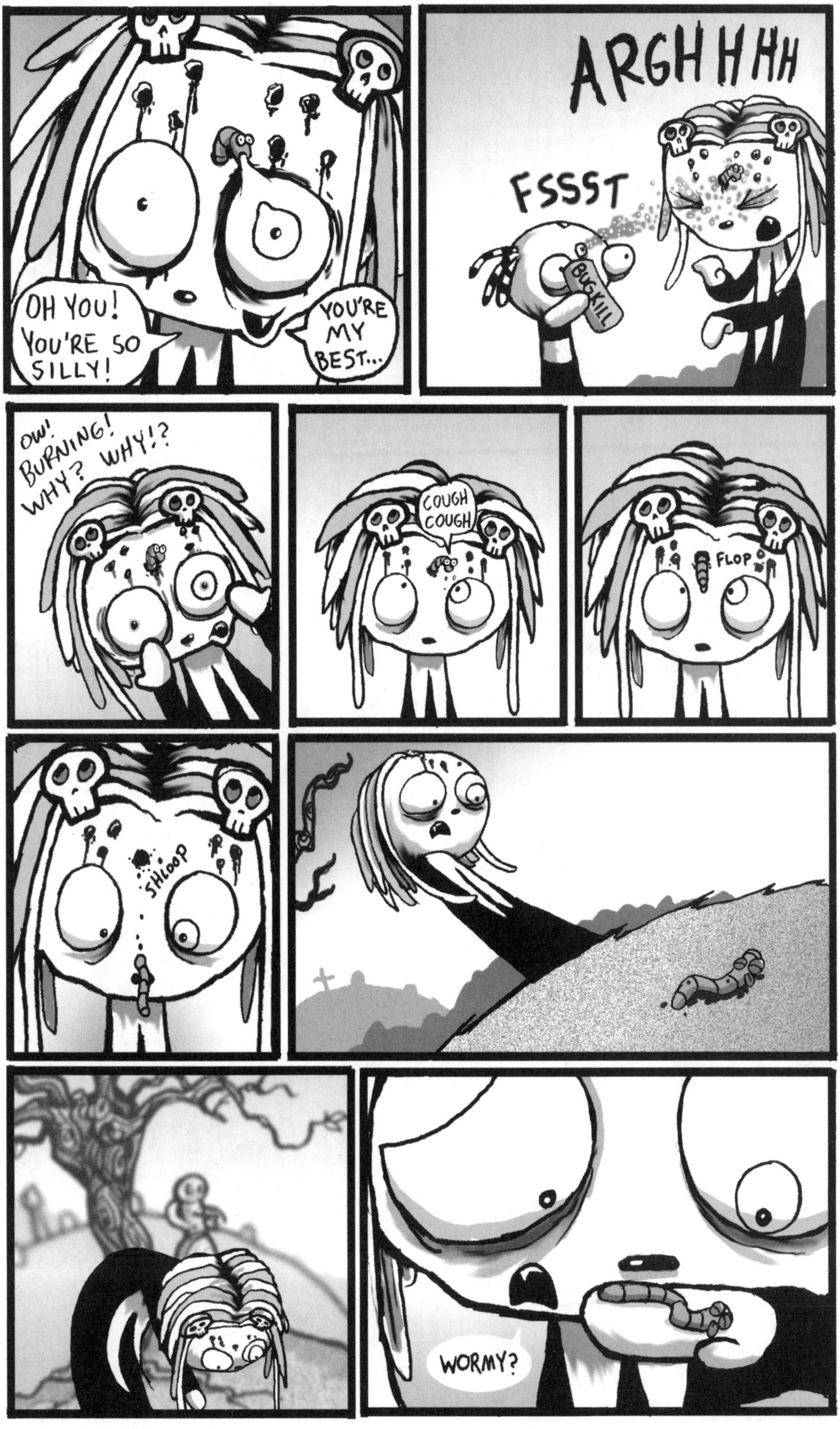

OH YOU! YOU'RE SO SILLY!
YOU'RE MY BEST...
ARGHHHH
FSSST
BUGKILL
OW! BURNING! WHY? WHY!?
COUGH COUGH
FLOP
SHLOOP
WORMY?

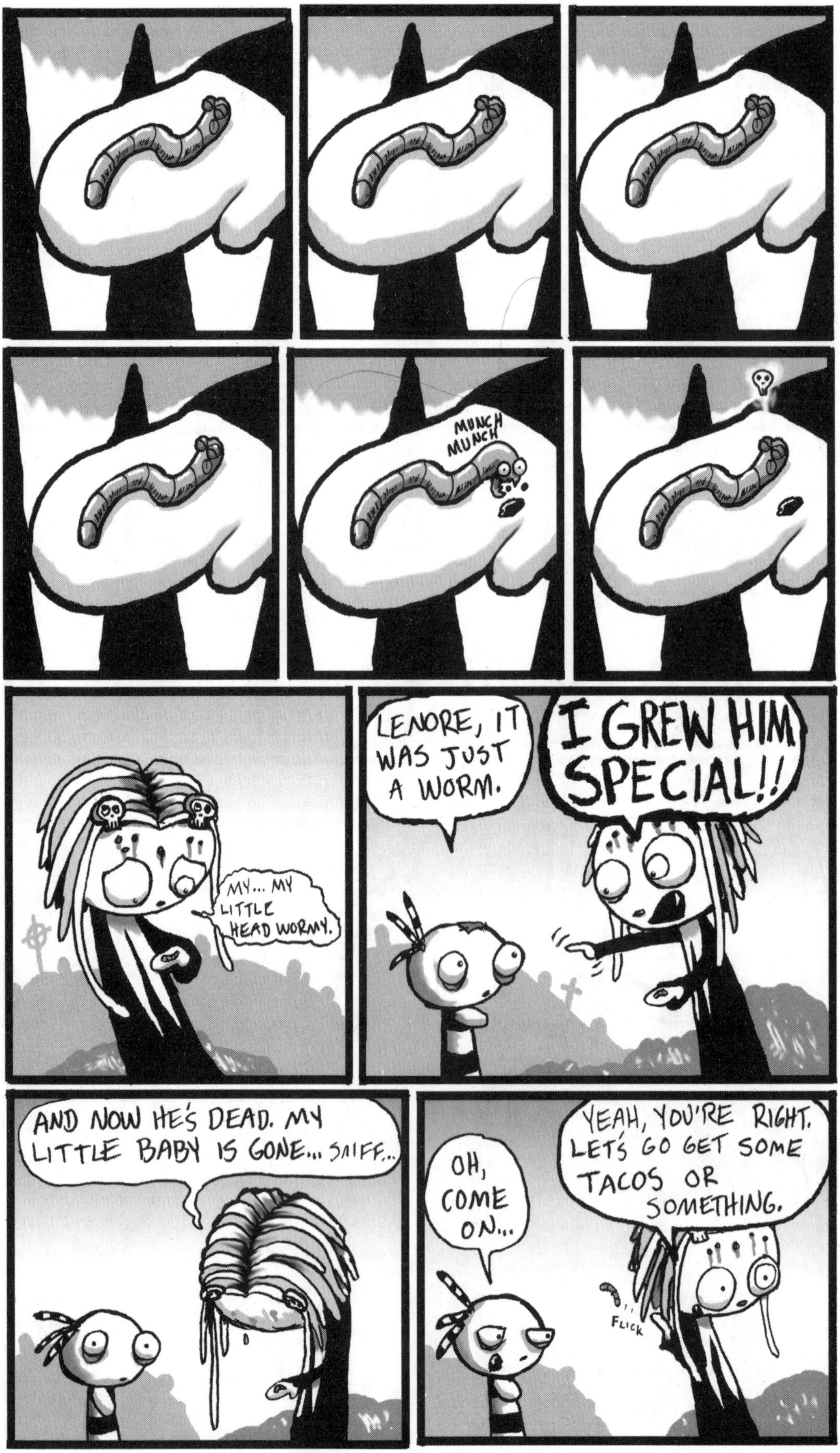
MUNCH MUNCH
MY... MY LITTLE HEAD WORMY.
LENORE, IT WAS JUST A WORM.
I GREW HIM SPECIAL!!
AND NOW HE'S DEAD. MY LITTLE BABY IS GONE... SNIFF...
OH, COME ON...
YEAH, YOU'RE RIGHT. LET'S GO GET SOME TACOS OR SOMETHING.
FLICK

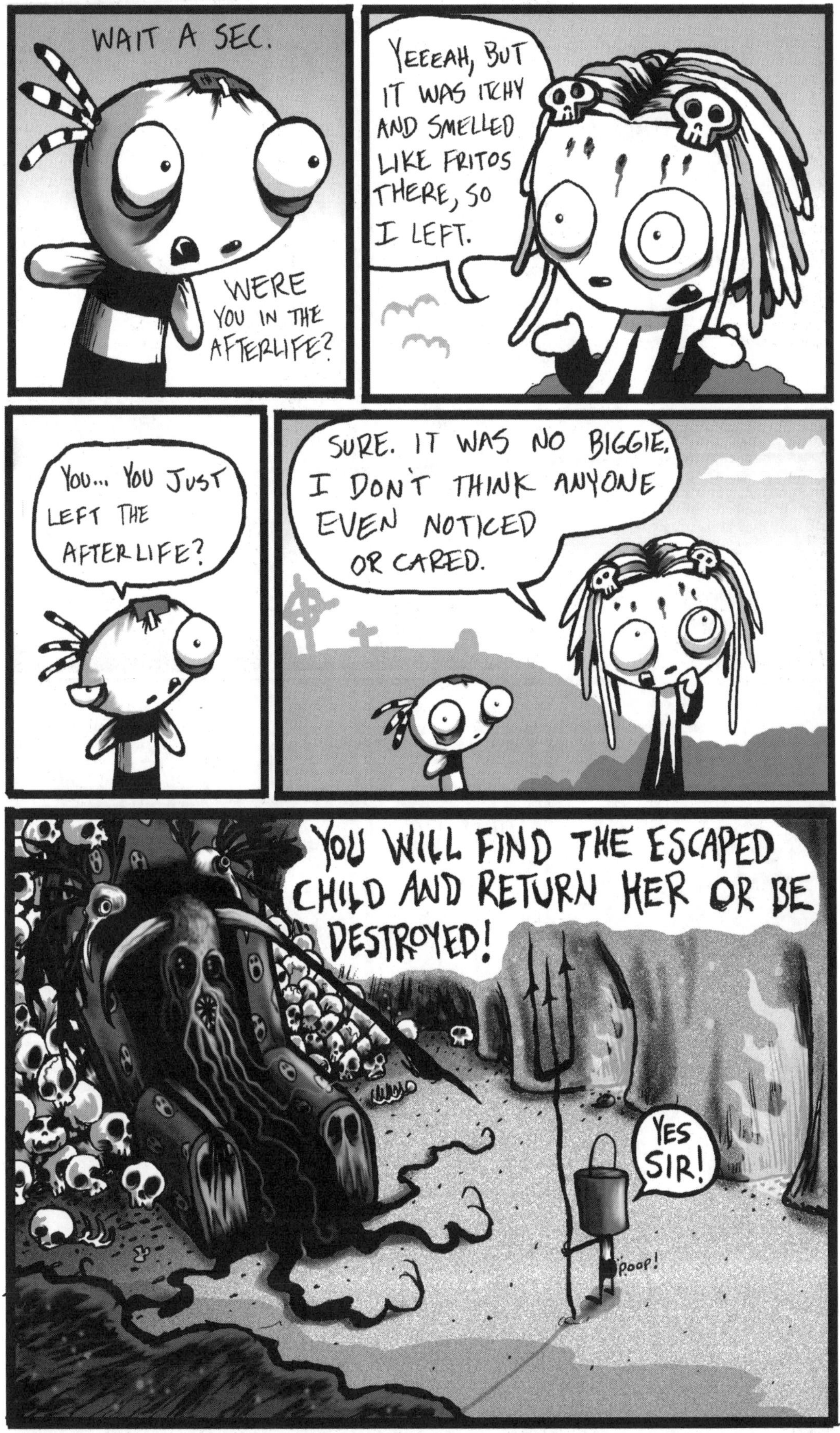
WAIT A SEC.
WERE YOU IN THE AFTERLIFE?
YEEEAH, BUT IT WAS ITCHY AND SMELLED LIKE FRITOS THERE, SO I LEFT.
YOU... YOU JUST LEFT THE AFTERLIFE?
SURE. IT WAS NO BIGGIE. I DON'T THINK ANYONE EVEN NOTICED OR CARED.
YOU WILL FIND THE ESCAPED CHILD AND RETURN HER OR BE DESTROYED!
YES SIR!
POOP!

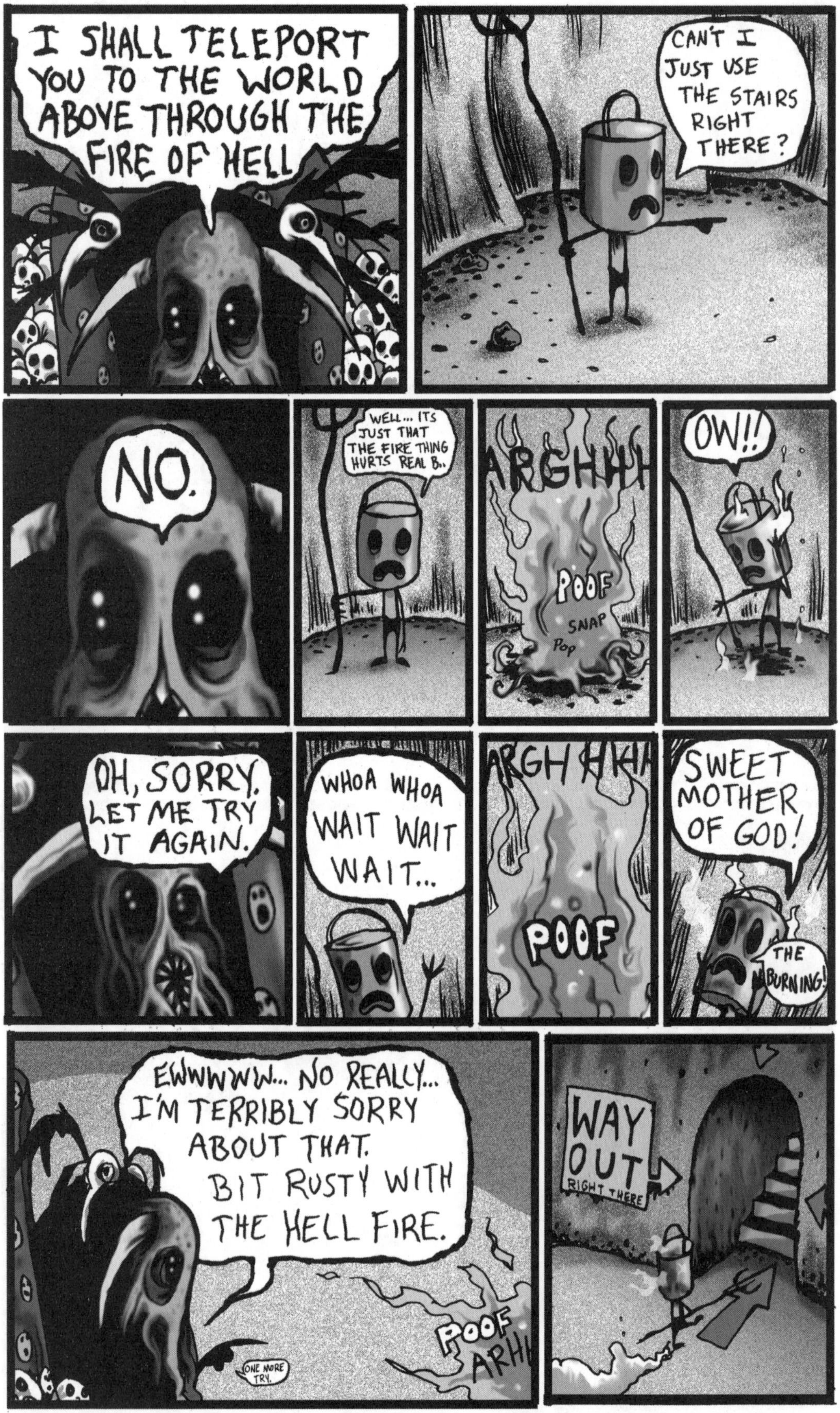
I SHALL TELEPORT YOU TO THE WORLD ABOVE THROUGH THE FIRE OF HELL
CAN'T I JUST USE THE STAIRS RIGHT THERE?
NO.
WELL... ITS JUST THAT THE FIRE THING HURTS REAL B..
ARGHHH
POOF
SNAP
POP
OW!!
OH, SORRY. LET ME TRY IT AGAIN.
WHOA WHOA WAIT WAIT WAIT...
ARGH HHH
POOF
SWEET MOTHER OF GOD!
THE BURNING!
EWWWWW... NO REALLY... I'M TERRIBLY SORRY ABOUT THAT. BIT RUSTY WITH THE HELL FIRE.
POOF
ARHH
ONE MORE TRY.
WAY OUT
RIGHT THERE

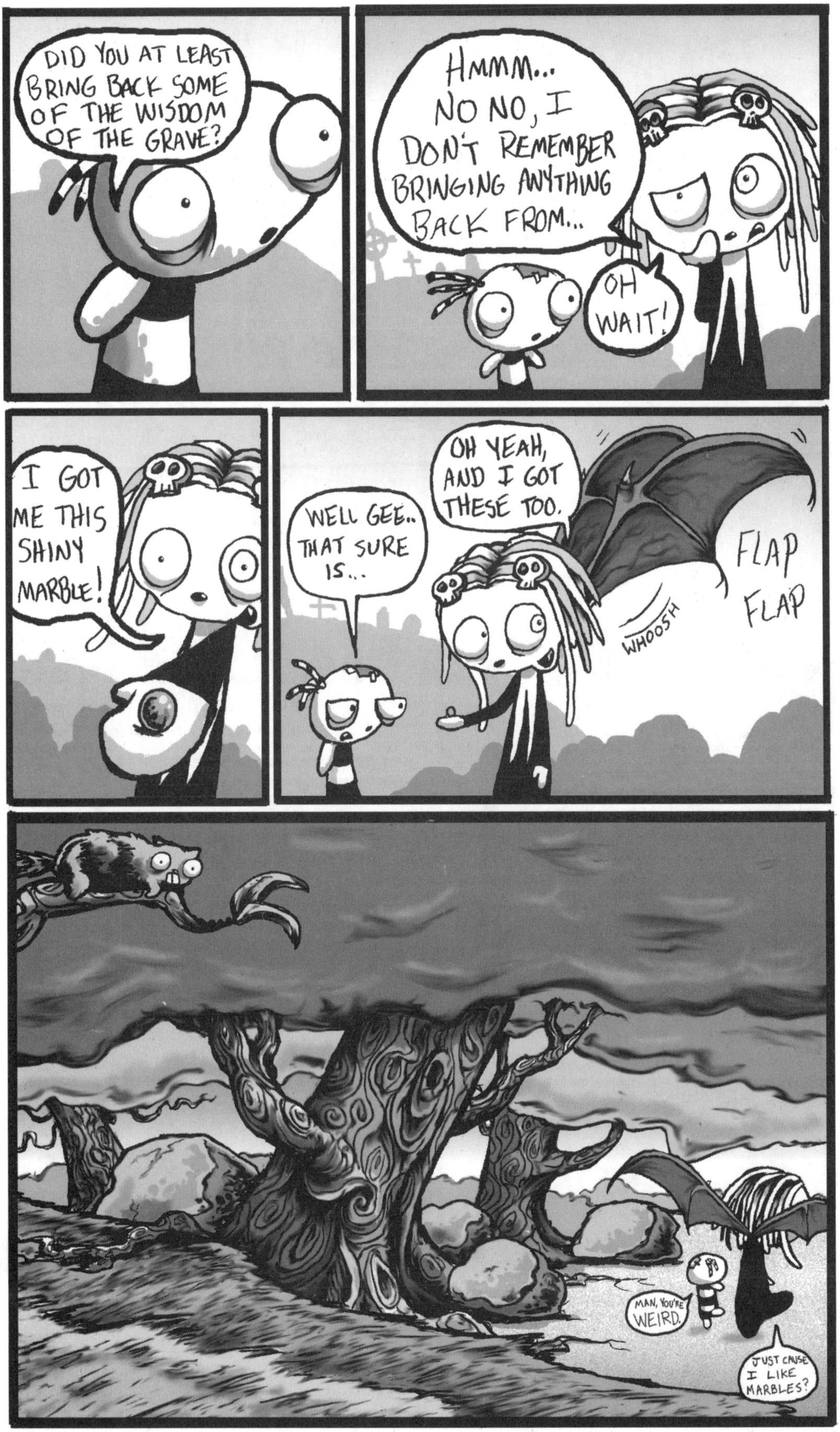
DID YOU AT LEAST BRING BACK SOME OF THE WISDOM OF THE GRAVE?
HMMM... NO NO, I DON'T REMEMBER BRINGING ANYTHING BACK FROM...
OH WAIT!
I GOT ME THIS SHINY MARBLE!
WELL GEE.. THAT SURE IS...
OH YEAH, AND I GOT THESE TOO.
FLAP
FLAP
WHOOSH
MAN, YOU'RE WEIRD.
JUST CAUSE I LIKE MARBLES?

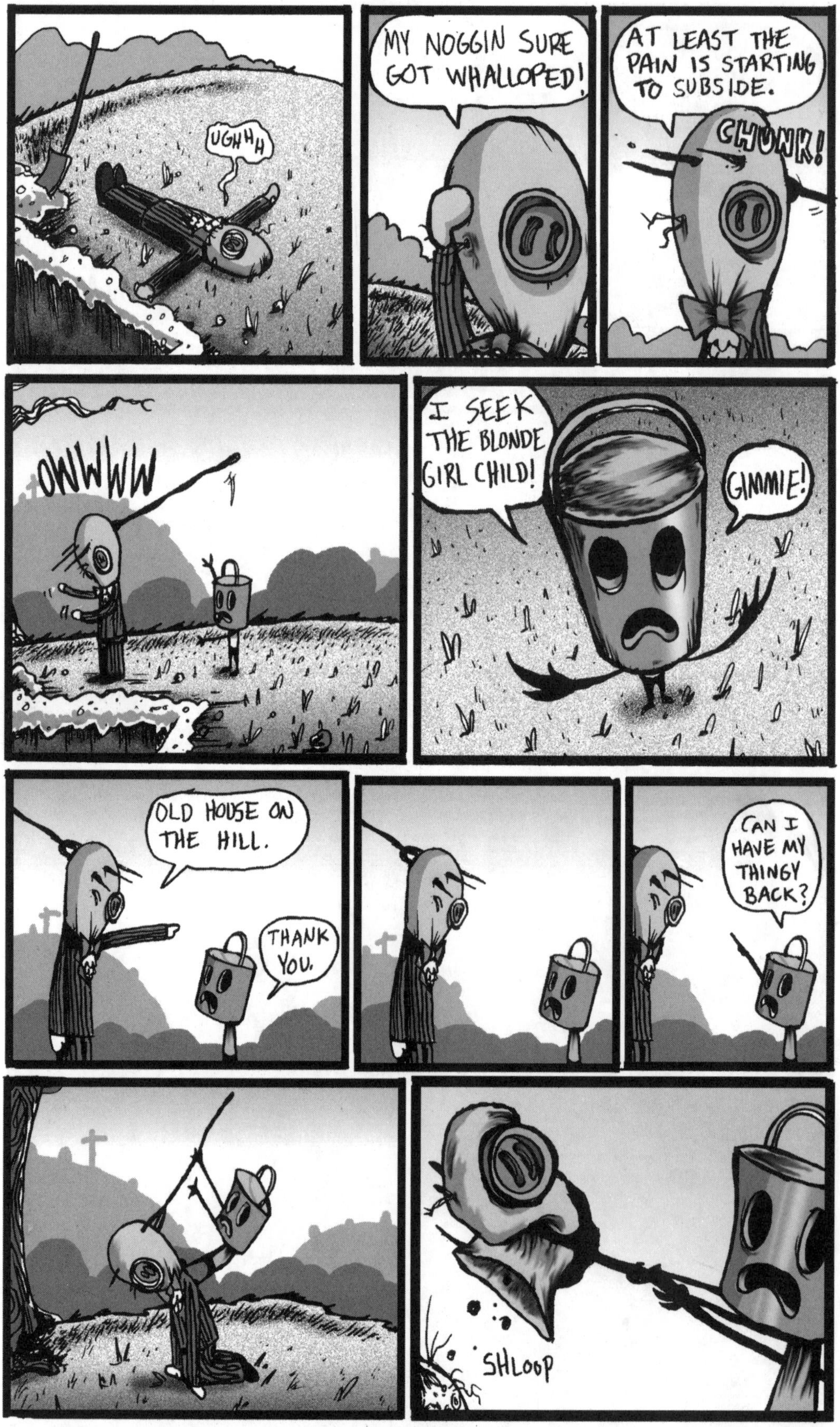
UGHHH
MY NOGGIN SURE GOT WHALLOPED!
AT LEAST THE PAIN IS STARTING TO SUBSIDE.
CHUNK!
OWWWW
I SEEK THE BLONDE GIRL CHILD!
GIMMIE!
OLD HOUSE ON THE HILL.
THANK YOU.
CAN I HAVE MY THINGY BACK?
SHLOOP

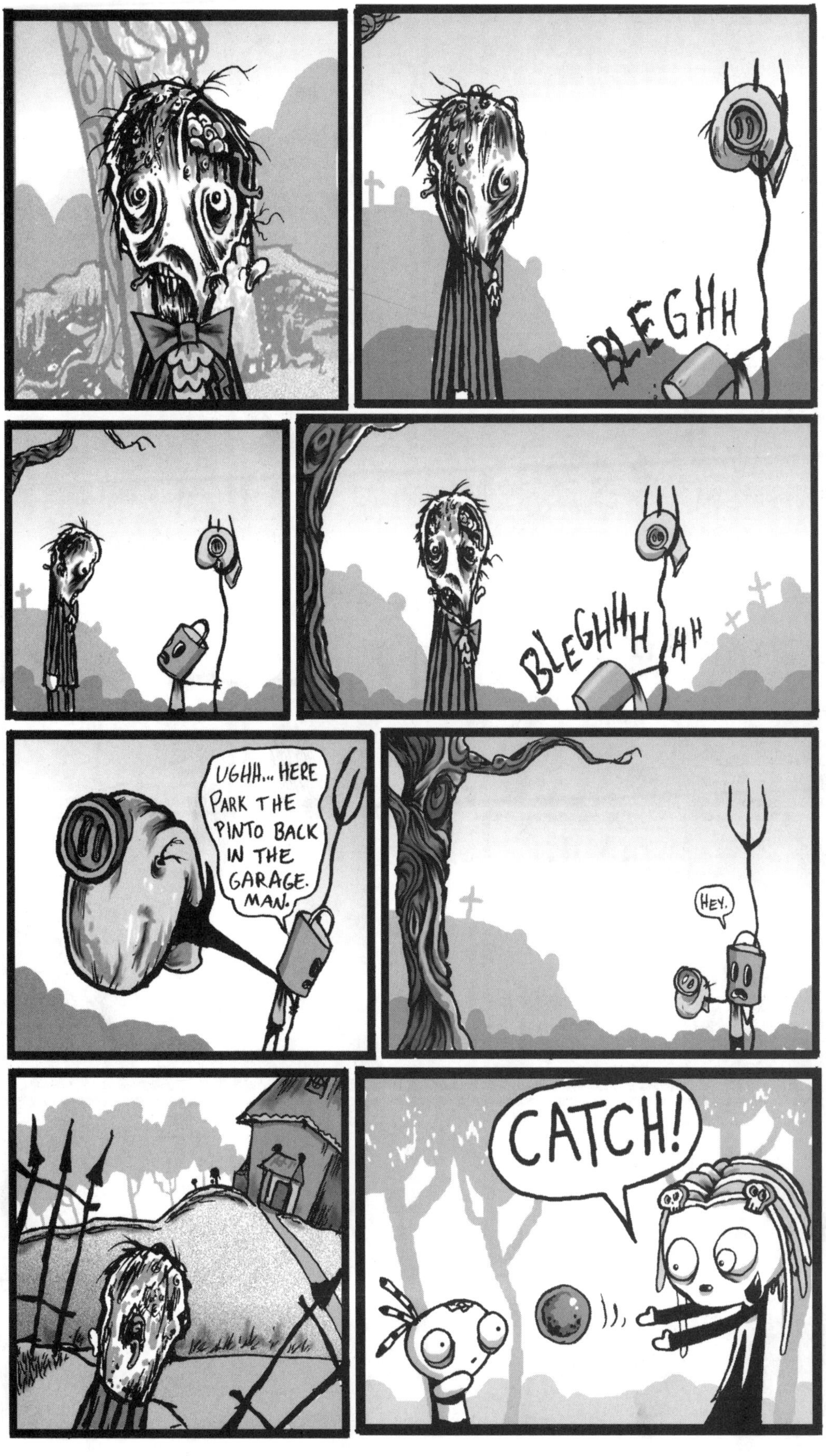
BLEGHH
BLEGHHHH HH
UGHH... HERE
PARK THE PINTO BACK IN THE GARAGE. MAN.
HEY.
CATCH!

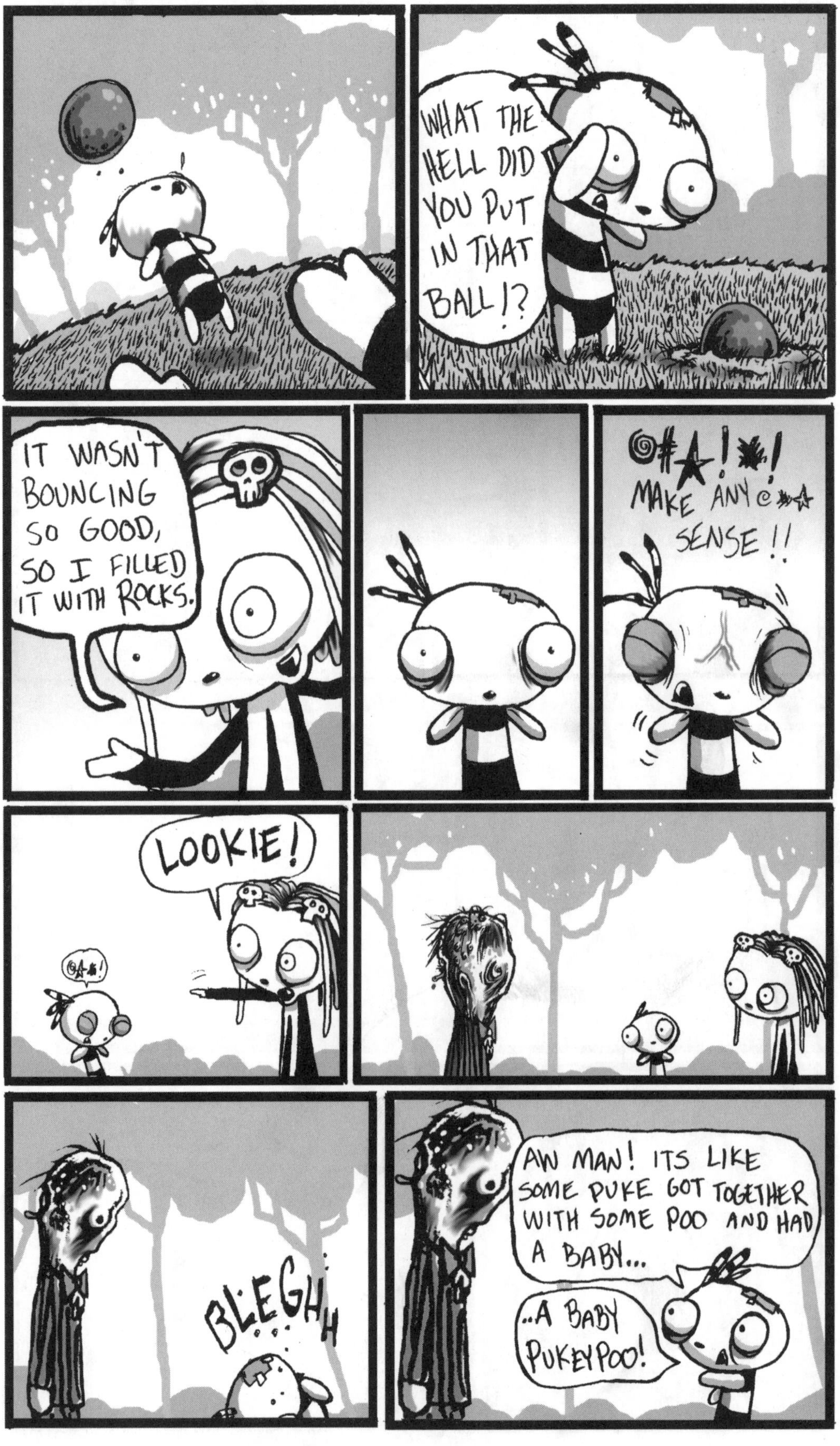

WHAT THE HELL DID YOU PUT IN THAT BALL!?
IT WASN'T BOUNCING SO GOOD, SO I FILLED IT WITH ROCKS.
MAKE ANY SENSE!!
LOOKIE!
BLEGHH
AW MAN! ITS LIKE SOME PUKE GOT TOGETHER WITH SOME POO AND HAD A BABY...
..A BABY PUKEYPOO!

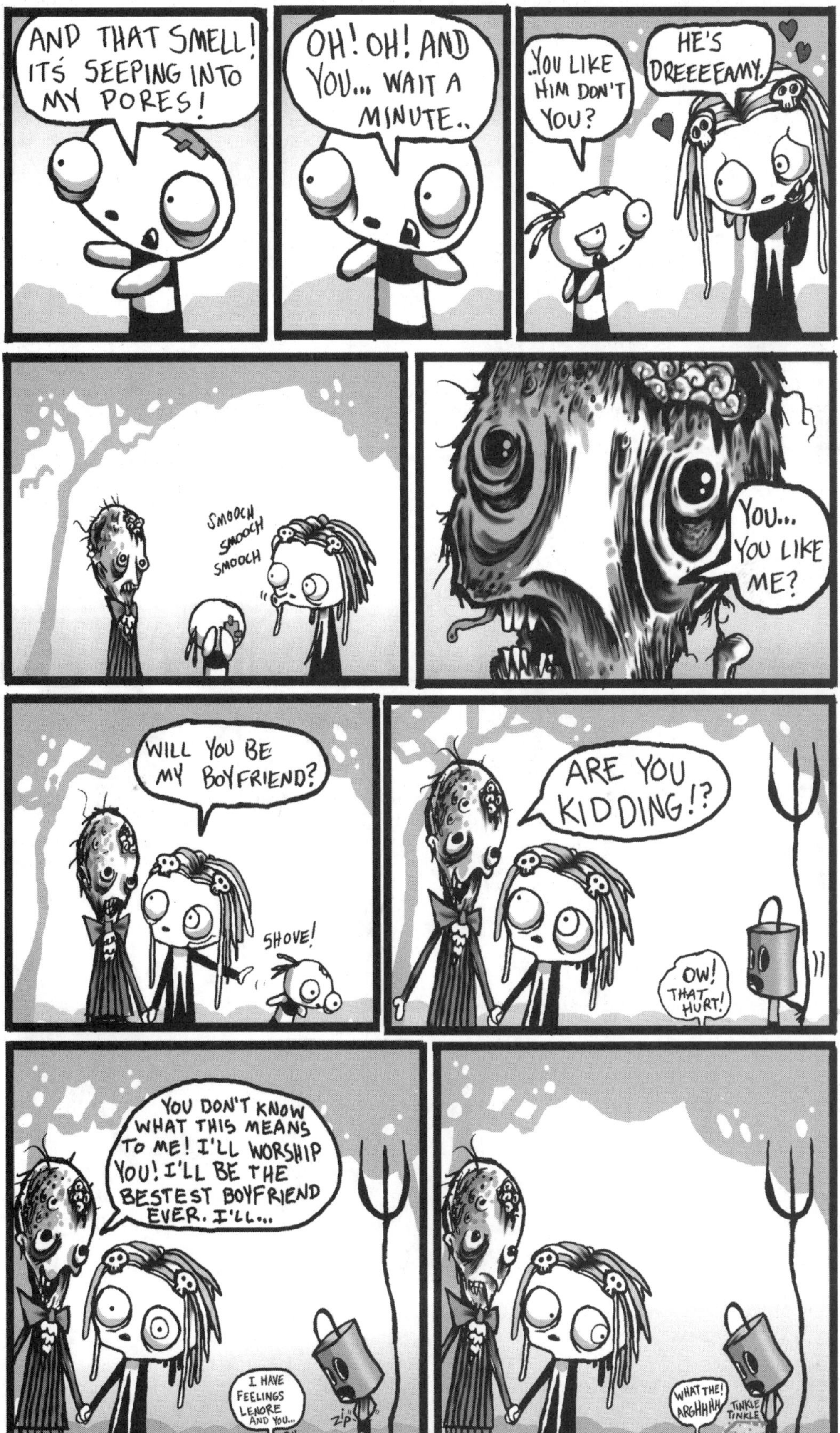
AND THAT SMELL! ITS SEEPING INTO MY PORES!
OH! OH! AND YOU... WAIT A MINUTE..
..YOU LIKE HIM DON'T YOU?
HE'S DREEEEAMY.
SMOOCH SMOOCH SMOOCH
YOU... YOU LIKE ME?
WILL YOU BE MY BOYFRIEND?
SHOVE!
ARE YOU KIDDING!?
OW! THAT HURT!
YOU DON'T KNOW WHAT THIS MEANS TO ME! I'LL WORSHIP YOU! I'LL BE THE BESTEST BOYFRIEND EVER. I'LL...
I HAVE FEELINGS LENORE AND YOU...
ZIP
WHAT THE! ARGHHHH
TINKLE TINKLE

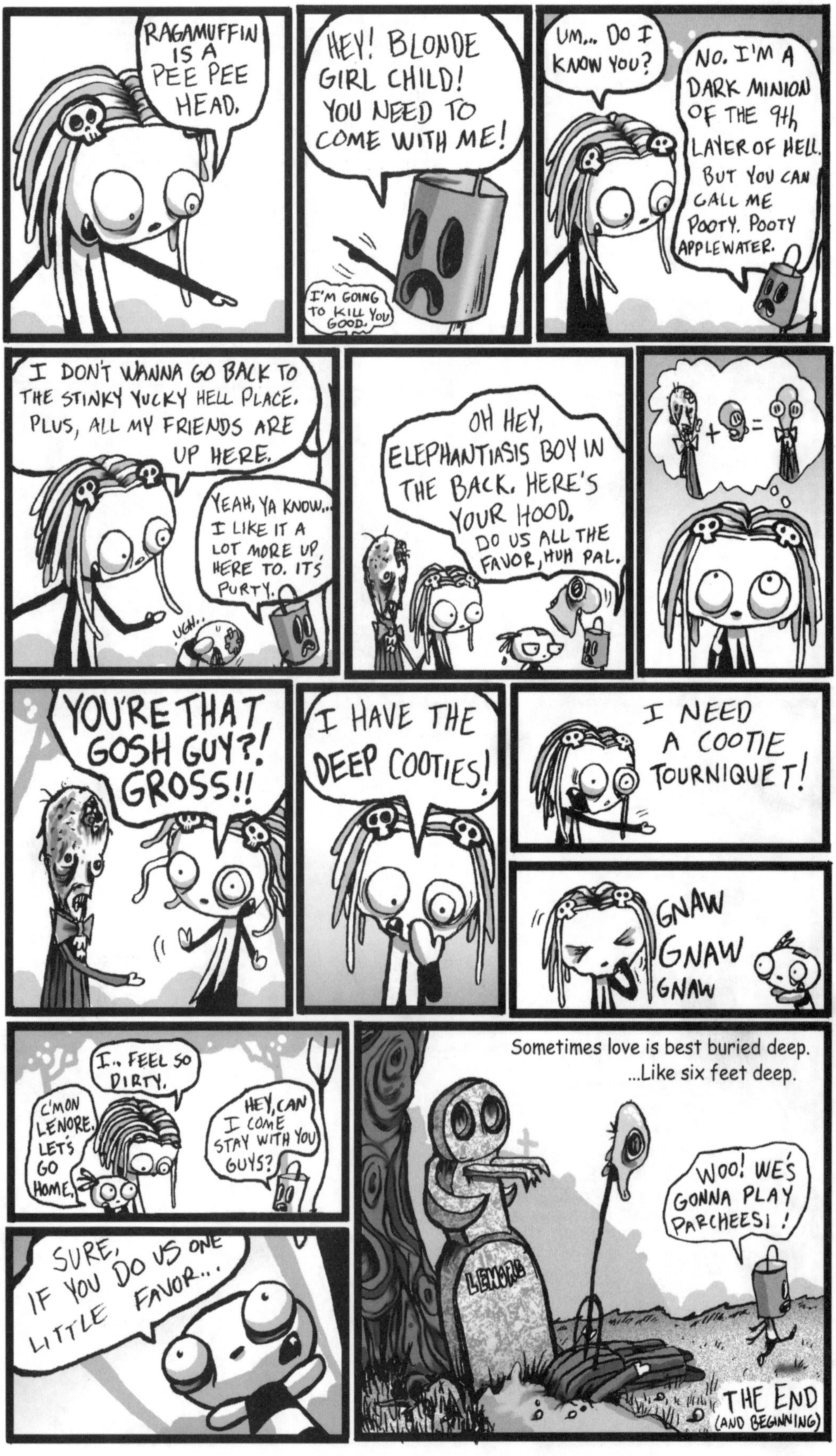
RAGAMUFFIN IS A PEE PEE HEAD.
HEY! BLONDE GIRL CHILD! YOU NEED TO COME WITH ME!
I'M GOING TO KILL YOU GOOD.
UM... DO I KNOW YOU?
NO. I'M A DARK MINION OF THE 9th LAYER OF HELL. BUT YOU CAN CALL ME POOTY. POOTY APPLEWATER.
I DON'T WANNA GO BACK TO THE STINKY YUCKY HELL PLACE. PLUS, ALL MY FRIENDS ARE UP HERE.
YEAH, YA KNOW... I LIKE IT A LOT MORE UP HERE TO. IT'S PURTY.
UGH..
OH HEY, ELEPHANTIASIS BOY IN THE BACK. HERE'S YOUR HOOD.
DO US ALL THE FAVOR, HUH PAL.
YOU'RE THAT GOSH GUY?! GROSS!!
I HAVE THE DEEP COOTIES!
I NEED A COOTIE TOURNIQUET!
GNAW GNAW GNAW
I.. FEEL SO DIRTY.
C'MON LENORE, LET'S GO HOME.
HEY, CAN I COME STAY WITH YOU GUYS?
SURE, IF YOU DO US ONE LITTLE FAVOR...
Sometimes love is best buried deep.
...Like six feet deep.
LENORE
WOO! WE'S GONNA PLAY PARCHEESI!
THE END
(AND BEGINNING)

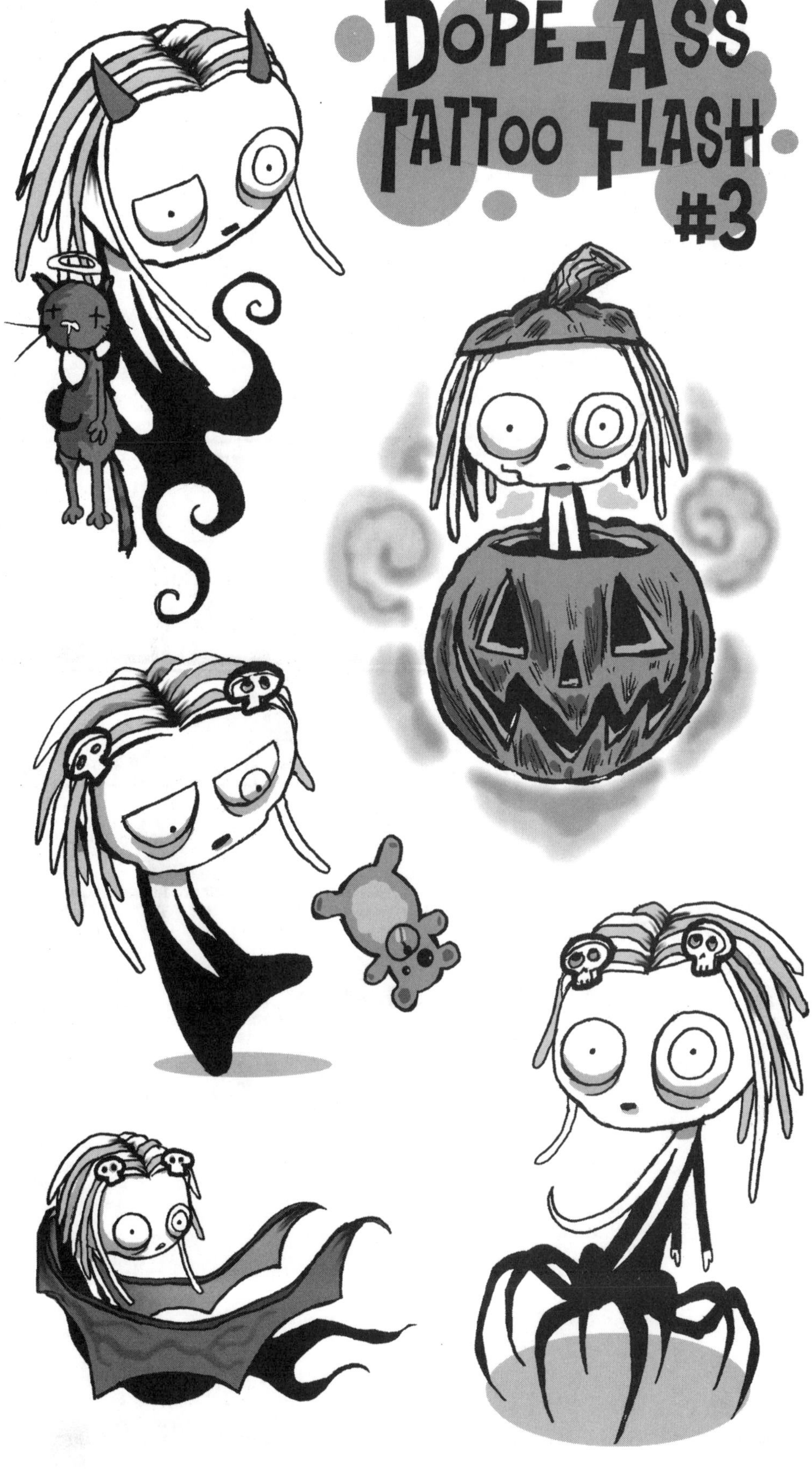
DOPE-ASS
TATTOO FLASH
#3

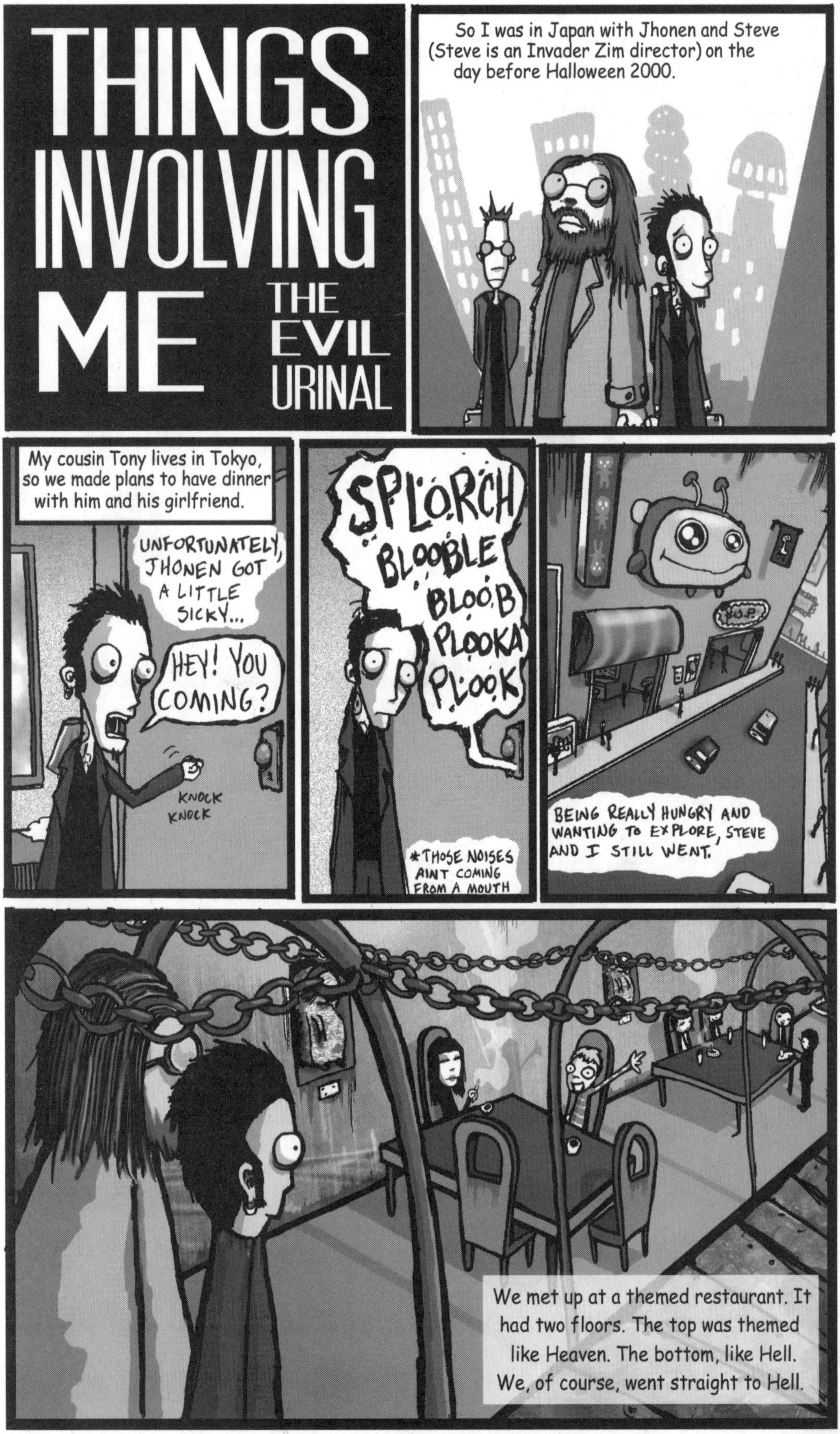
THINGS INVOLVING ME
THE EVIL URINAL
So I was in Japan with Jhonen and Steve (Steve is an Invader Zim director) on the day before Halloween 2000.
My cousin Tony lives in Tokyo, so we made plans to have dinner with him and his girlfriend.
UNFORTUNATELY, JHONEN GOT A LITTLE SICKY...
HEY! YOU COMING?
KNOCK KNOCK
SPLORCH BLOOBLE BLOOB PLOOKA PLOOK
*THOSE NOISES AINT COMING FROM A MOUTH
BEING REALLY HUNGRY AND WANTING TO EXPLORE, STEVE AND I STILL WENT.
We met up at a themed restaurant. It had two floors. The top was themed like Heaven. The bottom, like Hell. We, of course, went straight to Hell.

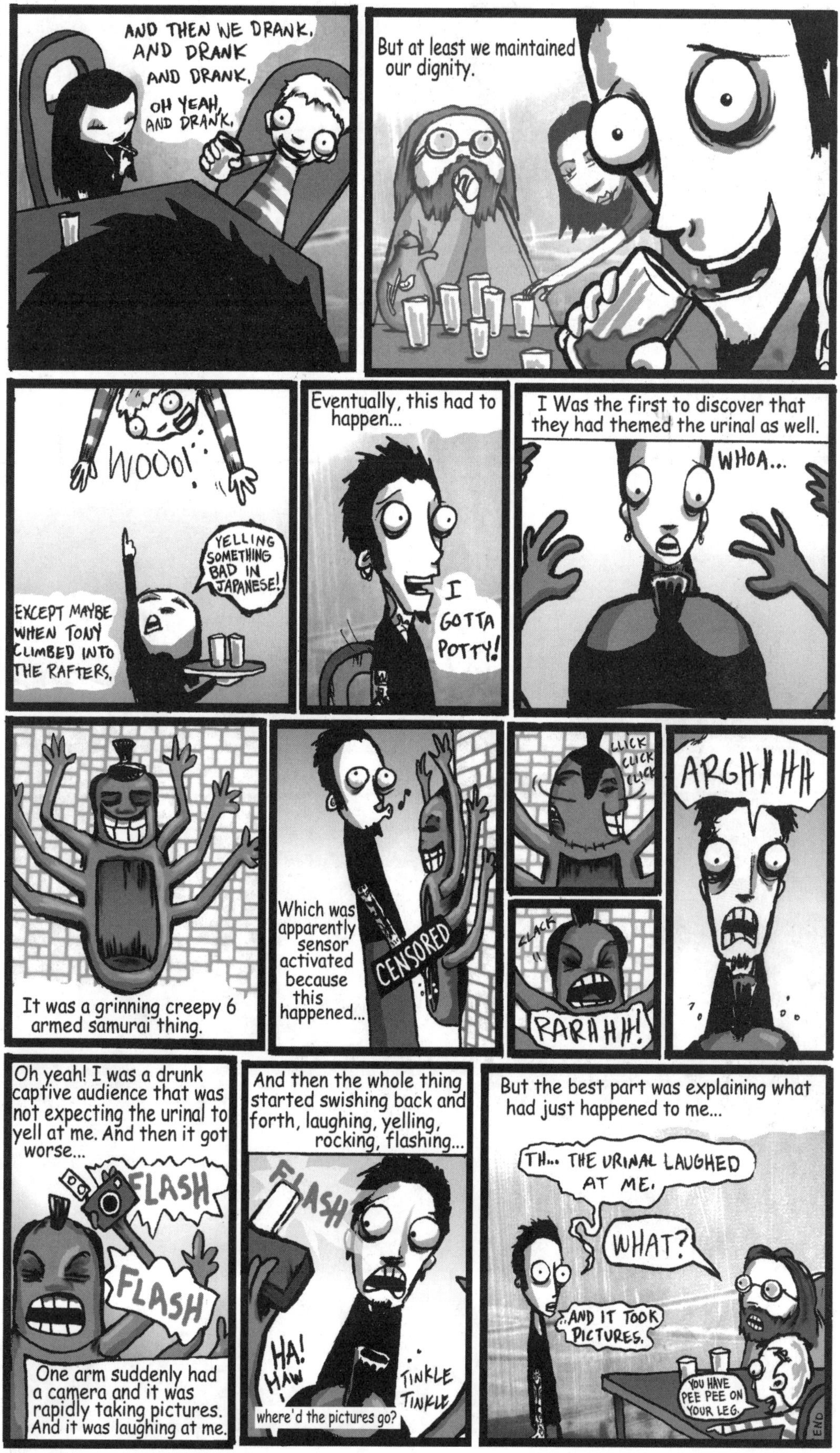
AND THEN WE DRANK. AND DRANK AND DRANK, OH YEAH, AND DRANK.
But at least we maintained our dignity.
WOOO!
EXCEPT MAYBE WHEN TONY CLIMBED INTO THE RAFTERS,
YELLING SOMETHING BAD IN JAPANESE!
Eventually, this had to happen...
I GOTTA POTTY!
I Was the first to discover that they had themed the urinal as well.
WHOA...
It was a grinning creepy 6 armed samurai thing.
Which was apparently sensor activated because this happened...
CENSORED
CLICK CLICK CLICK
CLACK
RARHHH!
ARGHHHH
Oh yeah! I was a drunk captive audience that was not expecting the urinal to yell at me. And then it got worse...
FLASH
FLASH
One arm suddenly had a camera and it was rapidly taking pictures. And it was laughing at me.
And then the whole thing started swishing back and forth, laughing, yelling, rocking, flashing...
FLASH
HA! HAW
TINKLE TINKLE
where'd the pictures go?
But the best part was explaining what had just happened to me...
TH... THE URINAL LAUGHED AT ME.
WHAT?
...AND IT TOOK PICTURES.
YOU HAVE PEE PEE ON YOUR LEG.
END

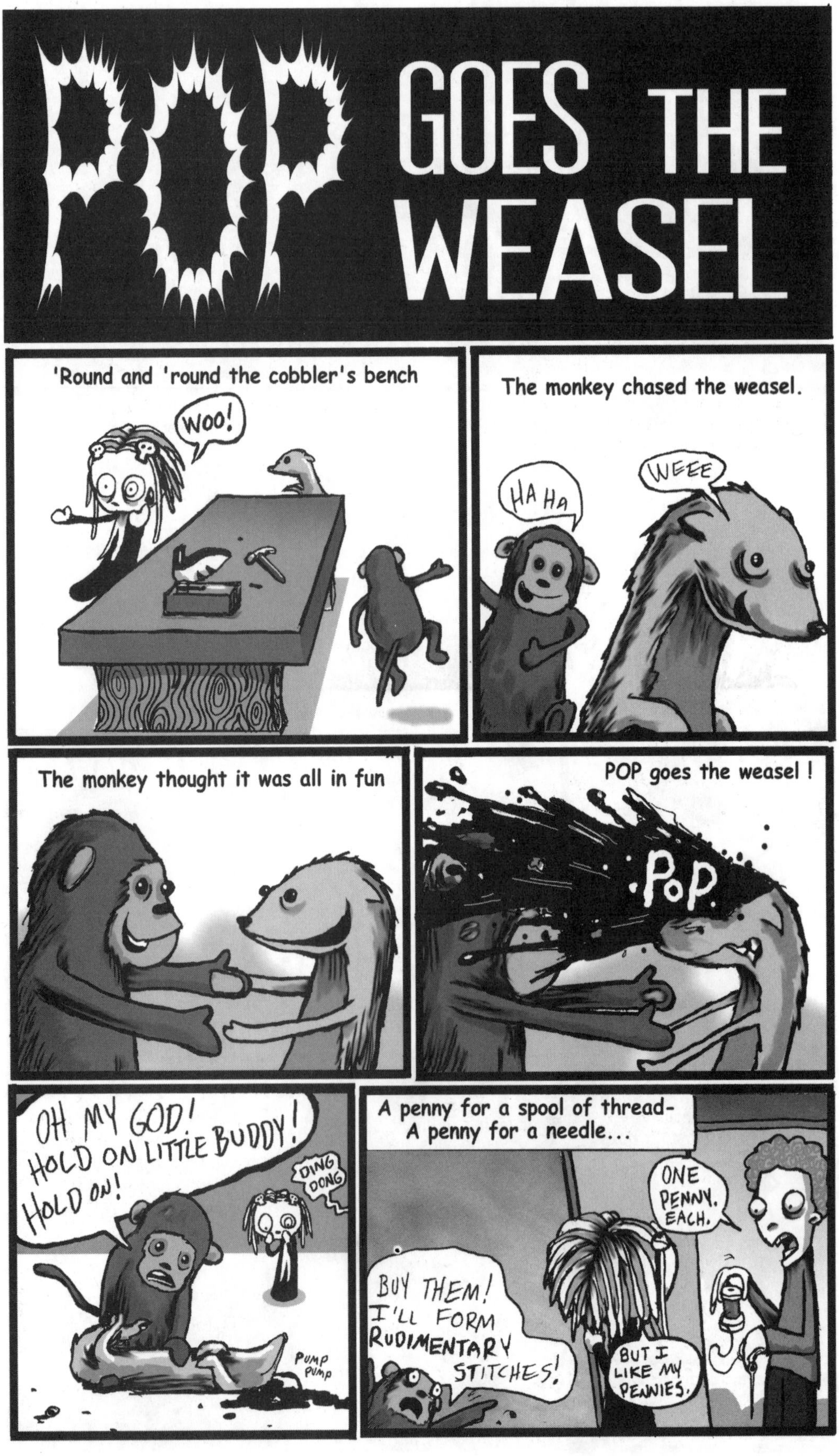
POP GOES THE WEASEL
'Round and 'round the cobbler's bench
WOO!
The monkey chased the weasel.
HA HA
WEEE
The monkey thought it was all in fun
POP goes the weasel !
POP
OH MY GOD! HOLD ON LITTLE BUDDY! HOLD ON!
DING DONG
PUMP PUMP
A penny for a spool of thread- A penny for a needle...
ONE PENNY. EACH.
BUY THEM! I'LL FORM RUDIMENTARY STITCHES!
BUT I LIKE MY PENNIES.

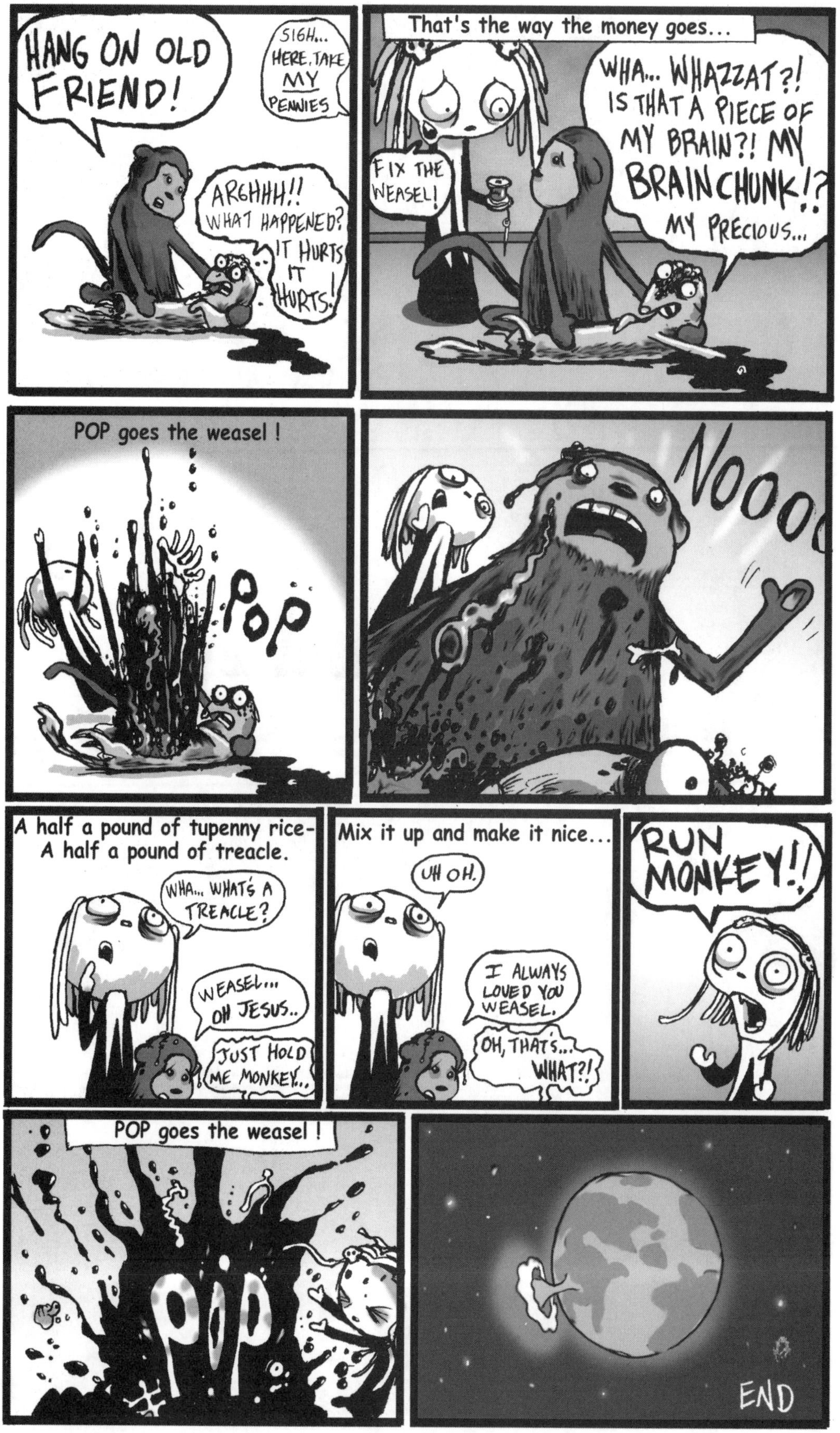
HANG ON OLD FRIEND!
SIGH... HERE, TAKE MY PENNIES
ARGHHH!! WHAT HAPPENED? IT HURTS IT HURTS!
That's the way the money goes...
FIX THE WEASEL!
WHA... WHAZZAT?! IS THAT A PIECE OF MY BRAIN?! MY BRAINCHUNK!? MY PRECIOUS...
POP goes the weasel !
POP
NOOOO
A half a pound of tupenny rice-
A half a pound of treacle.
WHA... WHAT'S A TREACLE?
WEASEL... OH JESUS..
JUST HOLD ME MONKEY...
Mix it up and make it nice...
UH OH.
I ALWAYS LOVED YOU WEASEL.
OH, THAT'S... WHAT?!
RUN MONKEY!!
POP goes the weasel !
POP
END

Three months twelve days and two hours after the first story ended...

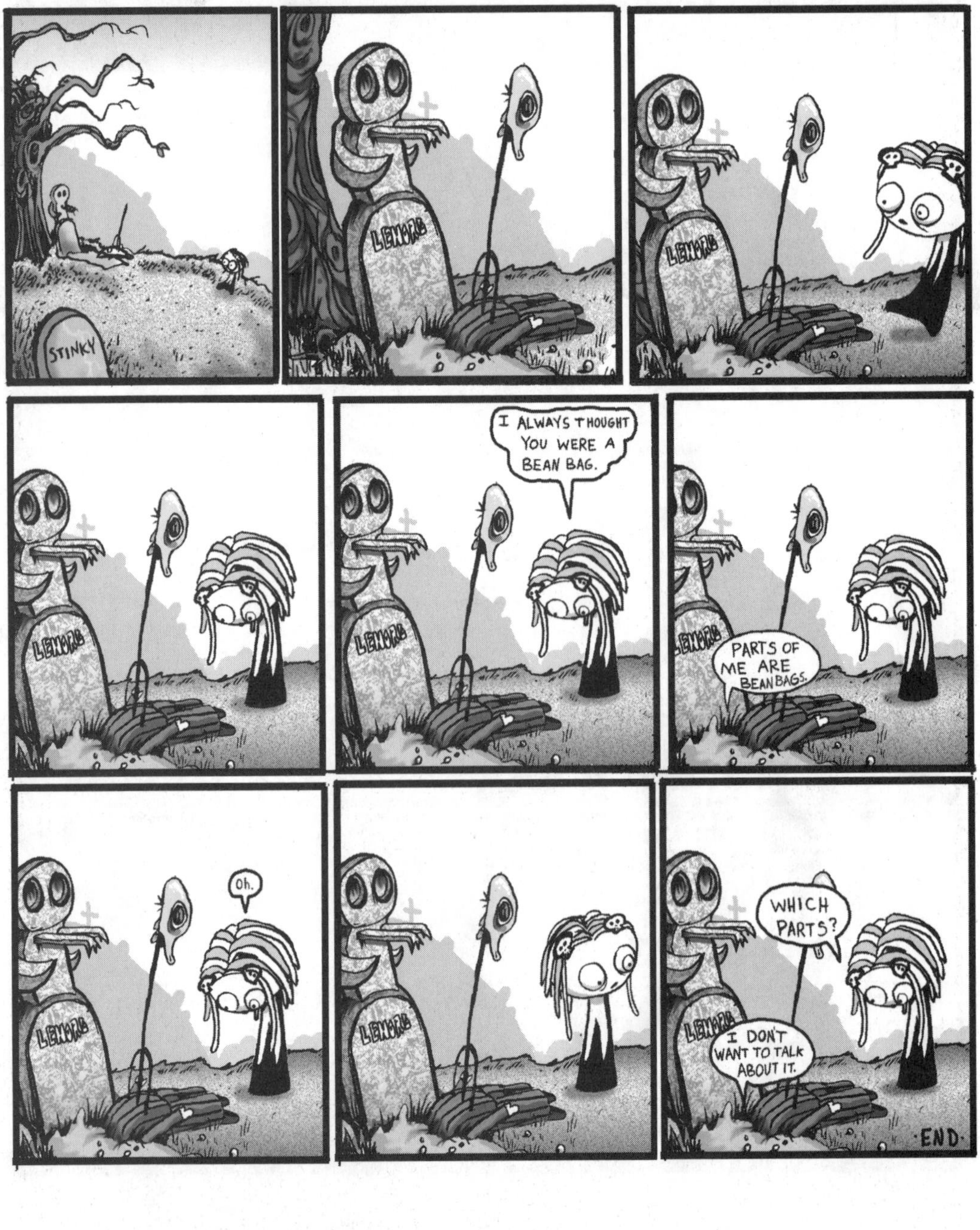
STINKY
LENORE
I ALWAYS THOUGHT YOU WERE A BEAN BAG.
PARTS OF ME ARE BEAN BAGS.
Oh.
WHICH PARTS?
I DON'T WANT TO TALK ABOUT IT.
END

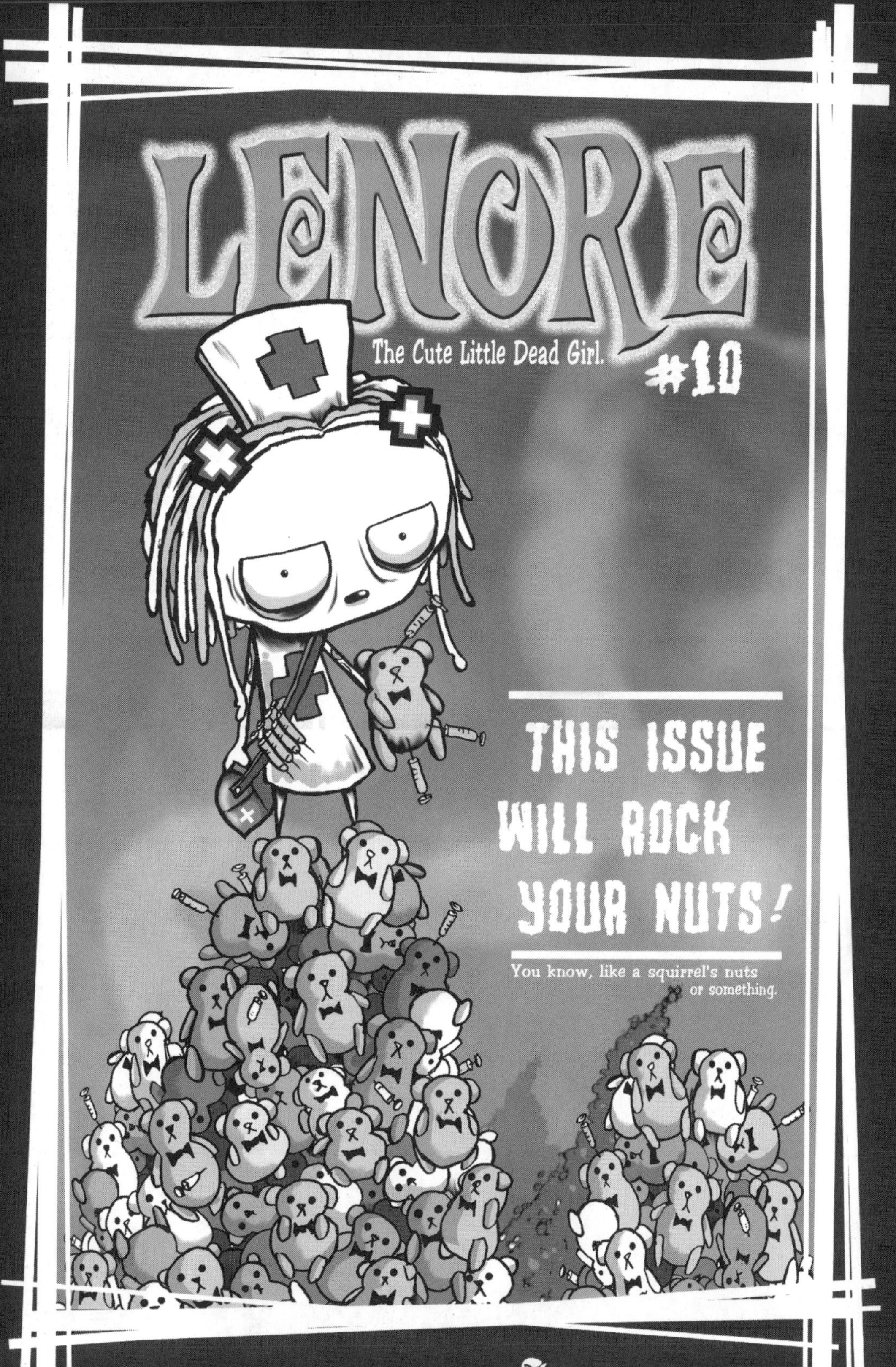
LENORE
The Cute Little Dead Girl.
#10
THIS ISSUE WILL ROCK YOUR NUTS!
You know, like a squirrel's nuts or something.

Issue #10

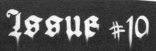

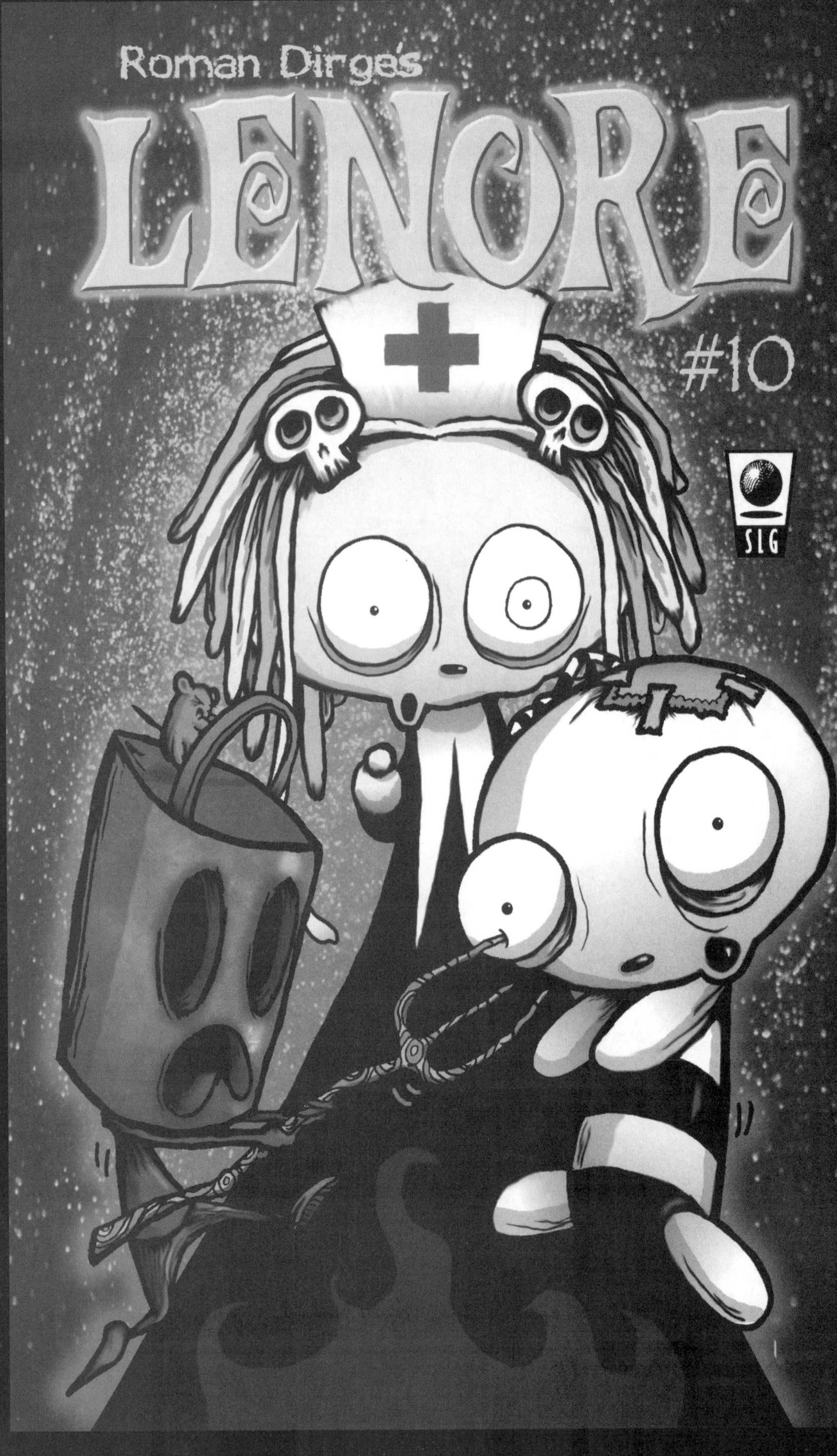
Roman Dirge's
LENORE
#10
SLG

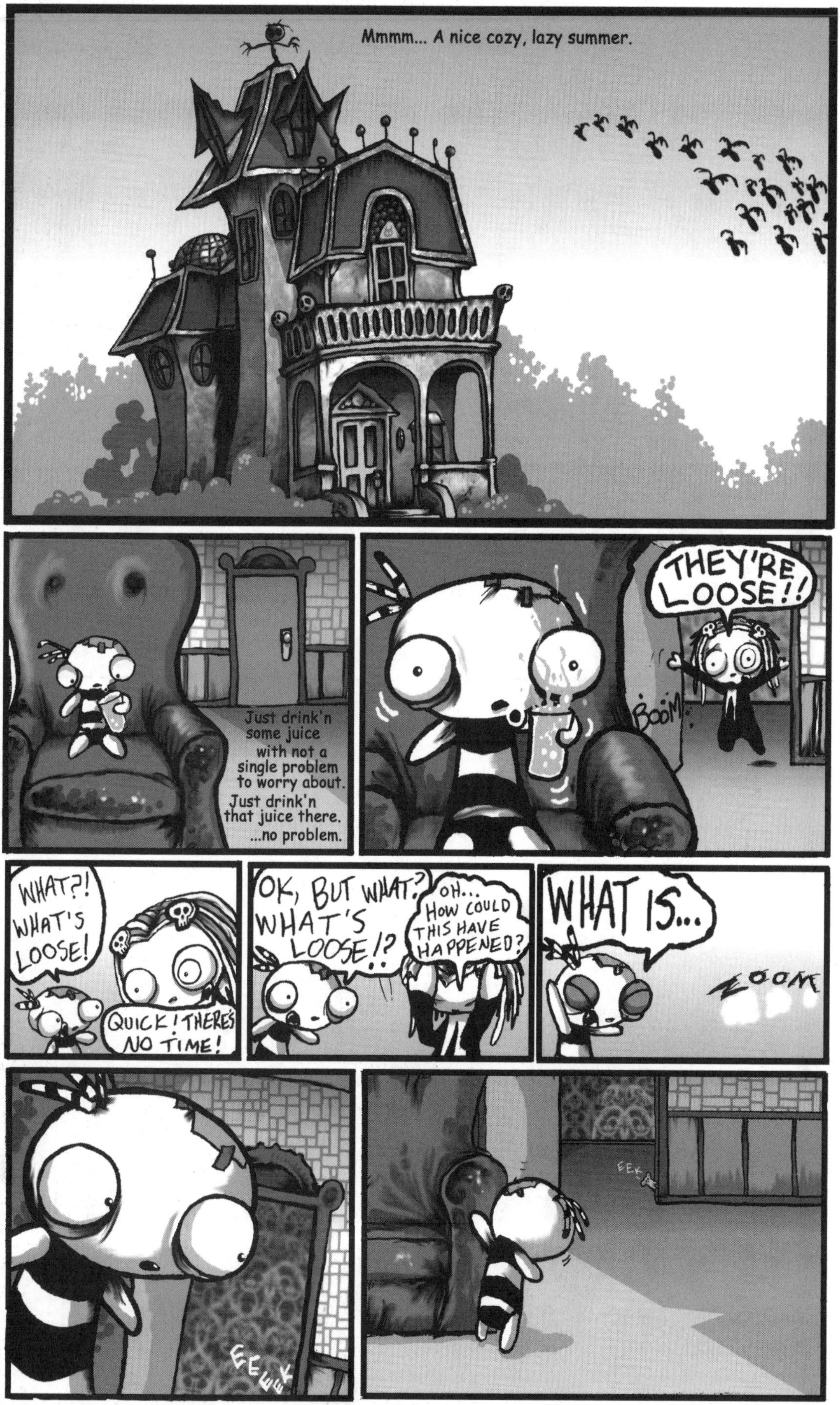

Mmmm... A nice cozy, lazy summer.
Just drink'n some juice with not a single problem to worry about. Just drink'n that juice there. ...no problem.
BOOM
THEY'RE LOOSE!!
WHAT?! WHAT'S LOOSE!
QUICK! THERE'S NO TIME!
OK, BUT WHAT? WHAT'S LOOSE!?
OH... HOW COULD THIS HAVE HAPPENED?
WHAT IS...
ZOOM
EEEK
EEK

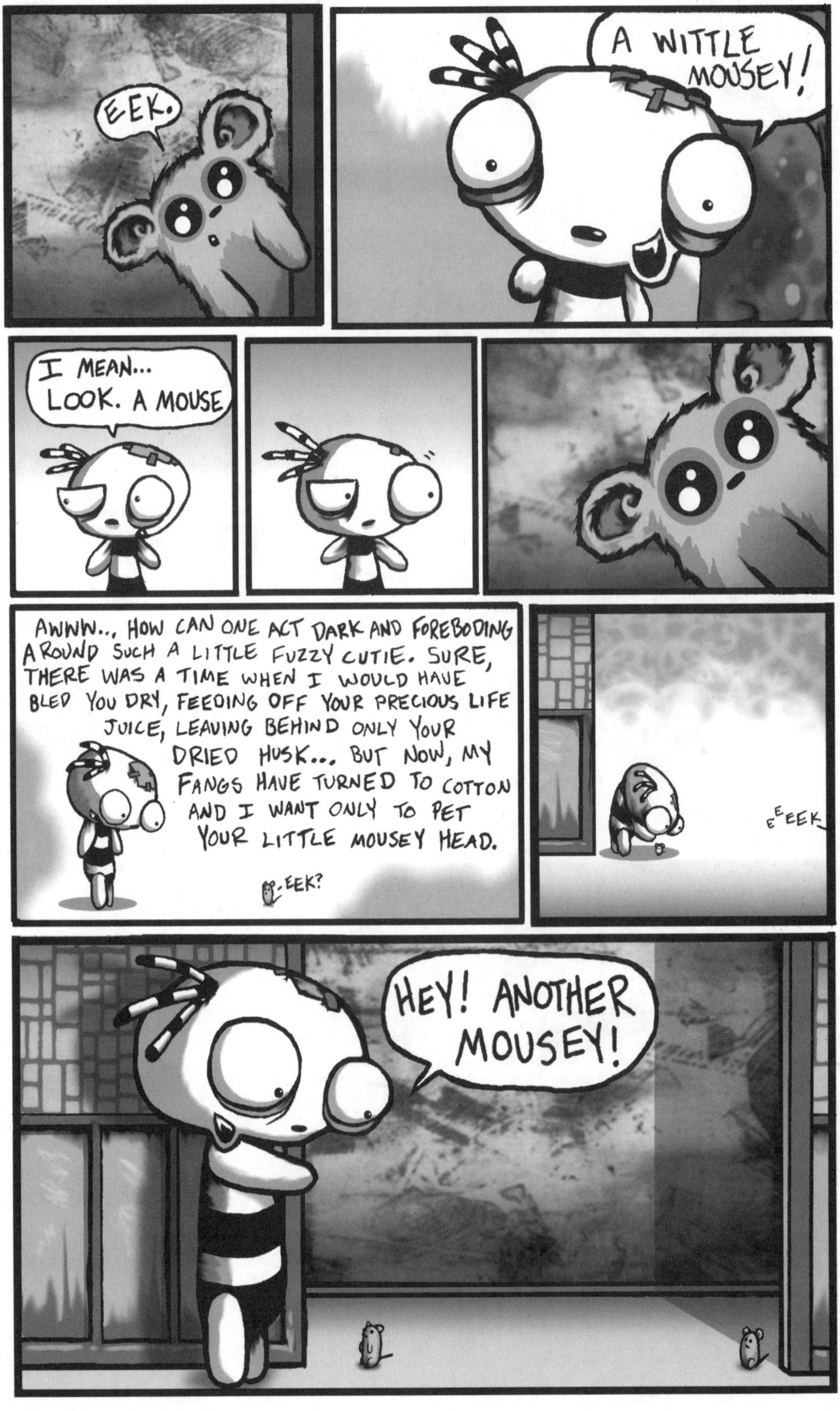
EEK.
A WITTLE MOUSEY!
I MEAN... LOOK. A MOUSE
AWWW.., HOW CAN ONE ACT DARK AND FOREBODING AROUND SUCH A LITTLE FUZZY CUTIE. SURE, THERE WAS A TIME WHEN I WOULD HAVE BLED YOU DRY, FEEDING OFF YOUR PRECIOUS LIFE JUICE, LEAVING BEHIND ONLY YOUR DRIED HUSK... BUT NOW, MY FANGS HAVE TURNED TO COTTON AND I WANT ONLY TO PET YOUR LITTLE MOUSEY HEAD.
-EEK?
EEEEK
HEY! ANOTHER MOUSEY!

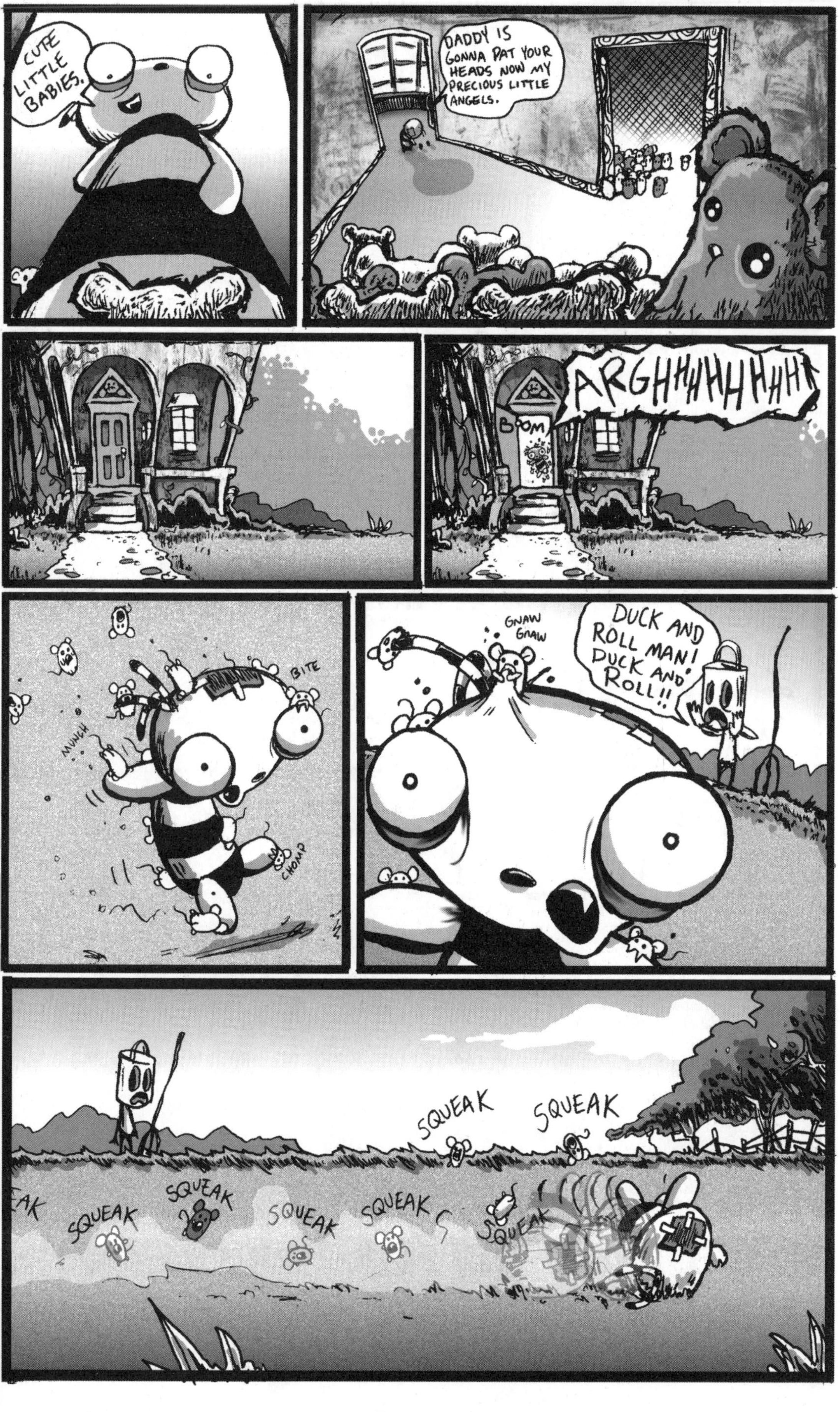
CUTE LITTLE BABIES.
DADDY IS GONNA PAT YOUR HEADS NOW MY PRECIOUS LITTLE ANGELS.
BOOM
ARGHHHHHHHH
BITE
MUNCH
CHOMP
GNAW GNAW
DUCK AND ROLL MAN! DUCK AND ROLL!!
SQUEAK
SQUEAK
EAK
SQUEAK
SQUEAK
SQUEAK
SQUEAK
SQUEAK

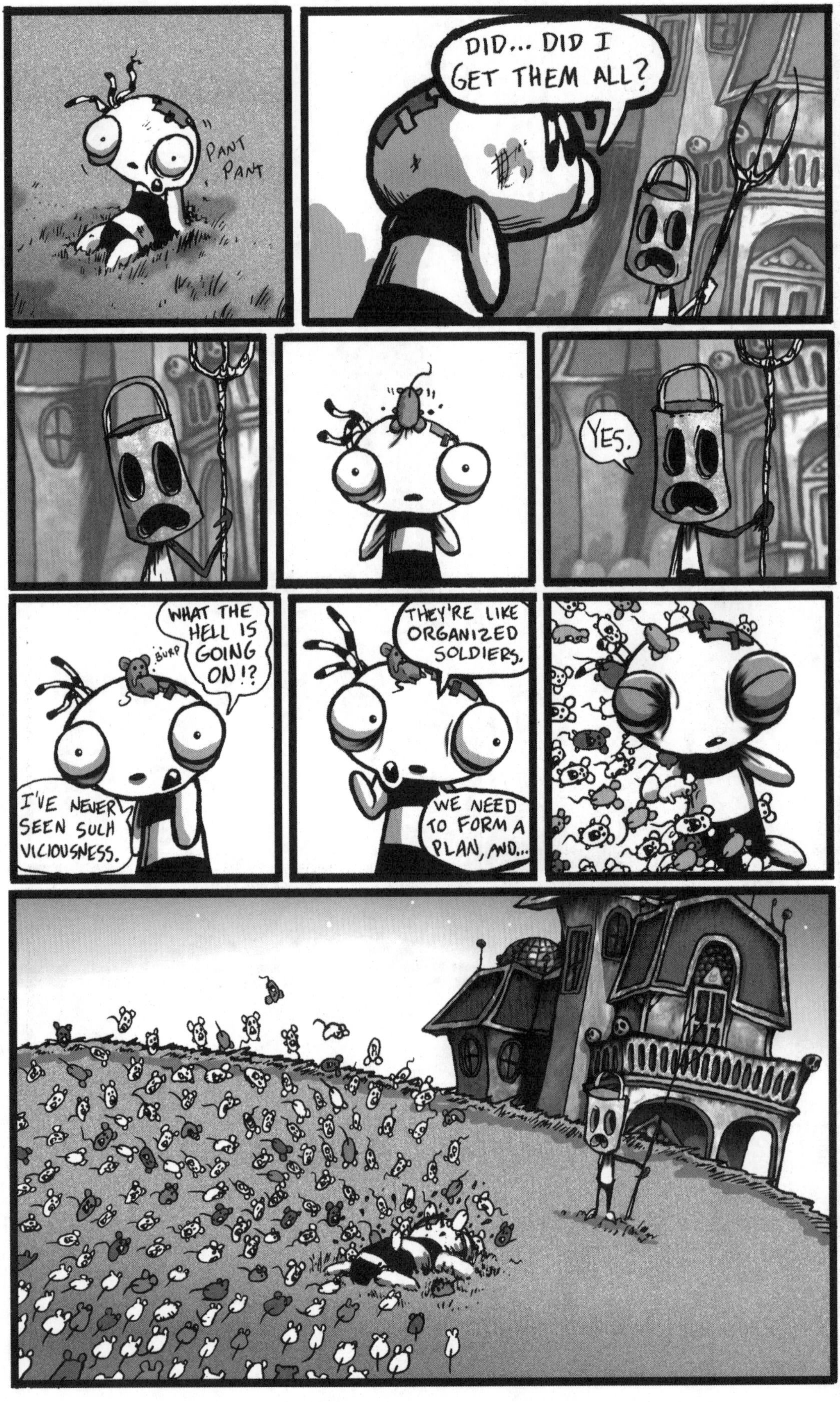
PANT
PANT
DID... DID I GET THEM ALL?
YES.
WHAT THE HELL IS GOING ON!?
BURP
I'VE NEVER SEEN SUCH VICIOUSNESS.
THEY'RE LIKE ORGANIZED SOLDIERS.
WE NEED TO FORM A PLAN, AND...

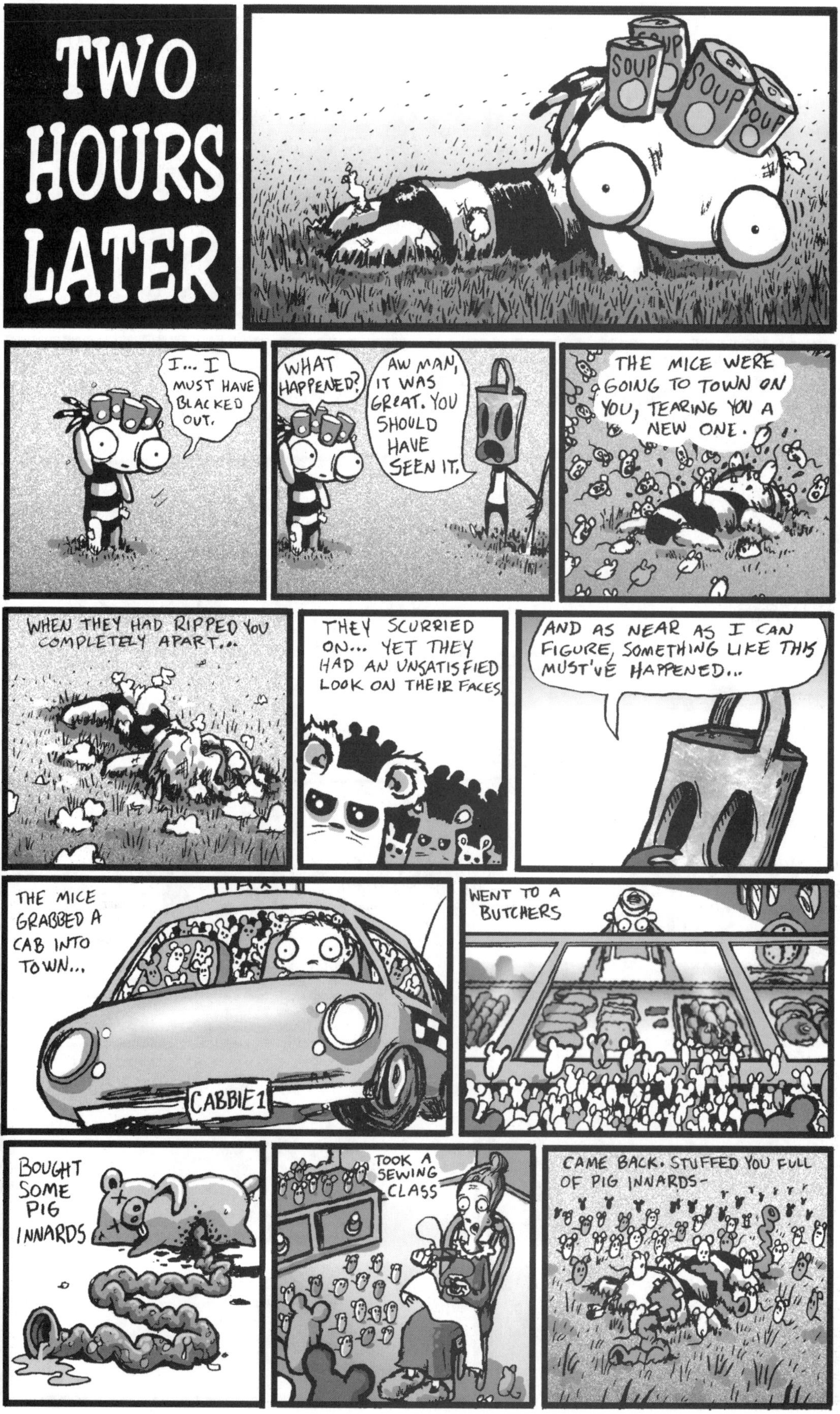
TWO HOURS LATER
SOUP
I... I MUST HAVE BLACKED OUT.
WHAT HAPPENED?
AW MAN, IT WAS GREAT. YOU SHOULD HAVE SEEN IT.
THE MICE WERE GOING TO TOWN ON YOU, TEARING YOU A NEW ONE.
WHEN THEY HAD RIPPED YOU COMPLETELY APART...
THEY SCURRIED ON... YET THEY HAD AN UNSATISFIED LOOK ON THEIR FACES.
AND AS NEAR AS I CAN FIGURE, SOMETHING LIKE THIS MUST'VE HAPPENED...
THE MICE GRABBED A CAB INTO TOWN...
CABBIE1
WENT TO A BUTCHERS
BOUGHT SOME PIG INNARDS
TOOK A SEWING CLASS
CAME BACK. STUFFED YOU FULL OF PIG INNARDS-

SEWED YOU BACK UP

ATE A SANDWICH

MUNCH MUNCH

AND THEN SAVAGELY RIPPED OUT YOUR INNARDS!!

WOO BOY, YOU SHOULD'VE SEEN IT! WHAT A BEAUTY!!

OH, C'MON! THAT DID NOT HAPPEN!

AND HOW COME NOTHING HAPPENED TO YOU?

THEY TRIED TO GET ME RIGHT AFTER FEASTING OFF YOUR PIGGY GUTS.

ARGH!

THUNK

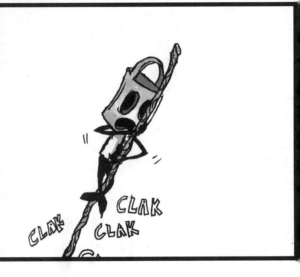

CLAK CLAK CLAK

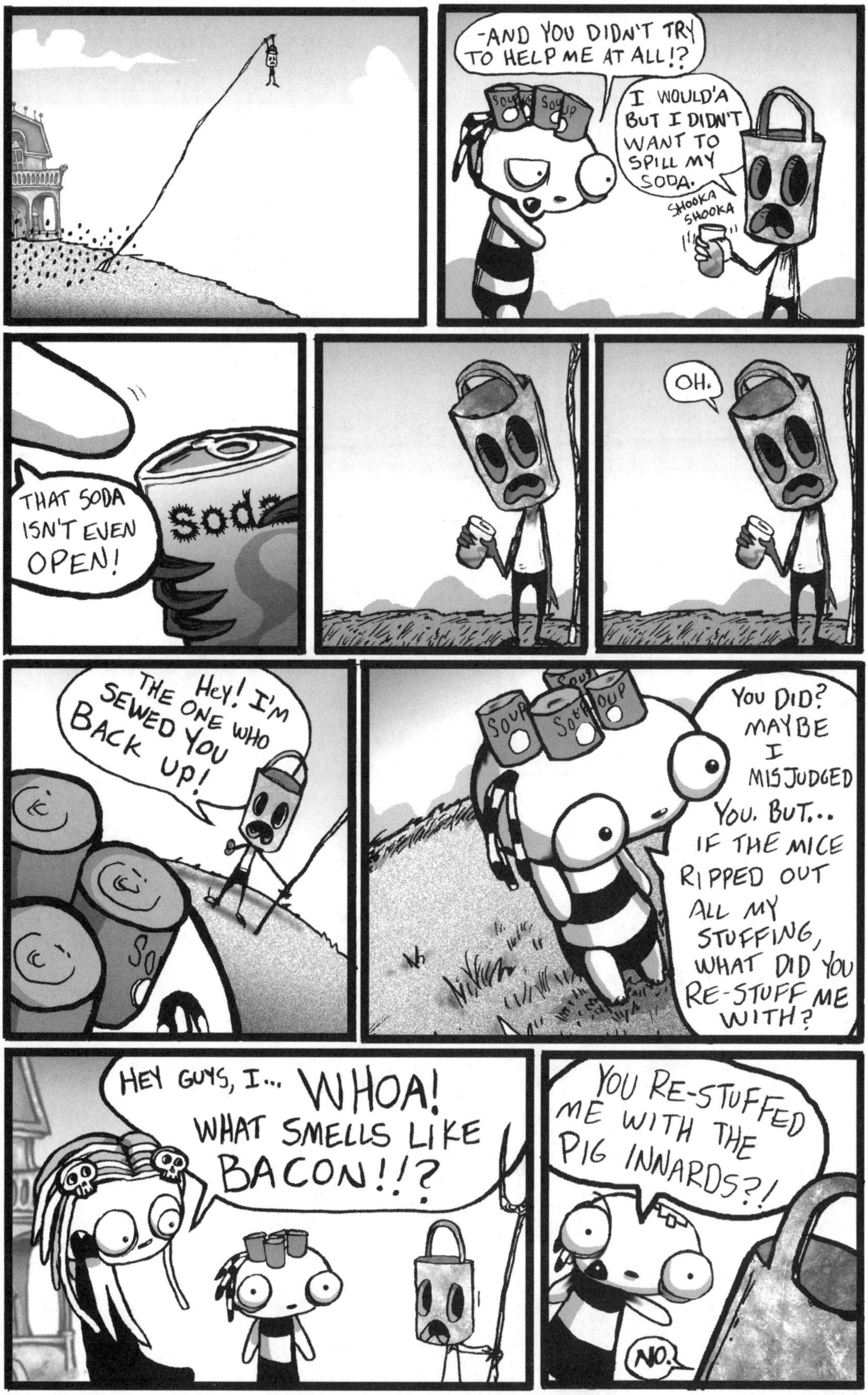

-AND YOU DIDN'T TRY TO HELP ME AT ALL!?
SOUP SOUP
I WOULD'A BUT I DIDN'T WANT TO SPILL MY SODA.
SHOOKA SHOOKA
THAT SODA ISN'T EVEN OPEN!
Soda
OH.
Hey! I'm THE ONE WHO SEWED YOU BACK UP!
You DID? MAYBE I MISJUDGED YOU. BUT... IF THE MICE RIPPED OUT ALL MY STUFFING, WHAT DID YOU RE-STUFF ME WITH?
HEY GUYS, I... WHOA! WHAT SMELLS LIKE BACON!!?
YOU RE-STUFFED ME WITH THE PIG INNARDS?!
NO.

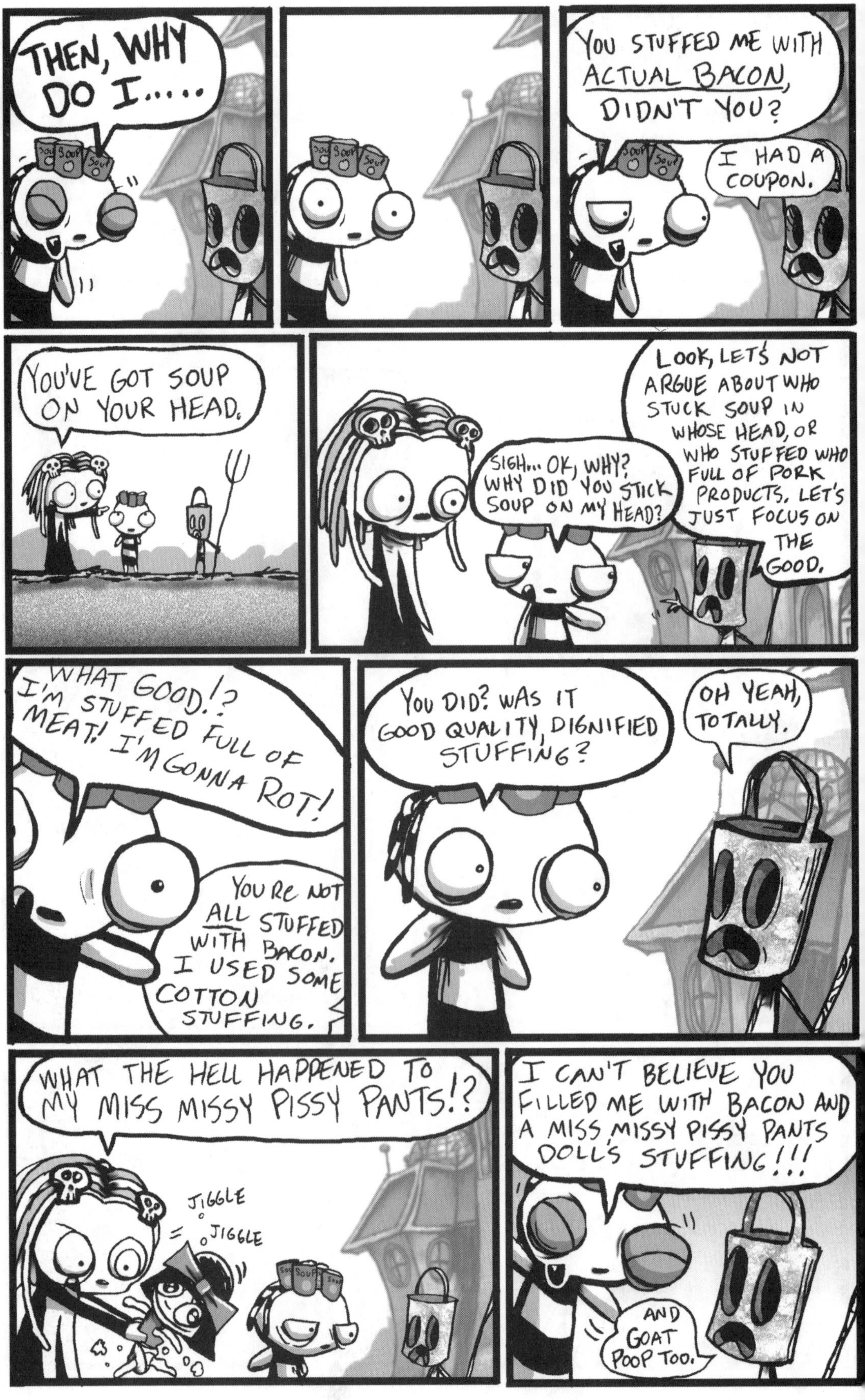
THEN, WHY DO I.....
SOUP SOUP SOUP
YOU STUFFED ME WITH ACTUAL BACON, DIDN'T YOU?
I HAD A COUPON.
YOU'VE GOT SOUP ON YOUR HEAD.
SIGH... OK, WHY? WHY DID YOU STICK SOUP ON MY HEAD?
LOOK, LET'S NOT ARGUE ABOUT WHO STUCK SOUP IN WHOSE HEAD, OR WHO STUFFED WHO FULL OF PORK PRODUCTS. LET'S JUST FOCUS ON THE GOOD.
WHAT GOOD!? I'M STUFFED FULL OF MEAT! I'M GONNA ROT!
YOU'RE NOT ALL STUFFED WITH BACON. I USED SOME COTTON STUFFING.
YOU DID? WAS IT GOOD QUALITY, DIGNIFIED STUFFING?
OH YEAH, TOTALLY.
WHAT THE HELL HAPPENED TO MY MISS MISSY PISSY PANTS!?
JIGGLE
JIGGLE
I CAN'T BELIEVE YOU FILLED ME WITH BACON AND A MISS MISSY PISSY PANTS DOLL'S STUFFING!!!
AND GOAT POOP TOO.

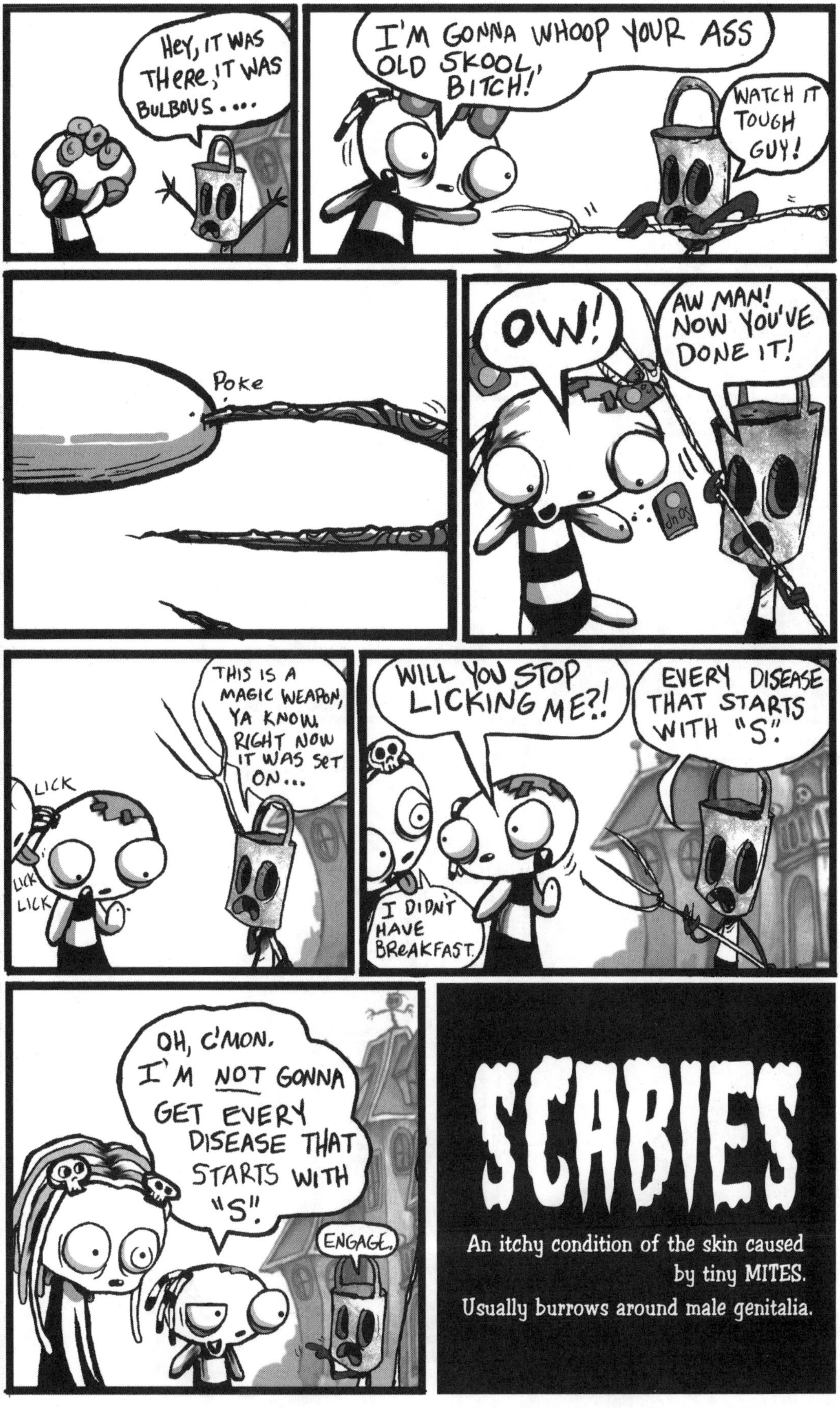
HEY, IT WAS THERE, IT WAS BULBOUS....
I'M GONNA WHOOP YOUR ASS OLD SKOOL, BITCH!
WATCH IT TOUGH GUY!
POKE
OW!
AW MAN! NOW YOU'VE DONE IT!
THIS IS A MAGIC WEAPON, YA KNOW. RIGHT NOW IT WAS SET ON...
LICK
LICK LICK
WILL YOU STOP LICKING ME?!
EVERY DISEASE THAT STARTS WITH "S".
I DIDN'T HAVE BREAKFAST.
OH, C'MON. I'M NOT GONNA GET EVERY DISEASE THAT STARTS WITH "S".
ENGAGE.
SCABIES
An itchy condition of the skin caused by tiny MITES.
Usually burrows around male genitalia.

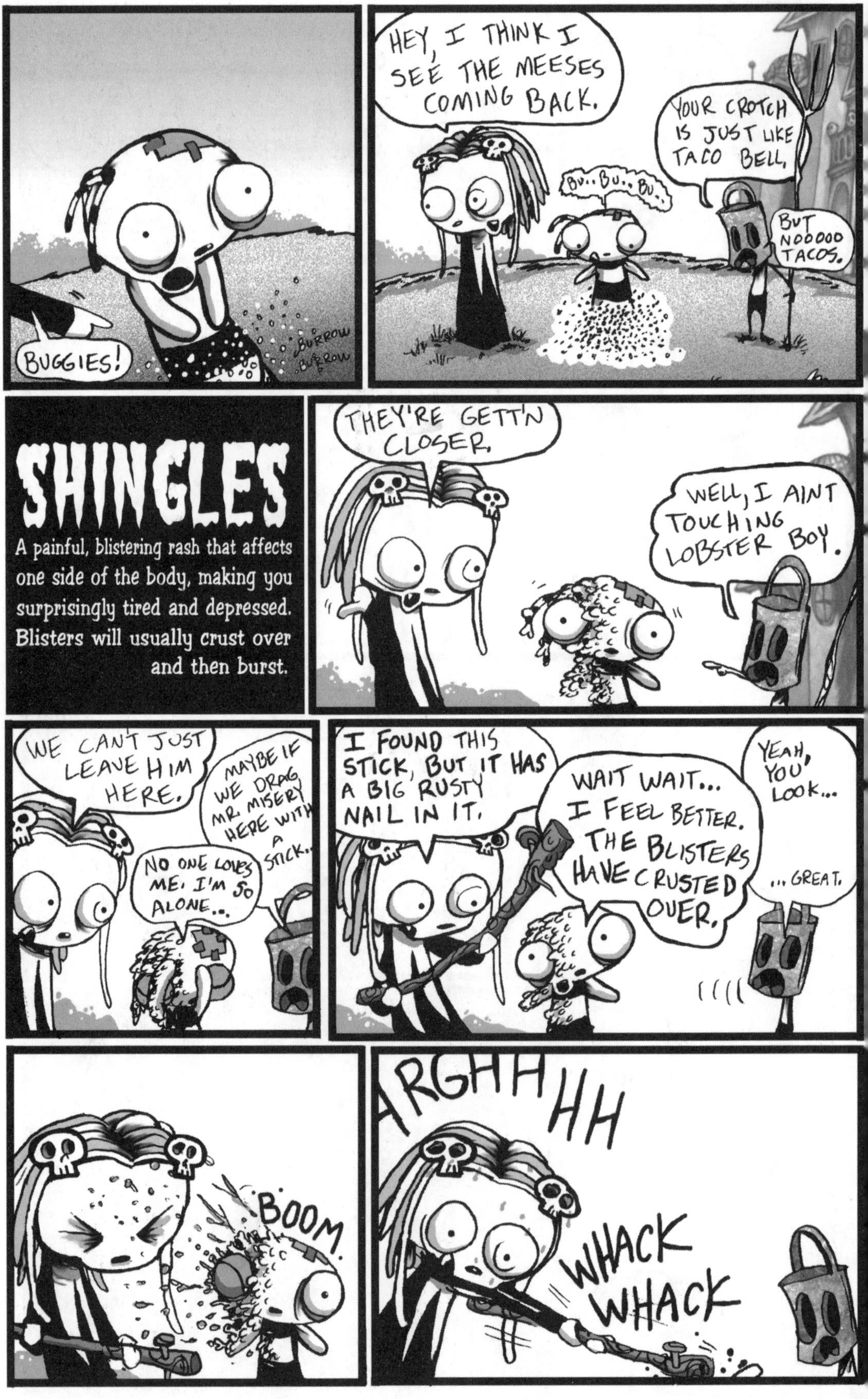
BUGGIES!
BURROW BURROW
HEY, I THINK I SEE THE MEESES COMING BACK.
BU.. BU.. BU..
YOUR CROTCH IS JUST LIKE TACO BELL,
BUT NOOOOO TACOS.
SHINGLES
A painful, blistering rash that affects one side of the body, making you surprisingly tired and depressed. Blisters will usually crust over and then burst.
THEY'RE GETT'N CLOSER.
WELL, I AINT TOUCHING LOBSTER BOY.
WE CAN'T JUST LEAVE HIM HERE.
MAYBE IF WE DRAG MR. MISERY HERE WITH A STICK...
NO ONE LOVES ME. I'M SO ALONE...
I FOUND THIS STICK, BUT IT HAS A BIG RUSTY NAIL IN IT.
WAIT WAIT... I FEEL BETTER. THE BLISTERS HAVE CRUSTED OVER.
YEAH, YOU LOOK...
...GREAT.
BOOM
ARGHHHH
WHACK
WHACK

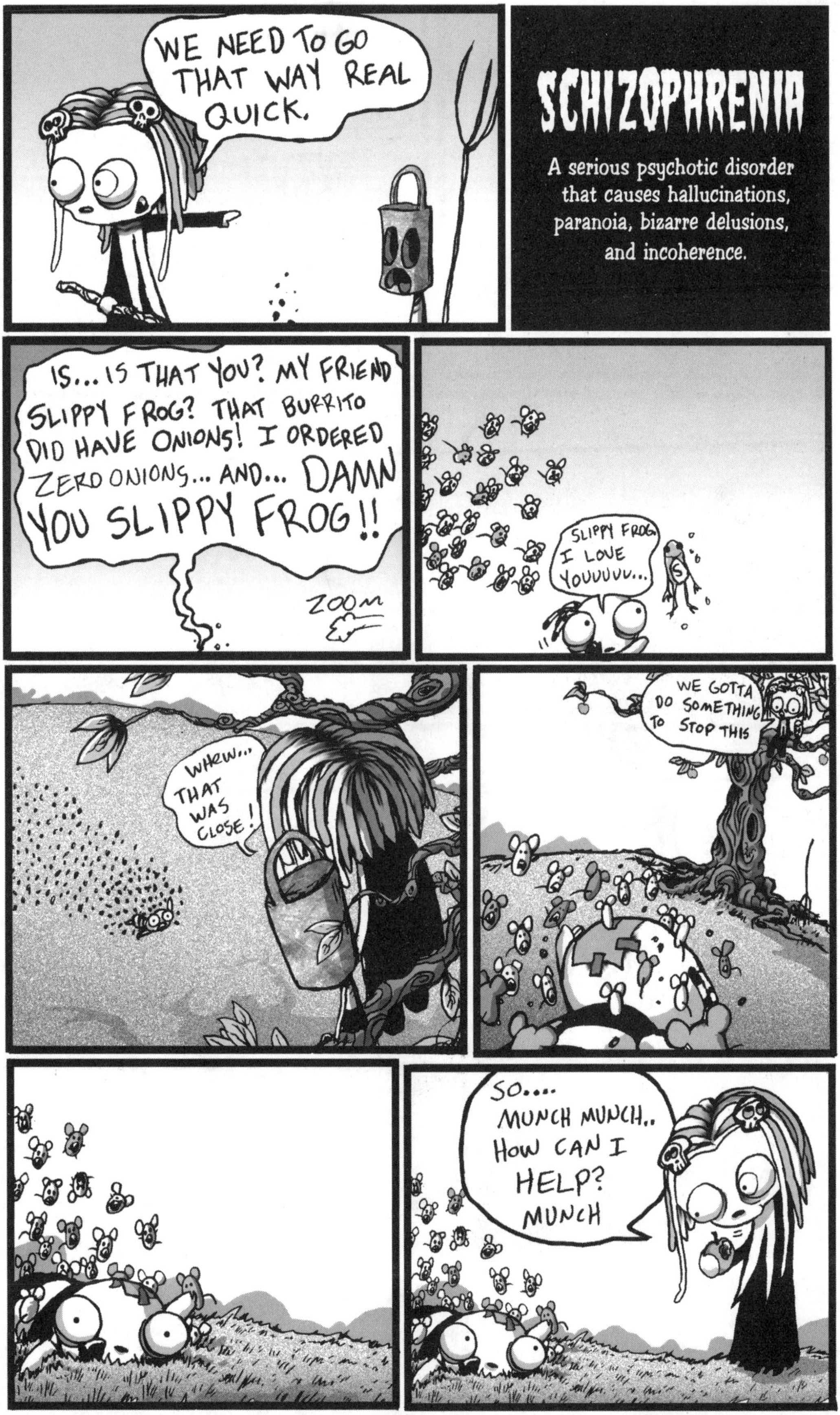
WE NEED TO GO THAT WAY REAL QUICK.
SCHIZOPHRENIA
A serious psychotic disorder that causes hallucinations, paranoia, bizarre delusions, and incoherence.
IS... IS THAT YOU? MY FRIEND SLIPPY FROG? THAT BURRITO DID HAVE ONIONS! I ORDERED ZERO ONIONS... AND... DAMN YOU SLIPPY FROG!!
ZOOM
SLIPPY FROG I LOVE YOUUUUU...
WHEW... THAT WAS CLOSE!
WE GOTTA DO SOMETHING TO STOP THIS
SO.... MUNCH MUNCH.. HOW CAN I HELP? MUNCH

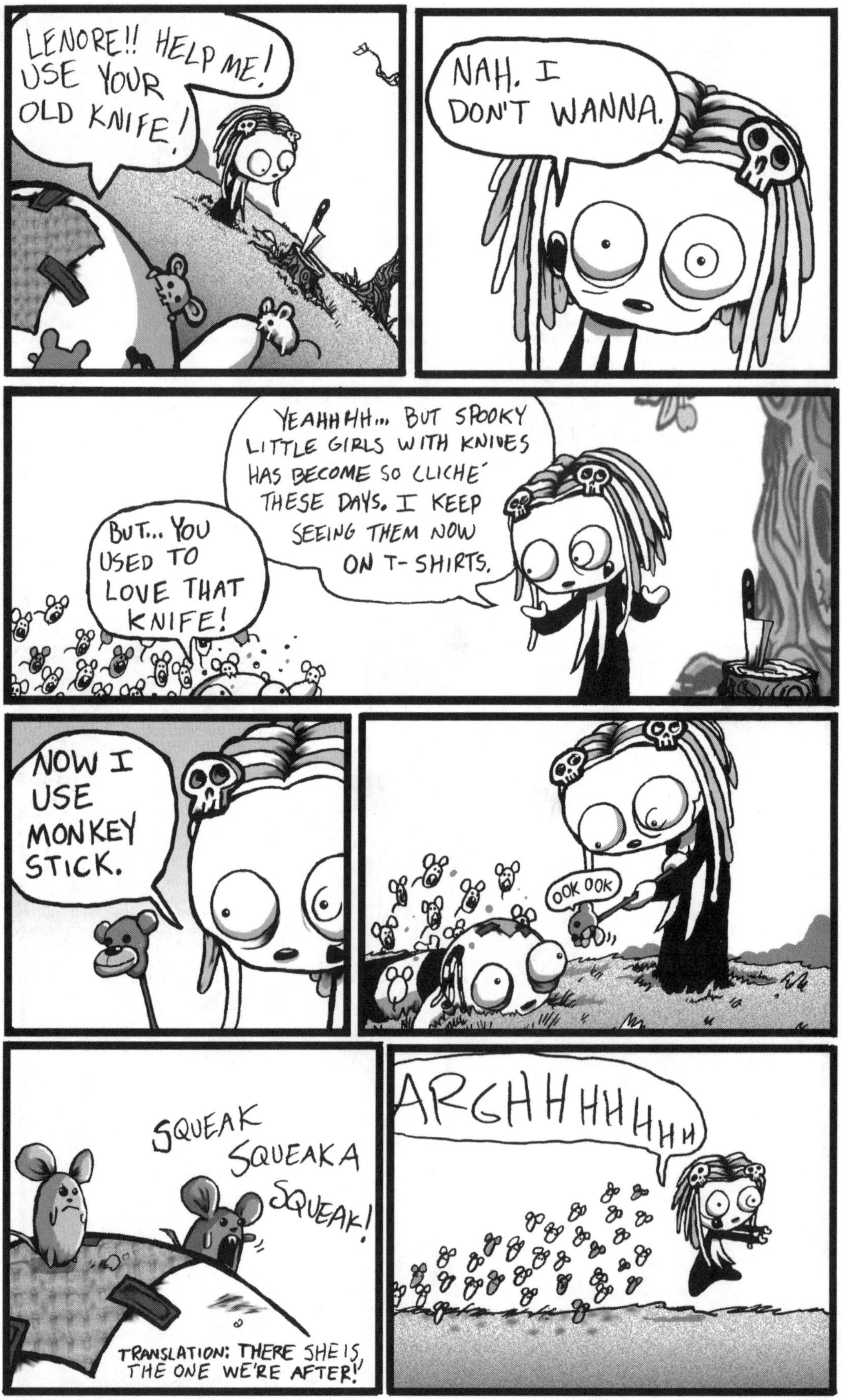
LENORE!! HELP ME! USE YOUR OLD KNIFE!
NAH. I DON'T WANNA.
BUT... YOU USED TO LOVE THAT KNIFE!
YEAHHHH... BUT SPOOKY LITTLE GIRLS WITH KNIVES HAS BECOME SO CLICHÉ THESE DAYS. I KEEP SEEING THEM NOW ON T-SHIRTS.
NOW I USE MONKEY STICK.
OOK OOK
SQUEAK SQUEAKA SQUEAK!
TRANSLATION: THERE SHE IS, THE ONE WE'RE AFTER!
ARGHHHHHHH

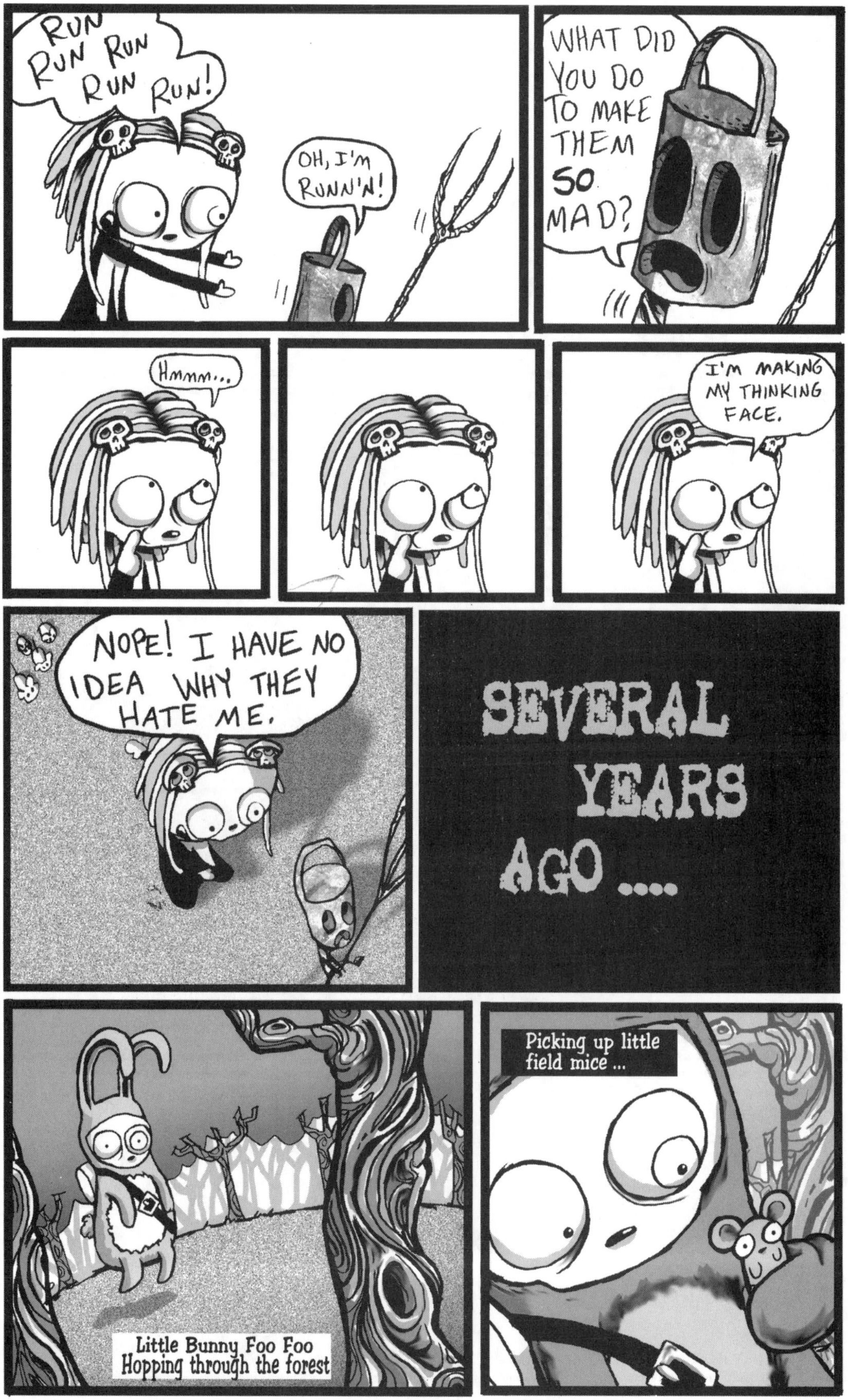
RUN RUN RUN RUN RUN RUN!
OH, I'M RUNN'N!
WHAT DID YOU DO TO MAKE THEM SO MAD?
Hmmm...
I'M MAKING MY THINKING FACE.
NOPE! I HAVE NO IDEA WHY THEY HATE ME.
SEVERAL YEARS AGO....
Little Bunny Foo Foo Hopping through the forest
Picking up little field mice ...

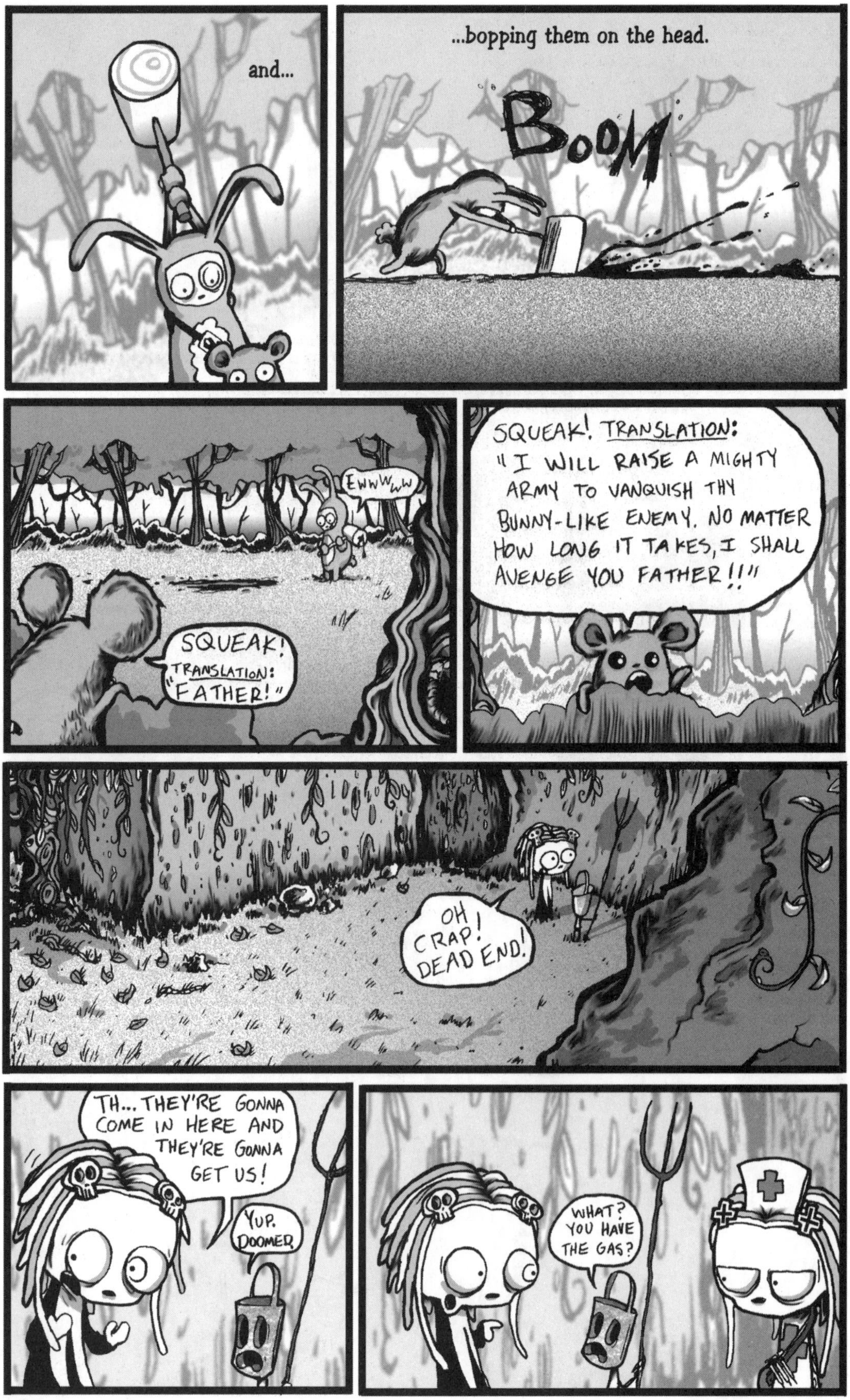
and...
...bopping them on the head.
BOOM
EWWWWW
SQUEAK! TRANSLATION: "FATHER!"
SQUEAK! TRANSLATION: "I WILL RAISE A MIGHTY ARMY TO VANQUISH THY BUNNY-LIKE ENEMY. NO MATTER HOW LONG IT TAKES, I SHALL AVENGE YOU FATHER!!"
OH CRAP! DEAD END!
TH... THEY'RE GONNA COME IN HERE AND THEY'RE GONNA GET US!
YUP. DOOMED.
WHAT? YOU HAVE THE GAS?

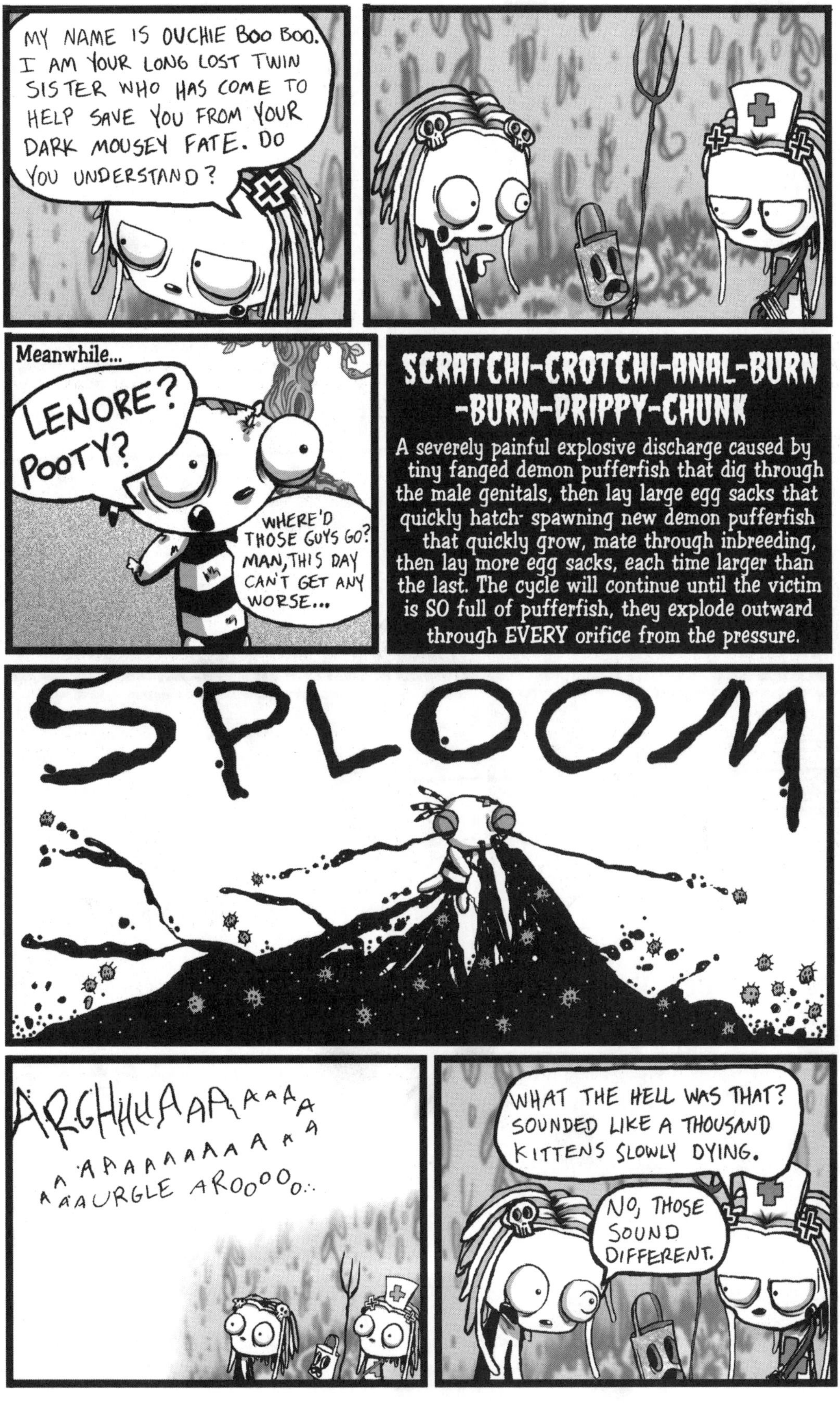
MY NAME IS OUCHIE BOO BOO. I AM YOUR LONG LOST TWIN SISTER WHO HAS COME TO HELP SAVE YOU FROM YOUR DARK MOUSEY FATE. DO YOU UNDERSTAND?
Meanwhile...
LENORE? POOTY?
WHERE'D THOSE GUYS GO? MAN, THIS DAY CAN'T GET ANY WORSE...
SCRATCHI-CROTCHI-ANAL-BURN -BURN-DRIPPY-CHUNK
A severely painful explosive discharge caused by tiny fanged demon pufferfish that dig through the male genitals, then lay large egg sacks that quickly hatch- spawning new demon pufferfish that quickly grow, mate through inbreeding, then lay more egg sacks, each time larger than the last. The cycle will continue until the victim is SO full of pufferfish, they explode outward through EVERY orifice from the pressure.
SPLOOM
ARGHHHAARAAAA AAAAAAAAAAAA AAAURGLE AROOOOO...
WHAT THE HELL WAS THAT? SOUNDED LIKE A THOUSAND KITTENS SLOWLY DYING.
NO, THOSE SOUND DIFFERENT.

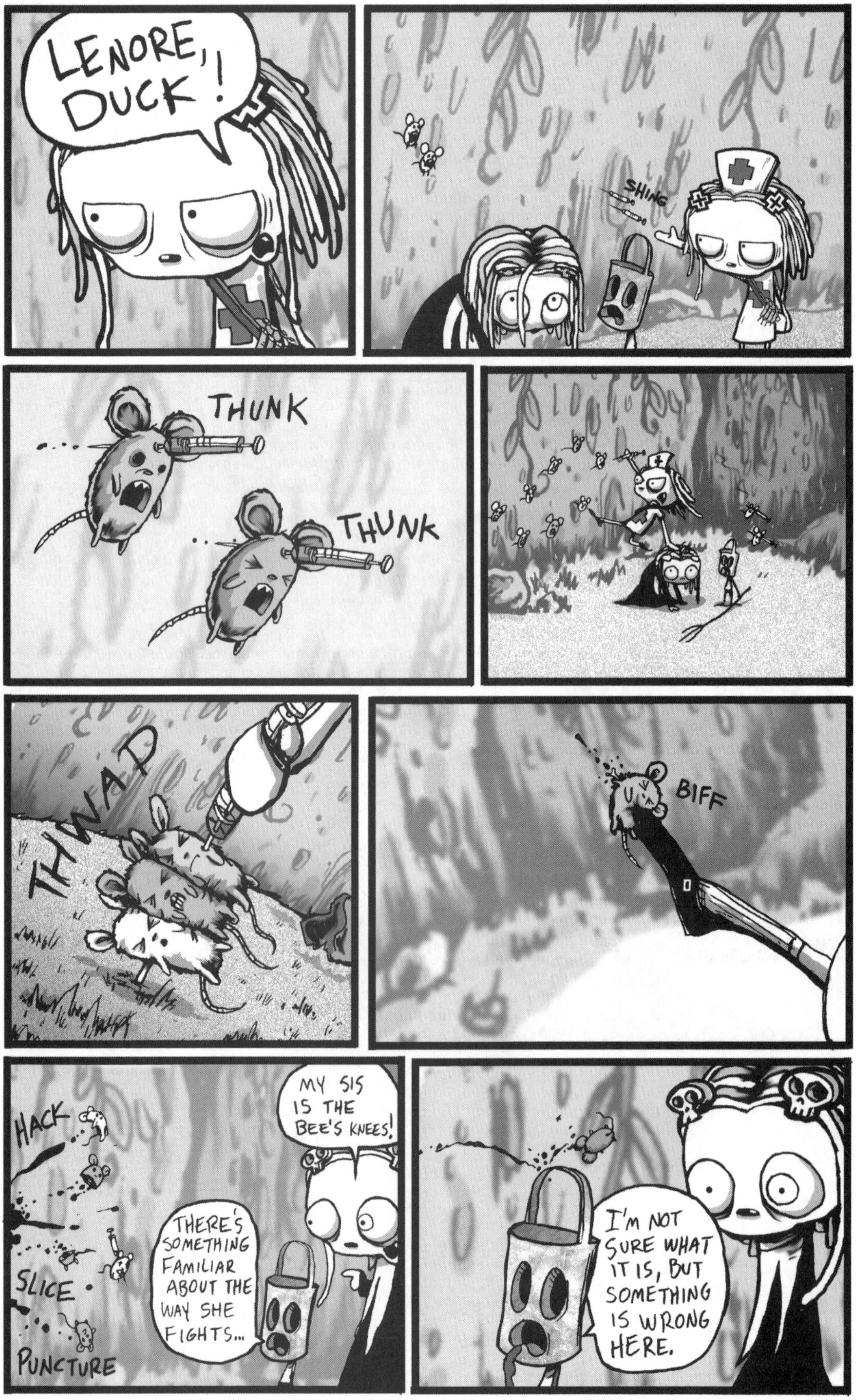
LENORE, DUCK!
SHING
THUNK
THUNK
THWAP
BIFF
HACK
SLICE
PUNCTURE
MY SIS IS THE BEE'S KNEES!
THERE'S SOMETHING FAMILIAR ABOUT THE WAY SHE FIGHTS...
I'M NOT SURE WHAT IT IS, BUT SOMETHING IS WRONG HERE.

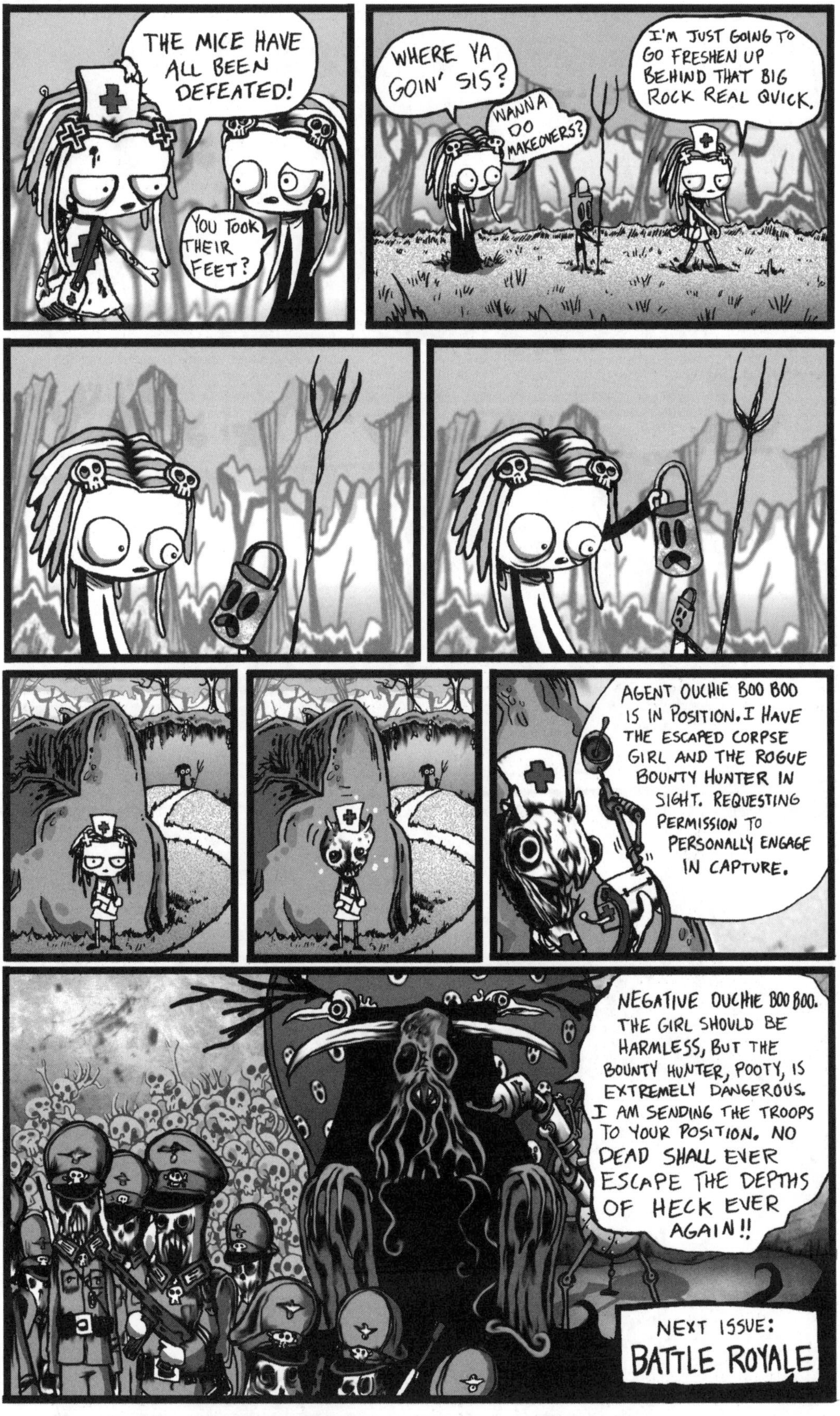
THE MICE HAVE ALL BEEN DEFEATED!
YOU TOOK THEIR FEET?
WHERE YA GOIN' SIS?
WANNA DO MAKEOVERS?
I'M JUST GOING TO GO FRESHEN UP BEHIND THAT BIG ROCK REAL QUICK.
AGENT OUCHIE BOO BOO IS IN POSITION. I HAVE THE ESCAPED CORPSE GIRL AND THE ROGUE BOUNTY HUNTER IN SIGHT. REQUESTING PERMISSION TO PERSONALLY ENGAGE IN CAPTURE.
NEGATIVE OUCHIE BOO BOO. THE GIRL SHOULD BE HARMLESS, BUT THE BOUNTY HUNTER, POOTY, IS EXTREMELY DANGEROUS. I AM SENDING THE TROOPS TO YOUR POSITION. NO DEAD SHALL EVER ESCAPE THE DEPTHS OF HECK EVER AGAIN!!
NEXT ISSUE:
BATTLE ROYALE

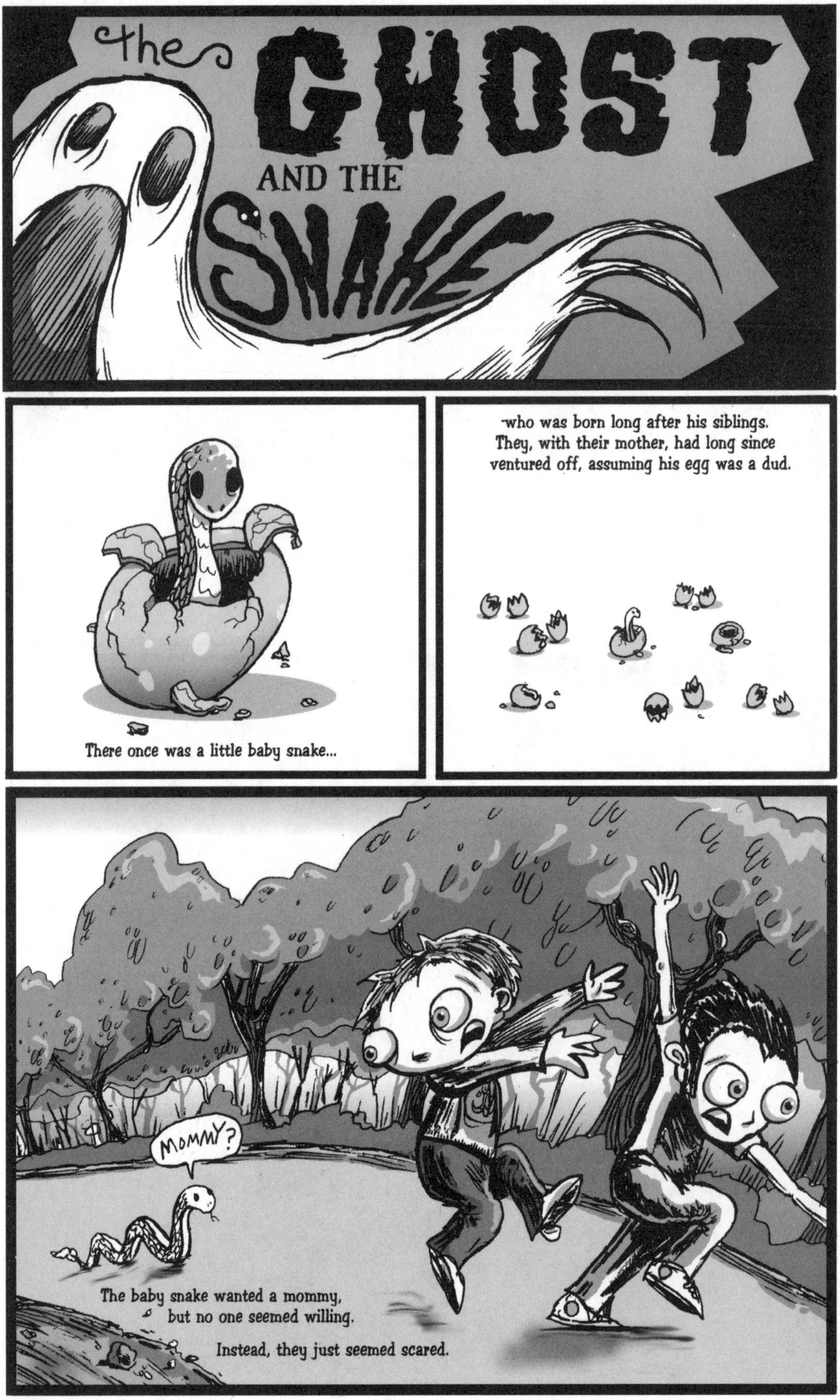

the GHOST AND THE SNAKE
There once was a little baby snake...
-who was born long after his siblings. They, with their mother, had long since ventured off, assuming his egg was a dud.
MOMMY?
The baby snake wanted a mommy, but no one seemed willing.
Instead, they just seemed scared.

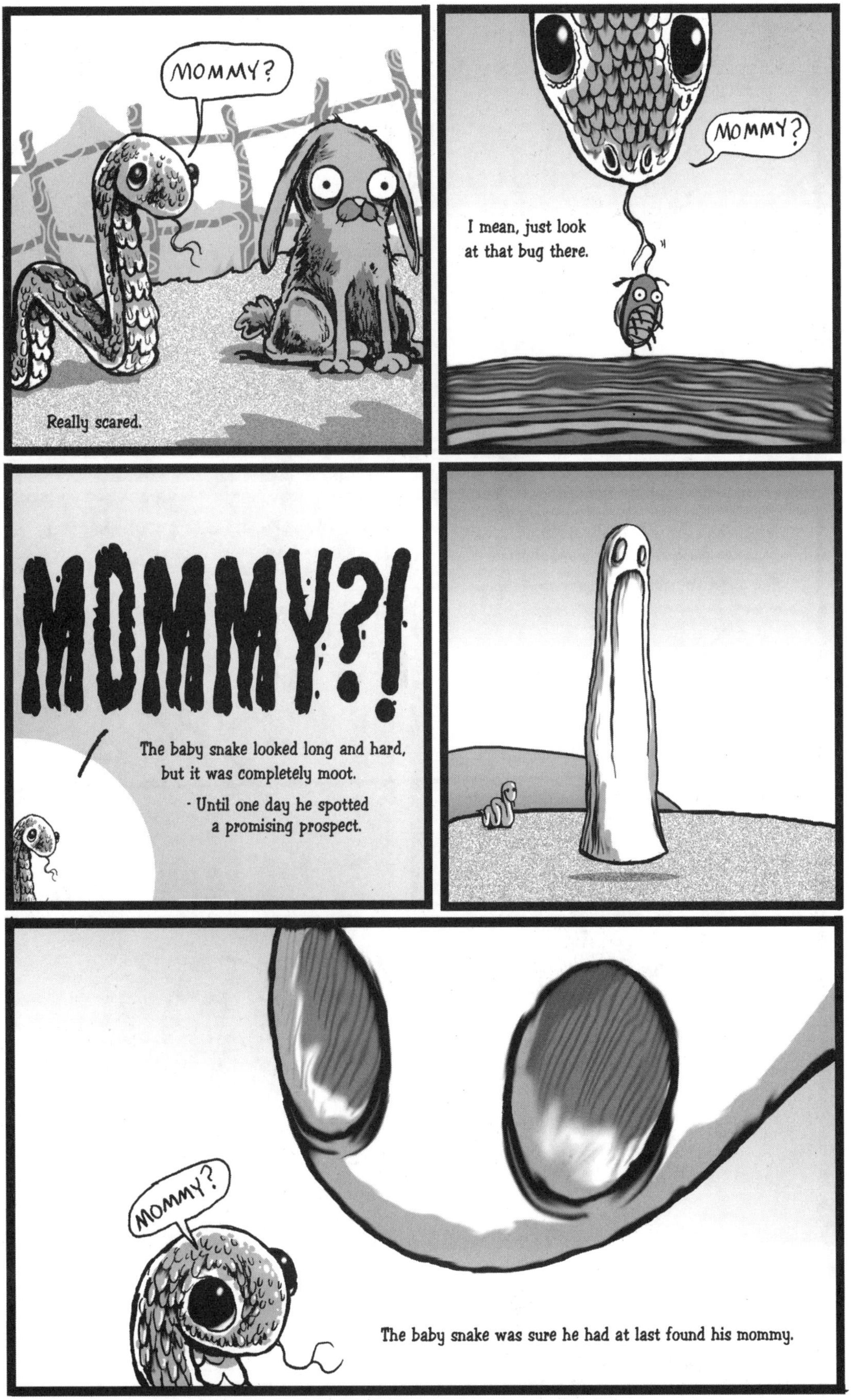
MOMMY?
Really scared.
I mean, just look at that bug there.
MOMMY?
MOMMY?!
The baby snake looked long and hard, but it was completely moot.
- Until one day he spotted a promising prospect.
MOMMY?
The baby snake was sure he had at last found his mommy.

The ghost had no arms, just like the baby snake.

Others were scared of the ghost, much like they were of the baby snake.

AIEEE

However, the ghost insisted the baby snake was wrong. The ghost is a floaty spectral creature, and the snake is a scaled living thing.

The ghost sent the baby snake on his way.

The baby snake was so busy pondering this, he did not see the car.

...And the baby snake was sure he had at last found his mommy.

MOMMY!!

AW 'CRAP...

oAT FLOAT FLOAT FLOAT FLOAT FLOAT

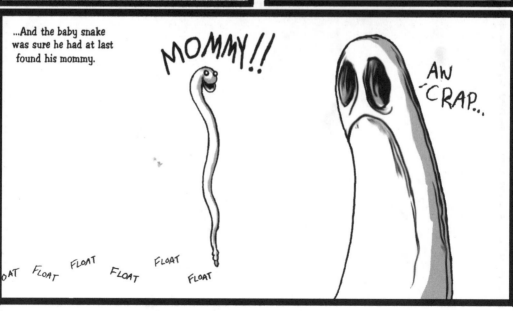

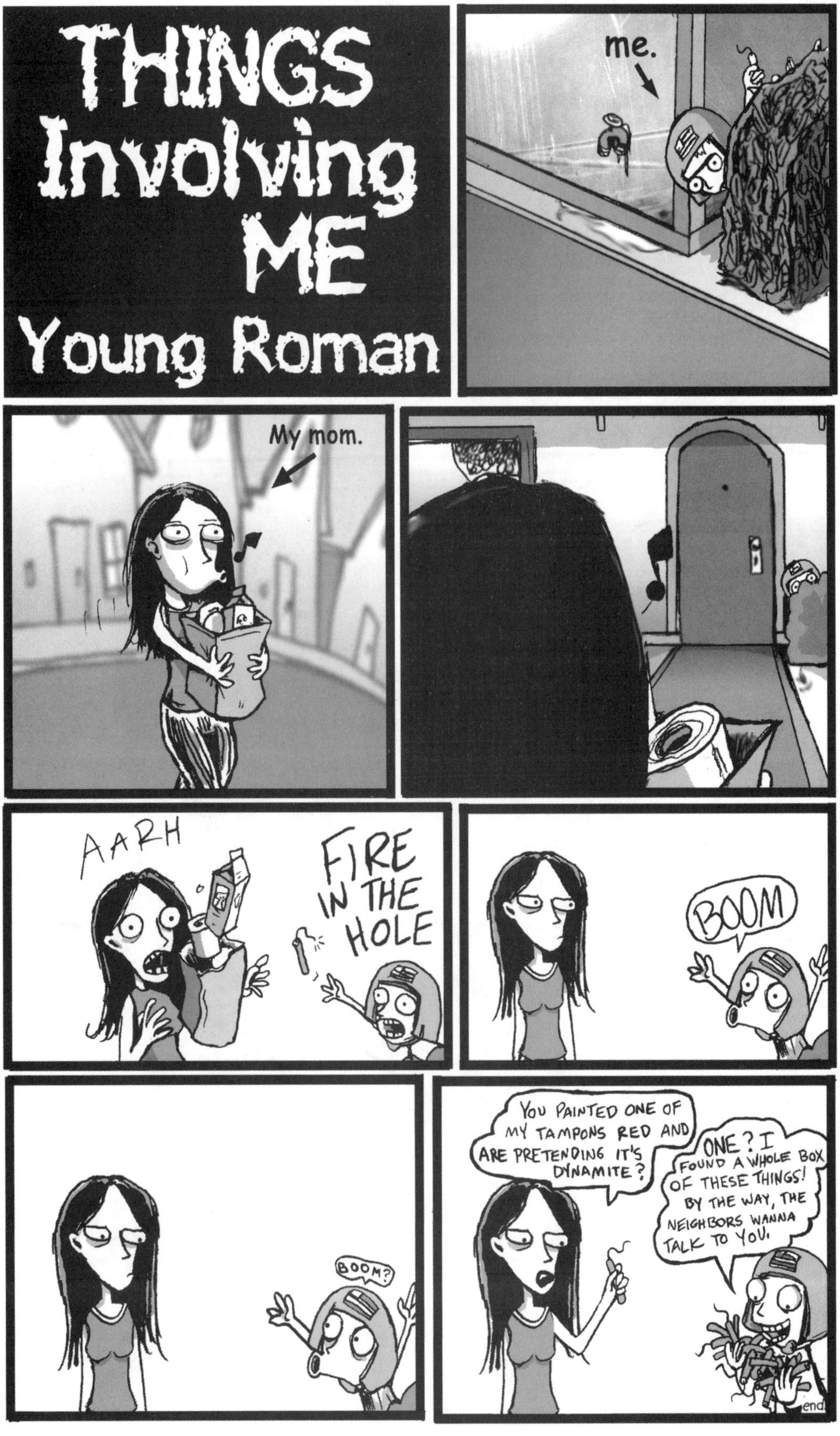
THINGS Involving ME
Young Roman
me.
My mom.
AARH
FIRE IN THE HOLE
BOOM
BOOM?
YOU PAINTED ONE OF MY TAMPONS RED AND ARE PRETENDING IT'S DYNAMITE?
ONE? I FOUND A WHOLE BOX OF THESE THINGS! BY THE WAY, THE NEIGHBORS WANNA TALK TO YOU.
end

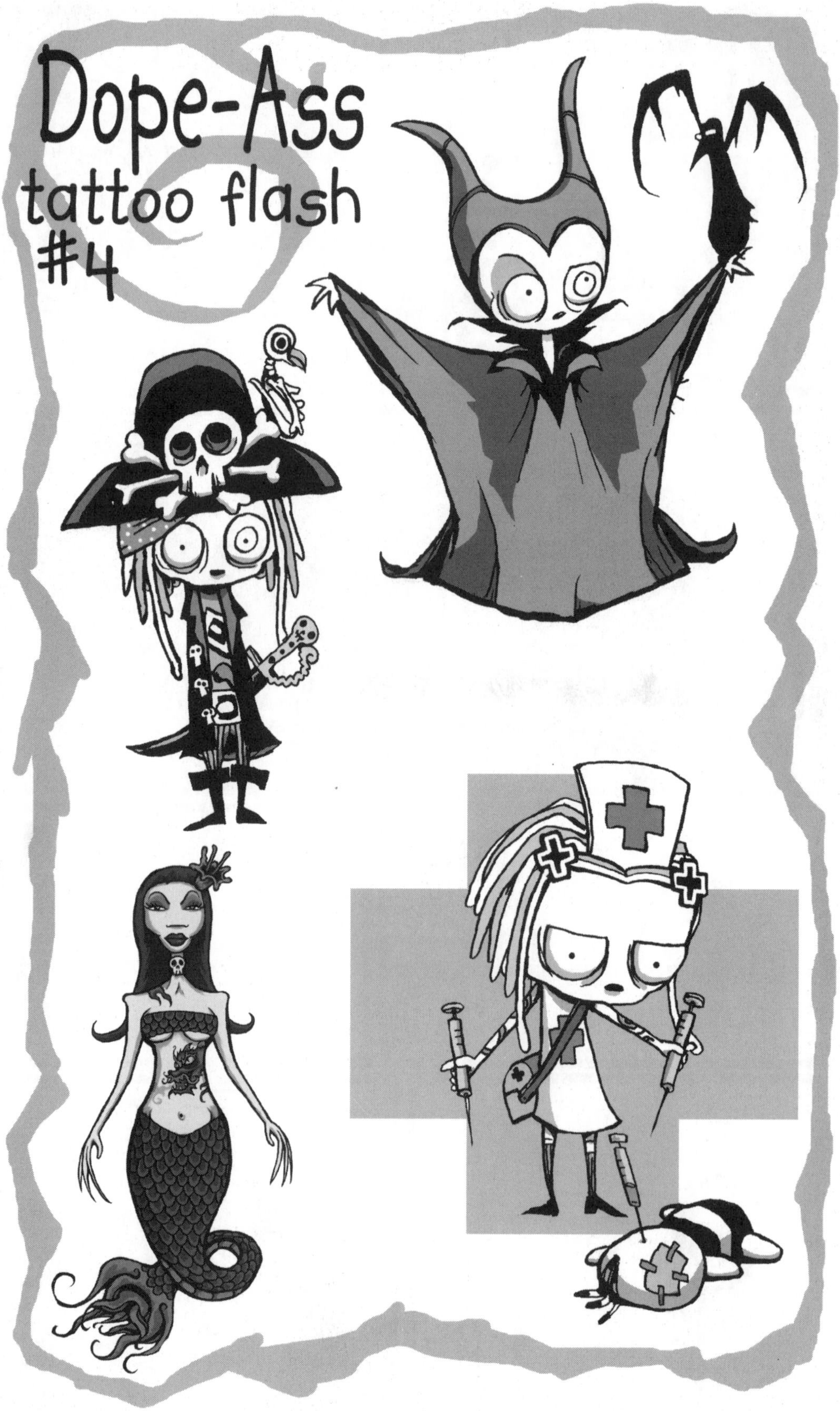
Dope-Ass
tattoo flash
#4

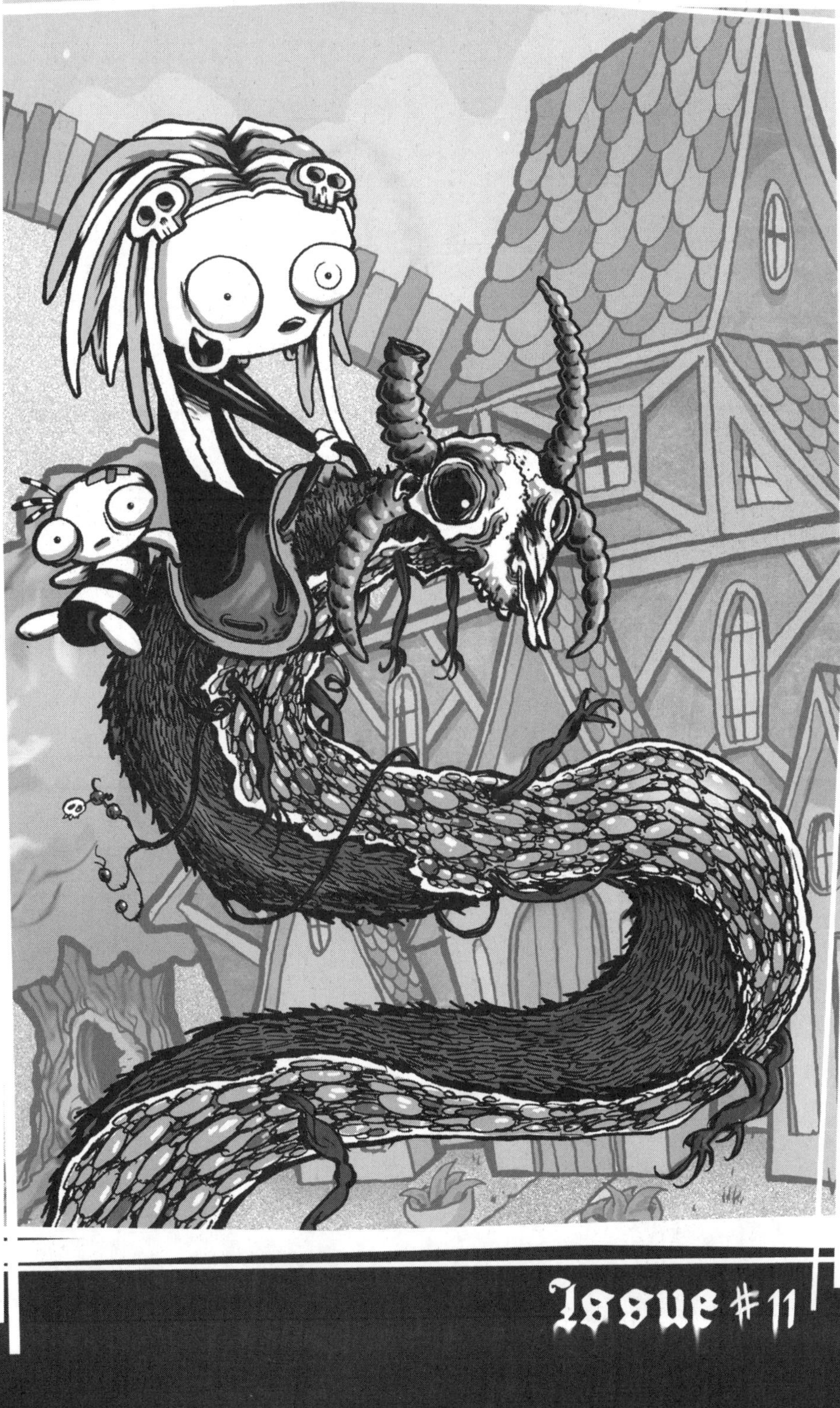

Issue #11

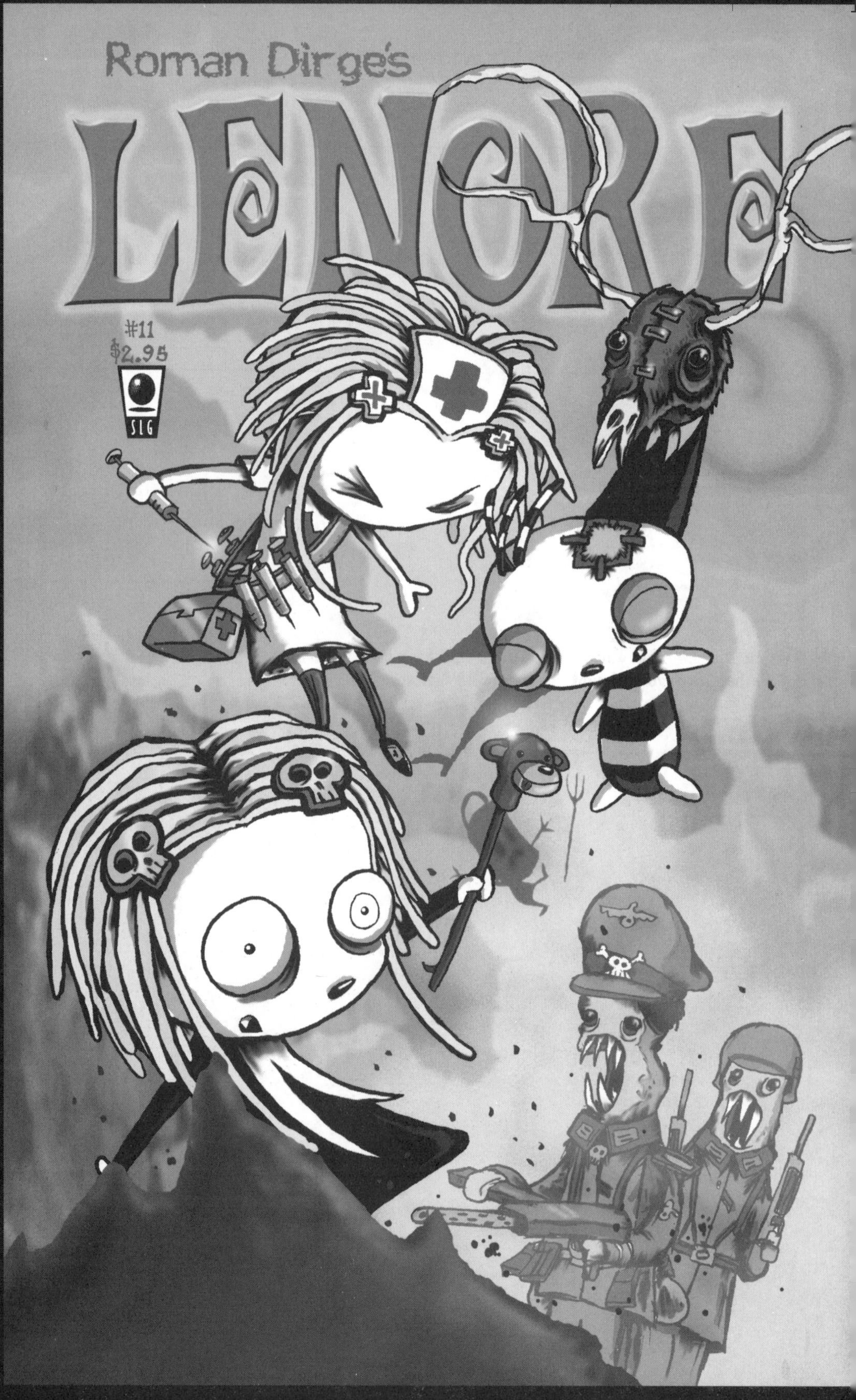

Roman Dirge's
LENORE
#11
$2.95
SLG

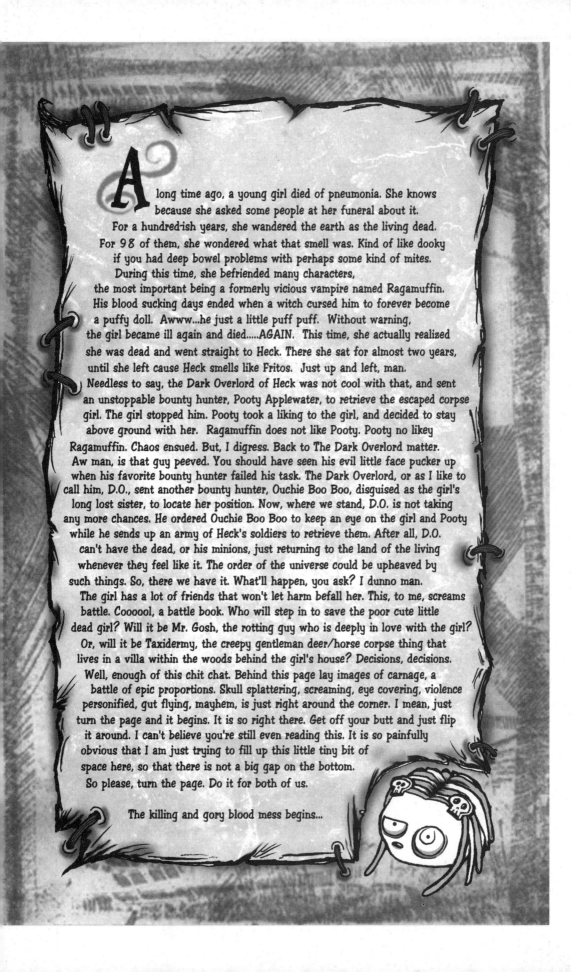

A long time ago, a young girl died of pneumonia. She knows because she asked some people at her funeral about it. For a hundred-ish years, she wandered the earth as the living dead. For 98 of them, she wondered what that smell was. Kind of like dooky if you had deep bowel problems with perhaps some kind of mites. During this time, she befriended many characters, the most important being a formerly vicious vampire named Ragamuffin. His blood sucking days ended when a witch cursed him to forever become a puffy doll. Awww...he just a little puff puff. Without warning, the girl became ill again and died.....AGAIN. This time, she actually realized she was dead and went straight to Heck. There she sat for almost two years, until she left cause Heck smells like Fritos. Just up and left, man. Needless to say, the Dark Overlord of Heck was not cool with that, and sent an unstoppable bounty hunter, Pooty Applewater, to retrieve the escaped corpse girl. The girl stopped him. Pooty took a liking to the girl, and decided to stay above ground with her. Ragamuffin does not like Pooty. Pooty no likey Ragamuffin. Chaos ensued. But, I digress. Back to The Dark Overlord matter. Aw man, is that guy peeved. You should have seen his evil little face pucker up when his favorite bounty hunter failed his task. The Dark Overlord, or as I like to call him, D.O., sent another bounty hunter, Ouchie Boo Boo, disguised as the girl's long lost sister, to locate her position. Now, where we stand, D.O. is not taking any more chances. He ordered Ouchie Boo Boo to keep an eye on the girl and Pooty while he sends up an army of Heck's soldiers to retrieve them. After all, D.O. can't have the dead, or his minions, just returning to the land of the living whenever they feel like it. The order of the universe could be upheaved by such things. So, there we have it. What'll happen, you ask? I dunno man. The girl has a lot of friends that won't let harm befall her. This, to me, screams battle. Coooool, a battle book. Who will step in to save the poor cute little dead girl? Will it be Mr. Gosh, the rotting guy who is deeply in love with the girl? Or, will it be Taxidermy, the creepy gentleman deer/horse corpse thing that lives in a villa within the woods behind the girl's house? Decisions, decisions. Well, enough of this chit chat. Behind this page lay images of carnage, a battle of epic proportions. Skull splattering, screaming, eye covering, violence personified, gut flying, mayhem, is just right around the corner. I mean, just turn the page and it begins. It is so right there. Get off your butt and just flip it around. I can't believe you're still even reading this. It is so painfully obvious that I am just trying to fill up this little tiny bit of space here, so that there is not a big gap on the bottom. So please, turn the page. Do it for both of us.

The killing and gory blood mess begins...

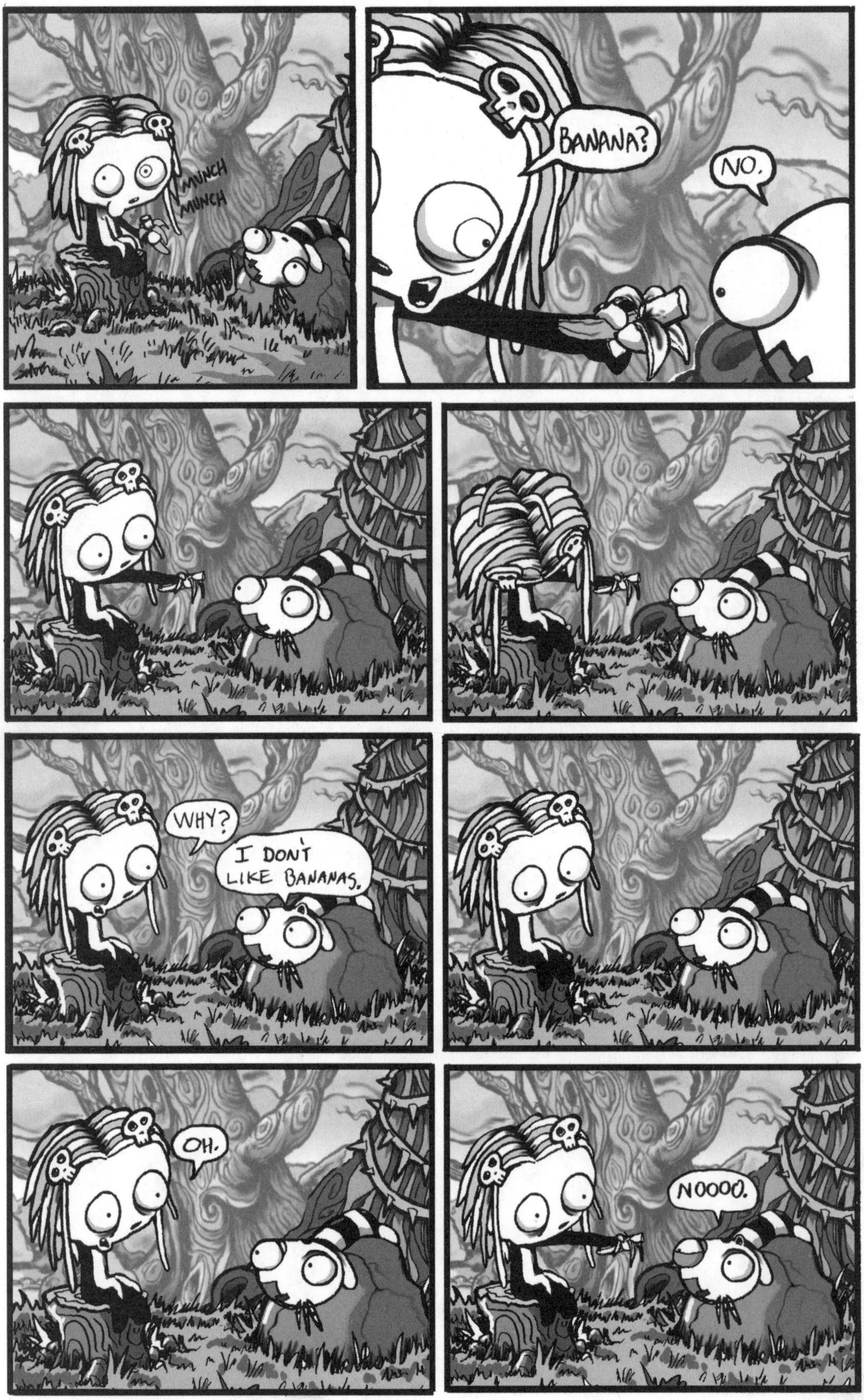
MUNCH
MUNCH
BANANA?
NO.
WHY?
I DON'T LIKE BANANAS.
OH.
NOOOO.

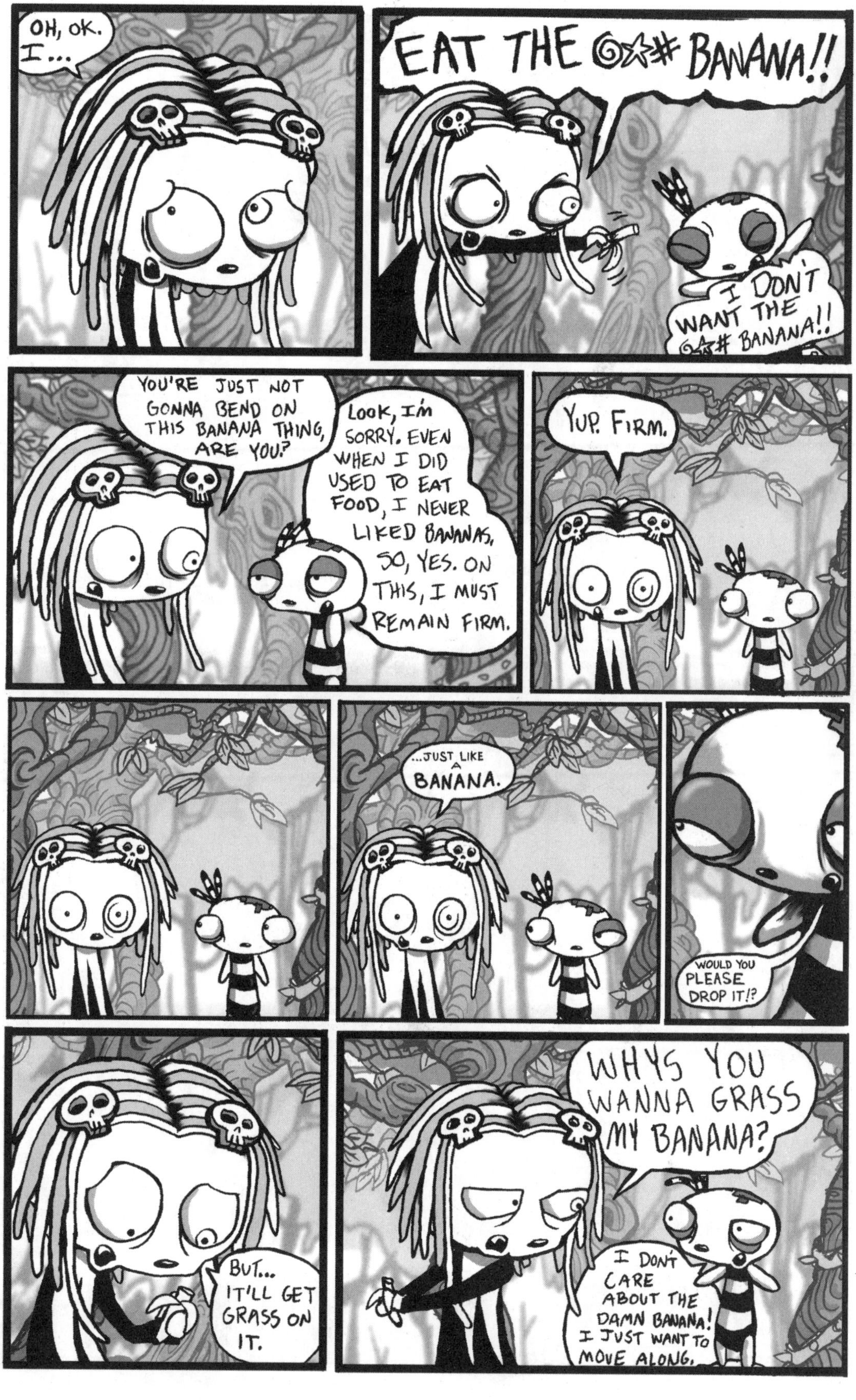
OH, OK. I...
EAT THE @☆# BANANA!!
I DON'T WANT THE @☆# BANANA!!
YOU'RE JUST NOT GONNA BEND ON THIS BANANA THING, ARE YOU?
LOOK, I'M SORRY. EVEN WHEN I DID USED TO EAT FOOD, I NEVER LIKED BANANAS. SO, YES. ON THIS, I MUST REMAIN FIRM.
YUP. FIRM.
...JUST LIKE A BANANA.
WOULD YOU PLEASE DROP IT!?
BUT... IT'LL GET GRASS ON IT.
WHYS YOU WANNA GRASS MY BANANA?
I DON'T CARE ABOUT THE DAMN BANANA! I JUST WANT TO MOVE ALONG.

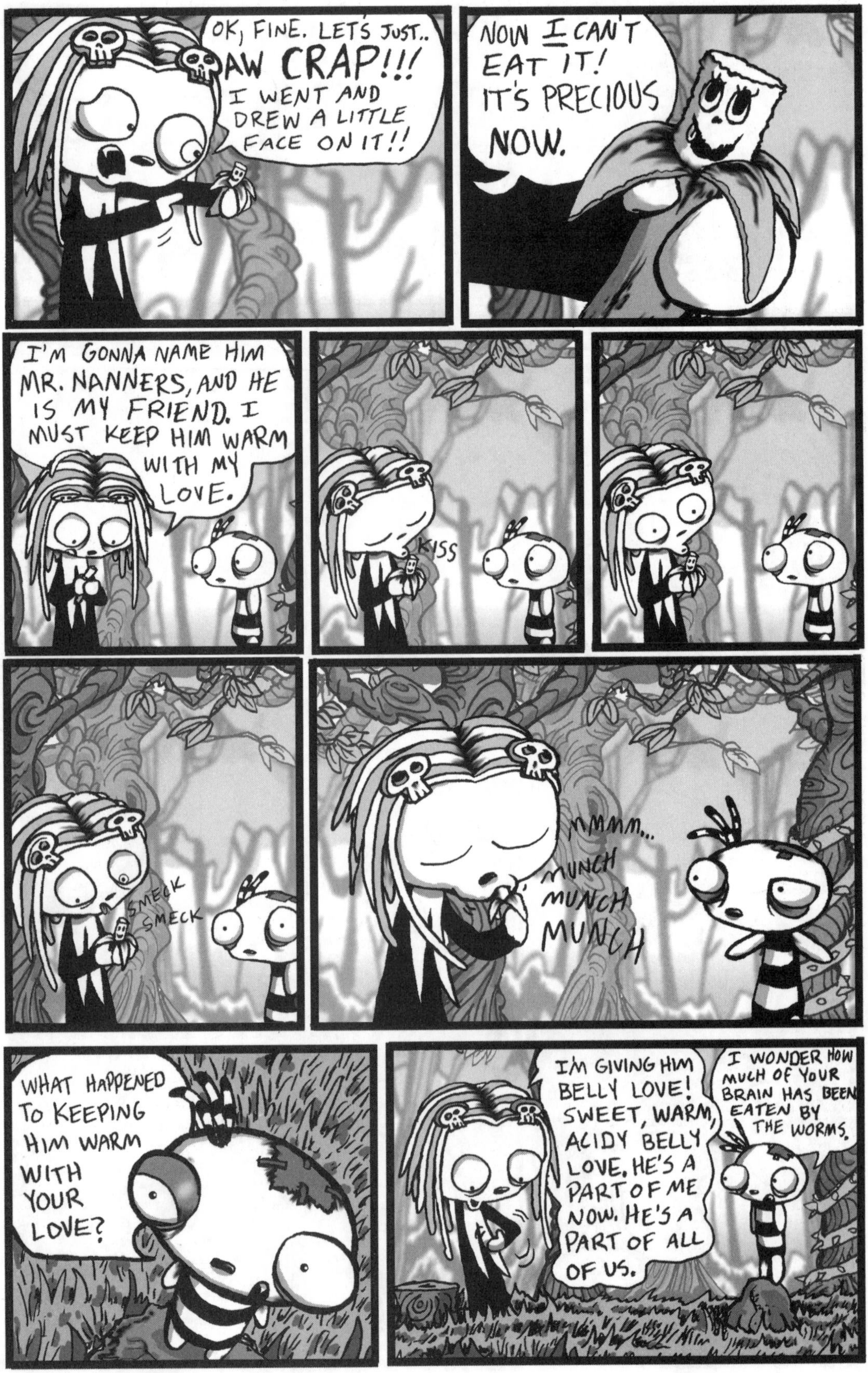

OK, FINE. LET'S JUST.. AW CRAP!!! I WENT AND DREW A LITTLE FACE ON IT!!
NOW I CAN'T EAT IT! IT'S PRECIOUS NOW.
I'M GONNA NAME HIM MR. NANNERS, AND HE IS MY FRIEND. I MUST KEEP HIM WARM WITH MY LOVE.
KISS
SMECK SMECK
MMMM...
MUNCH MUNCH MUNCH
WHAT HAPPENED TO KEEPING HIM WARM WITH YOUR LOVE?
I'M GIVING HIM BELLY LOVE! SWEET, WARM, ACIDY BELLY LOVE. HE'S A PART OF ME NOW. HE'S A PART OF ALL OF US.
I WONDER HOW MUCH OF YOUR BRAIN HAS BEEN EATEN BY THE WORMS.

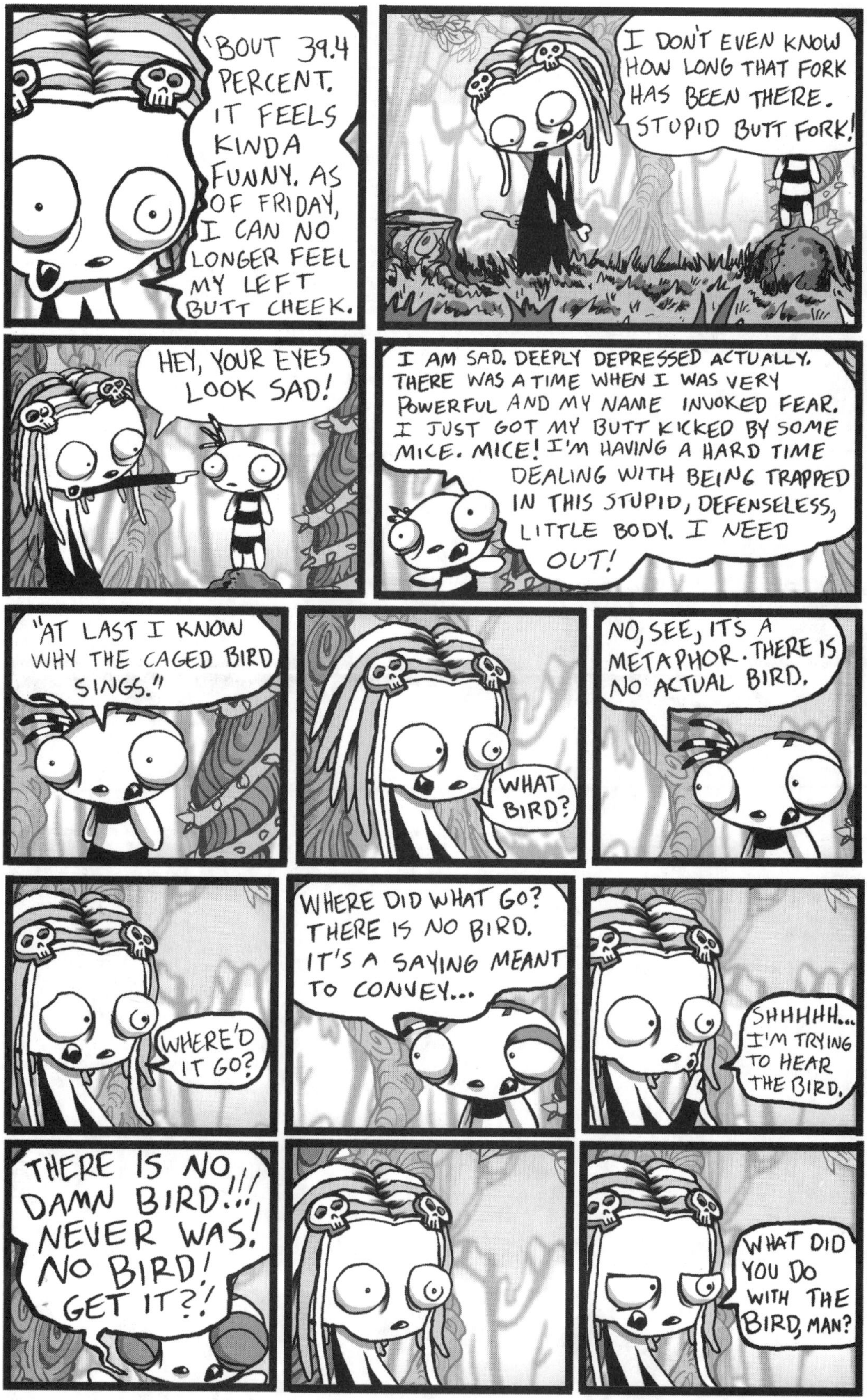
'BOUT 39.4 PERCENT. IT FEELS KINDA FUNNY. AS OF FRIDAY, I CAN NO LONGER FEEL MY LEFT BUTT CHEEK.
I DON'T EVEN KNOW HOW LONG THAT FORK HAS BEEN THERE. STUPID BUTT FORK!
HEY, YOUR EYES LOOK SAD!
I AM SAD. DEEPLY DEPRESSED ACTUALLY. THERE WAS A TIME WHEN I WAS VERY POWERFUL AND MY NAME INVOKED FEAR. I JUST GOT MY BUTT KICKED BY SOME MICE. MICE! I'M HAVING A HARD TIME DEALING WITH BEING TRAPPED IN THIS STUPID, DEFENSELESS, LITTLE BODY. I NEED OUT!
"AT LAST I KNOW WHY THE CAGED BIRD SINGS."
WHAT BIRD?
NO, SEE, ITS A METAPHOR. THERE IS NO ACTUAL BIRD.
WHERE'D IT GO?
WHERE DID WHAT GO? THERE IS NO BIRD. IT'S A SAYING MEANT TO CONVEY...
SHHHHH... I'M TRYING TO HEAR THE BIRD.
THERE IS NO DAMN BIRD!!! NEVER WAS! NO BIRD! GET IT?!
WHAT DID YOU DO WITH THE BIRD, MAN?

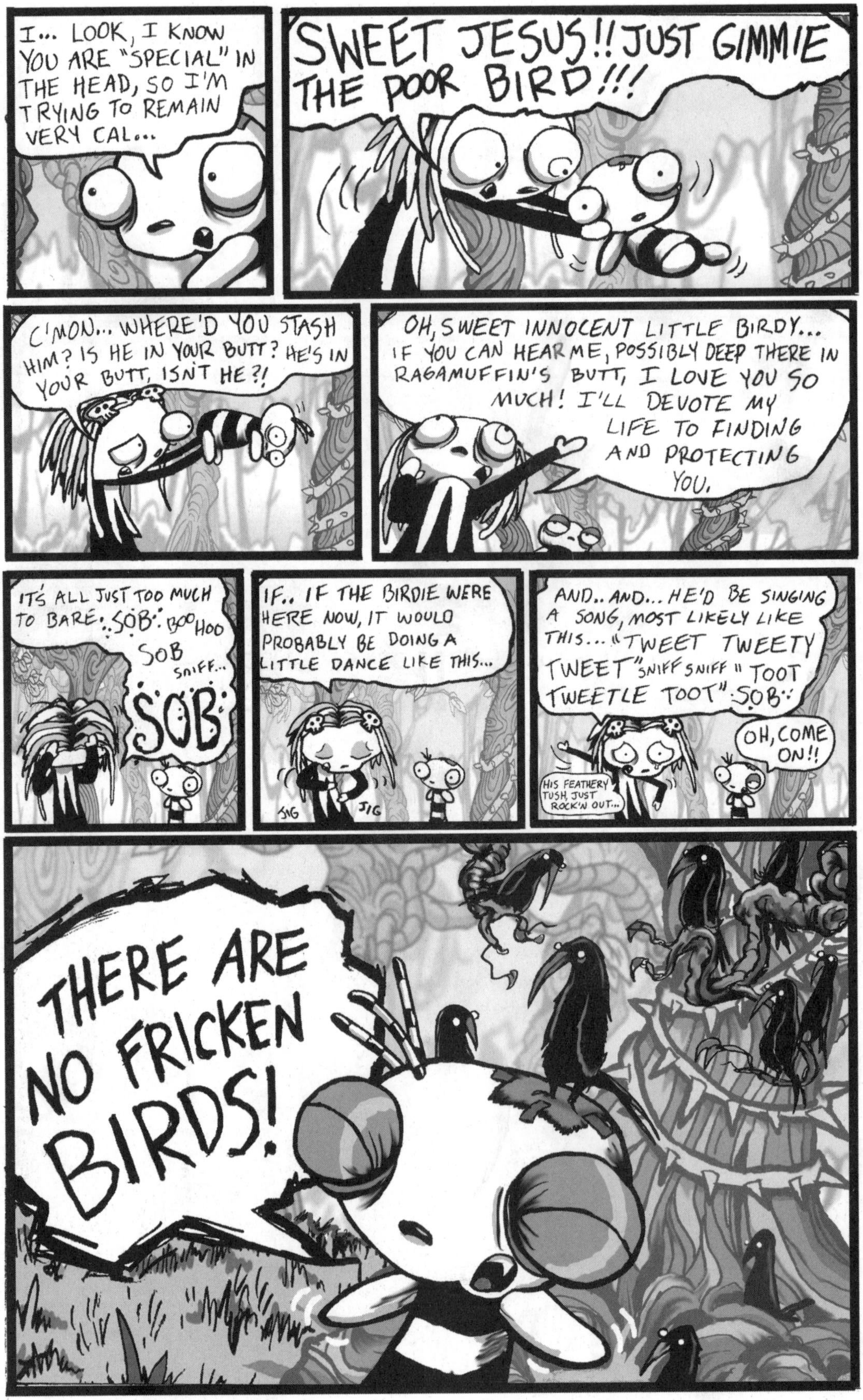

I... LOOK, I KNOW YOU ARE "SPECIAL" IN THE HEAD, SO I'M TRYING TO REMAIN VERY CAL...
SWEET JESUS!! JUST GIMMIE THE POOR BIRD!!!
C'MON... WHERE'D YOU STASH HIM? IS HE IN YOUR BUTT? HE'S IN YOUR BUTT, ISN'T HE?!
OH, SWEET INNOCENT LITTLE BIRDY... IF YOU CAN HEAR ME, POSSIBLY DEEP THERE IN RAGAMUFFIN'S BUTT, I LOVE YOU SO MUCH! I'LL DEVOTE MY LIFE TO FINDING AND PROTECTING YOU.
IT'S ALL JUST TOO MUCH TO BARE. SOB BOO HOO SOB SNIFF...
SOB
IF.. IF THE BIRDIE WERE HERE NOW, IT WOULD PROBABLY BE DOING A LITTLE DANCE LIKE THIS...
JIG JIG
AND.. AND... HE'D BE SINGING A SONG, MOST LIKELY LIKE THIS... "TWEET TWEETY TWEET" SNIFF SNIFF "TOOT TWEETLE TOOT" SOB
HIS FEATHERY TUSH, JUST ROCK'N OUT...
OH, COME ON!!
THERE ARE NO FRICKEN BIRDS!

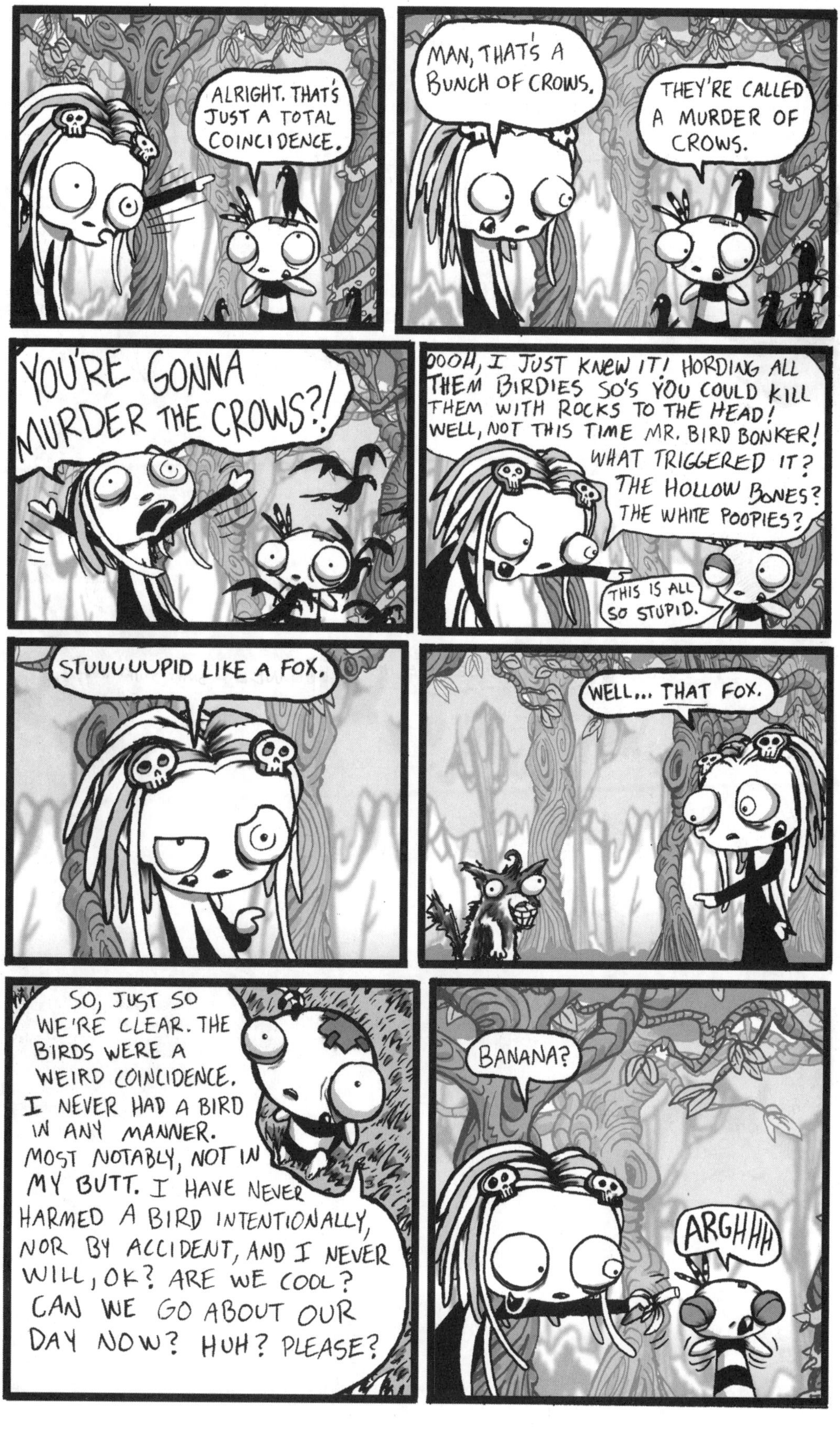
ALRIGHT. THAT'S JUST A TOTAL COINCIDENCE.
MAN, THAT'S A BUNCH OF CROWS.
THEY'RE CALLED A MURDER OF CROWS.
YOU'RE GONNA MURDER THE CROWS?!
OOOH, I JUST KNEW IT! HORDING ALL THEM BIRDIES SO'S YOU COULD KILL THEM WITH ROCKS TO THE HEAD! WELL, NOT THIS TIME MR. BIRD BONKER! WHAT TRIGGERED IT? THE HOLLOW BONES? THE WHITE POOPIES?
THIS IS ALL SO STUPID.
STUUUUUPID LIKE A FOX.
WELL... THAT FOX.
SO, JUST SO WE'RE CLEAR. THE BIRDS WERE A WEIRD COINCIDENCE. I NEVER HAD A BIRD IN ANY MANNER. MOST NOTABLY, NOT IN MY BUTT. I HAVE NEVER HARMED A BIRD INTENTIONALLY, NOR BY ACCIDENT, AND I NEVER WILL, OK? ARE WE COOL? CAN WE GO ABOUT OUR DAY NOW? HUH? PLEASE?
BANANA?
ARGHHH

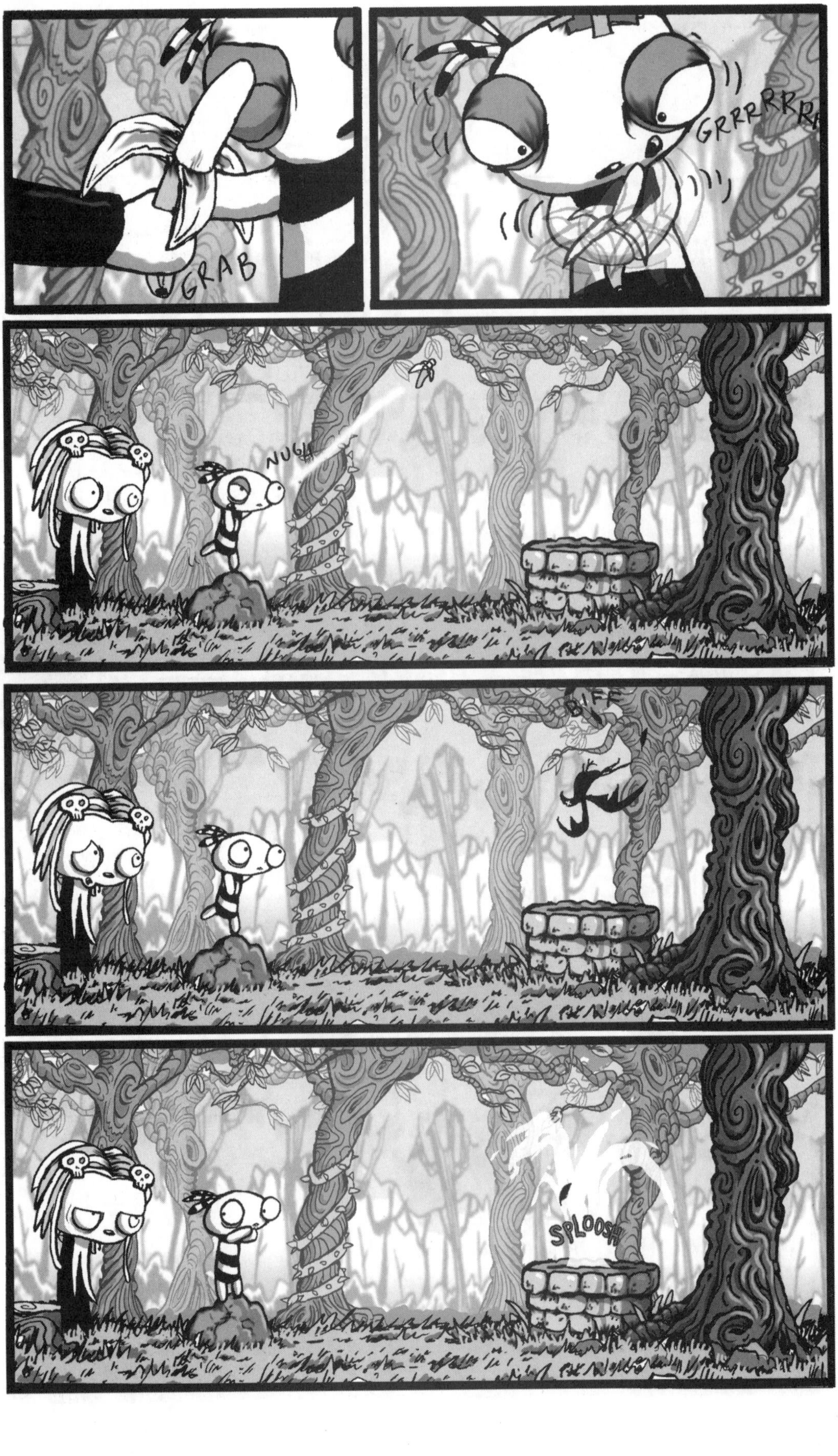
GRAB
GRRRRRRR
NUGH
BIFF
SPLOOSH

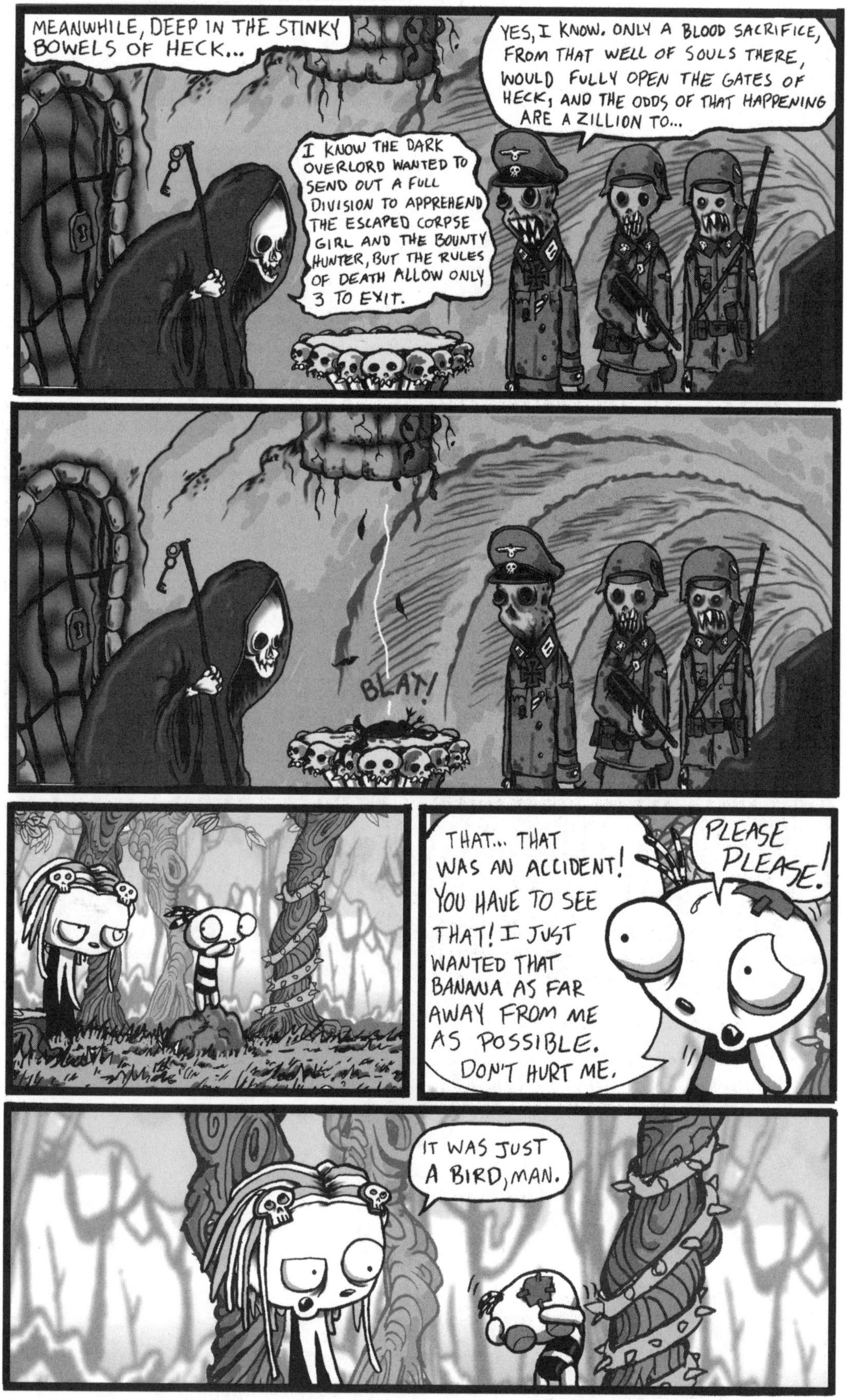
MEANWHILE, DEEP IN THE STINKY BOWELS OF HECK...
I KNOW THE DARK OVERLORD WANTED TO SEND OUT A FULL DIVISION TO APPREHEND THE ESCAPED CORPSE GIRL AND THE BOUNTY HUNTER, BUT THE RULES OF DEATH ALLOW ONLY 3 TO EXIT.
YES, I KNOW. ONLY A BLOOD SACRIFICE, FROM THAT WELL OF SOULS THERE, WOULD FULLY OPEN THE GATES OF HECK, AND THE ODDS OF THAT HAPPENING ARE A ZILLION TO...
BLAT!
THAT... THAT WAS AN ACCIDENT! YOU HAVE TO SEE THAT! I JUST WANTED THAT BANANA AS FAR AWAY FROM ME AS POSSIBLE. DON'T HURT ME.
PLEASE PLEASE!
IT WAS JUST A BIRD, MAN.

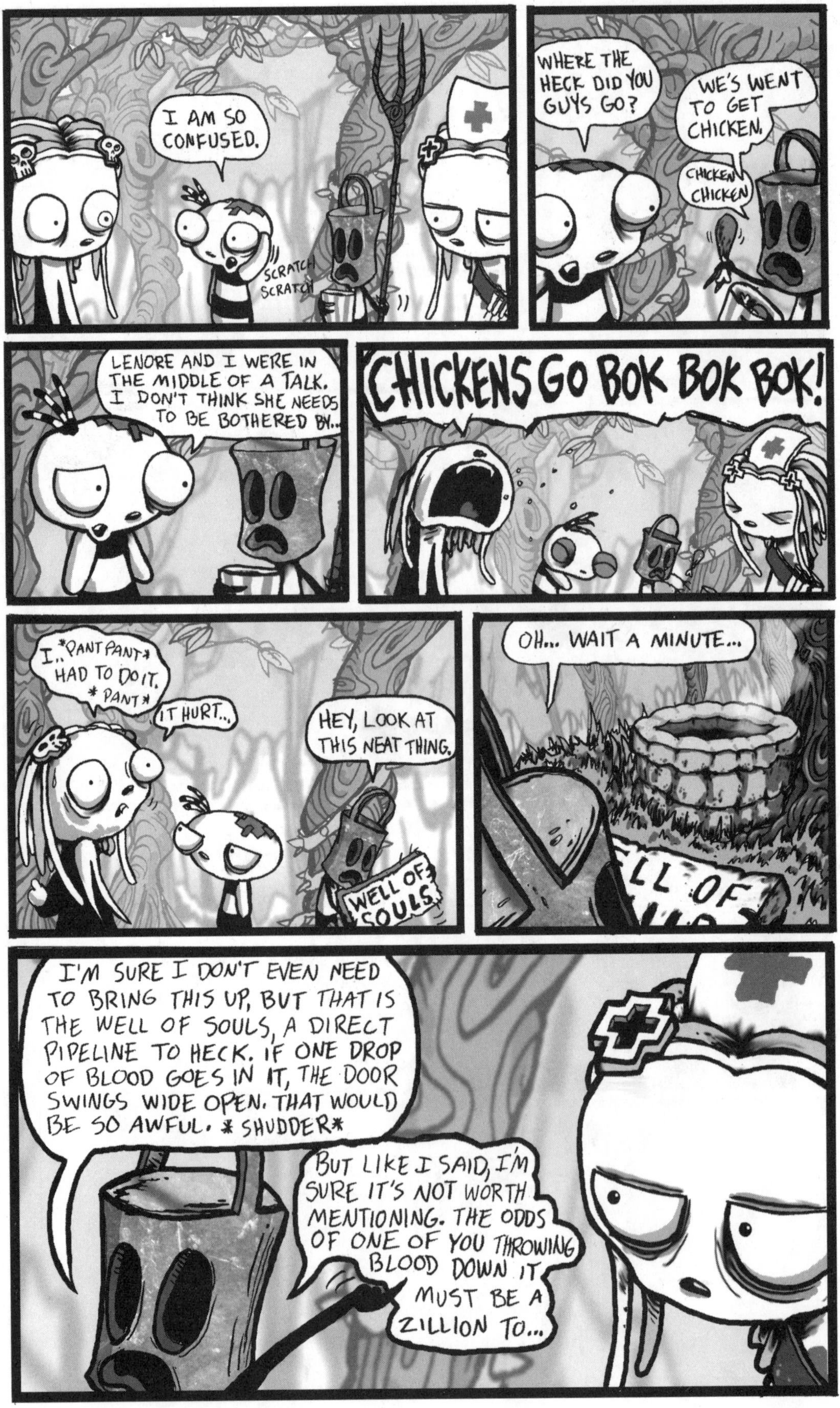

I AM SO CONFUSED.
SCRATCH SCRATCH
WHERE THE HECK DID YOU GUYS GO?
WE'S WENT TO GET CHICKEN.
CHICKEN CHICKEN
LENORE AND I WERE IN THE MIDDLE OF A TALK. I DON'T THINK SHE NEEDS TO BE BOTHERED BY...
CHICKENS GO BOK BOK BOK!
I.. *PANT PANT* HAD TO DO IT. *PANT*
IT HURT...
HEY, LOOK AT THIS NEAT THING.
WELL OF SOULS
OH... WAIT A MINUTE...
LL OF
I'M SURE I DON'T EVEN NEED TO BRING THIS UP, BUT THAT IS THE WELL OF SOULS, A DIRECT PIPELINE TO HECK. IF ONE DROP OF BLOOD GOES IN IT, THE DOOR SWINGS WIDE OPEN. THAT WOULD BE SO AWFUL. *SHUDDER*
BUT LIKE I SAID, I'M SURE IT'S NOT WORTH MENTIONING. THE ODDS OF ONE OF YOU THROWING BLOOD DOWN IT MUST BE A ZILLION TO...

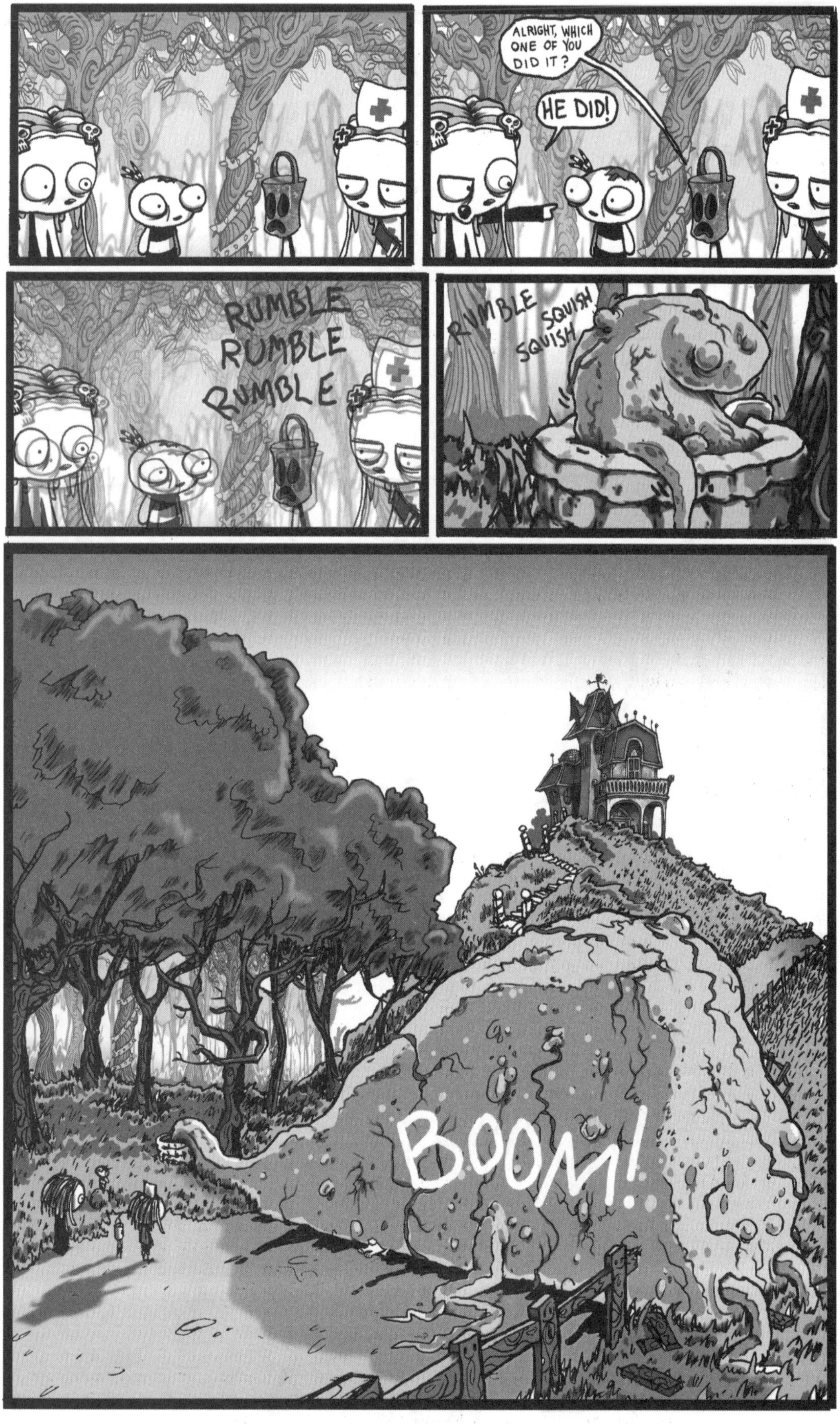

ALRIGHT, WHICH ONE OF YOU DID IT?
HE DID!
RUMBLE RUMBLE RUMBLE
RUMBLE
SQUISH SQUISH
BOOM!

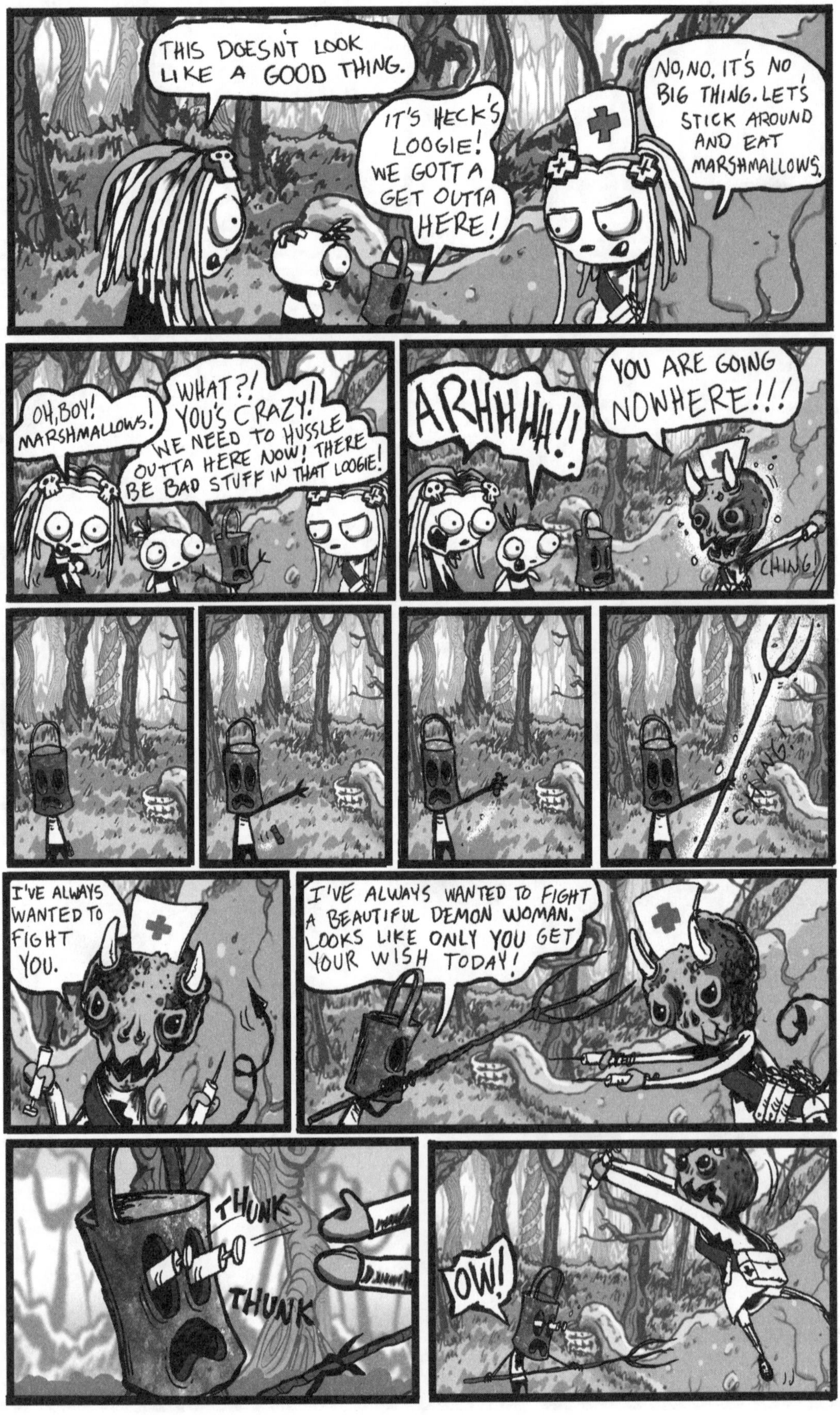

THIS DOESN'T LOOK LIKE A GOOD THING.
IT'S HECK'S LOOGIE! WE GOTTA GET OUTTA HERE!
NO, NO. IT'S NO BIG THING. LET'S STICK AROUND AND EAT MARSHMALLOWS.
OH, BOY! MARSHMALLOWS!
WHAT?! YOU'S CRAZY! WE NEED TO HUSSLE OUTTA HERE NOW! THERE BE BAD STUFF IN THAT LOOGIE!
ARHHHA!!
YOU ARE GOING NOWHERE!!!
CHING!
CHING!
I'VE ALWAYS WANTED TO FIGHT YOU.
I'VE ALWAYS WANTED TO FIGHT A BEAUTIFUL DEMON WOMAN. LOOKS LIKE ONLY YOU GET YOUR WISH TODAY!
THUNK
THUNK
OW!

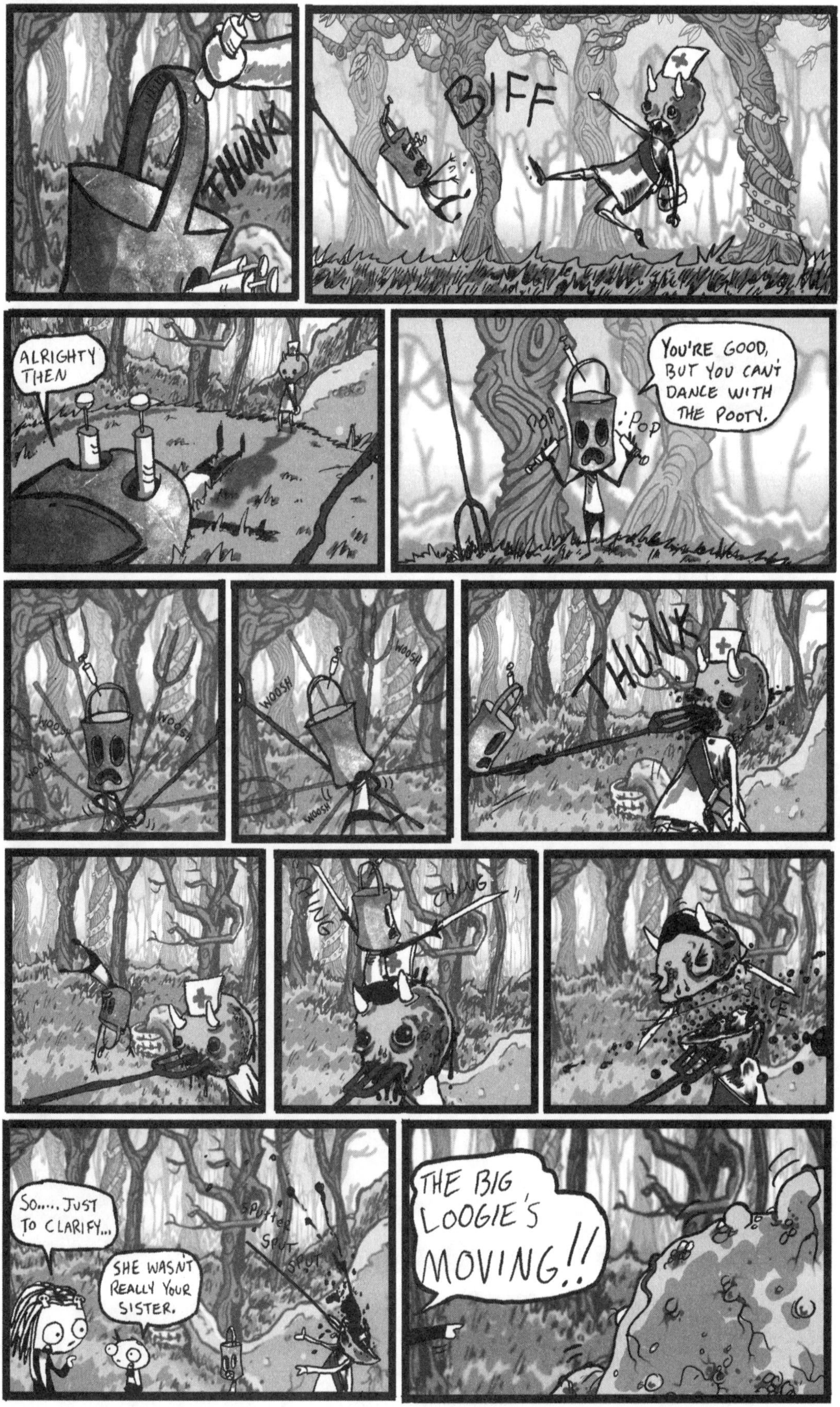

THUNK
BIFF
ALRIGHTY THEN
YOU'RE GOOD, BUT YOU CAN'T DANCE WITH THE POOTY.
POP
POP
WOOSH
WOOSH
WOOSH
WOOSH
WOOSH
WOOSH
THUNK
CHING
CHING
SLICE
SO..... JUST TO CLARIFY...
SHE WASN'T REALLY YOUR SISTER.
SPUTTER
SPUT
SPUT
THE BIG LOOGIE'S MOVING!!

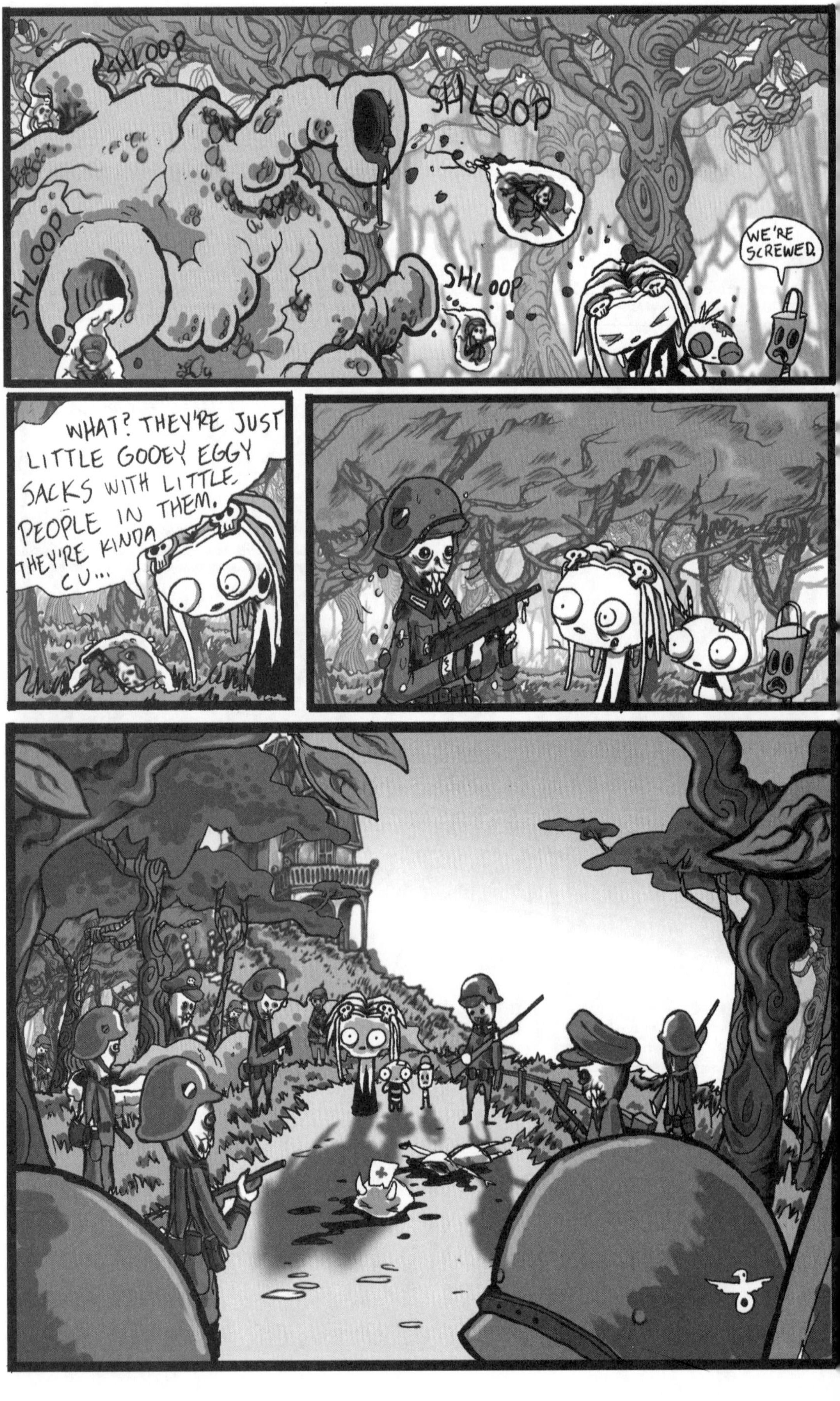
SHLOOP
SHLOOP
SHLOOP
SHLOOP
WE'RE SCREWED.
WHAT? THEY'RE JUST LITTLE GOOEY EGGY SACKS WITH LITTLE PEOPLE IN THEM. THEY'RE KINDA CU...

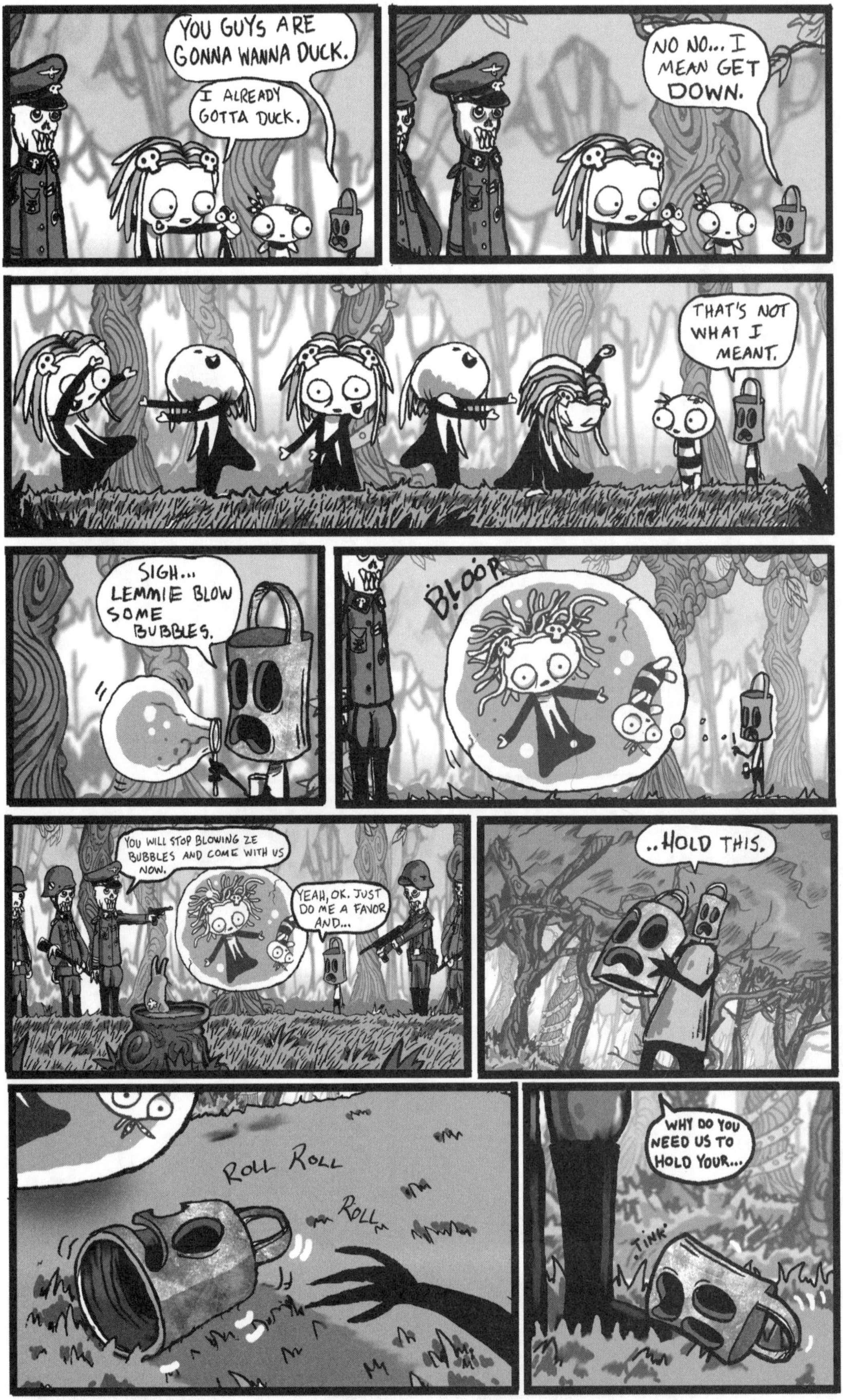

YOU GUYS ARE GONNA WANNA DUCK.
I ALREADY GOTTA DUCK.
NO NO... I MEAN GET DOWN.
THAT'S NOT WHAT I MEANT.
SIGH... LEMMIE BLOW SOME BUBBLES.
BLOOP
YOU WILL STOP BLOWING ZE BUBBLES AND COME WITH US NOW.
YEAH, OK. JUST DO ME A FAVOR AND...
..HOLD THIS.
ROLL ROLL
ROLL
WHY DO YOU NEED US TO HOLD YOUR...
TINK

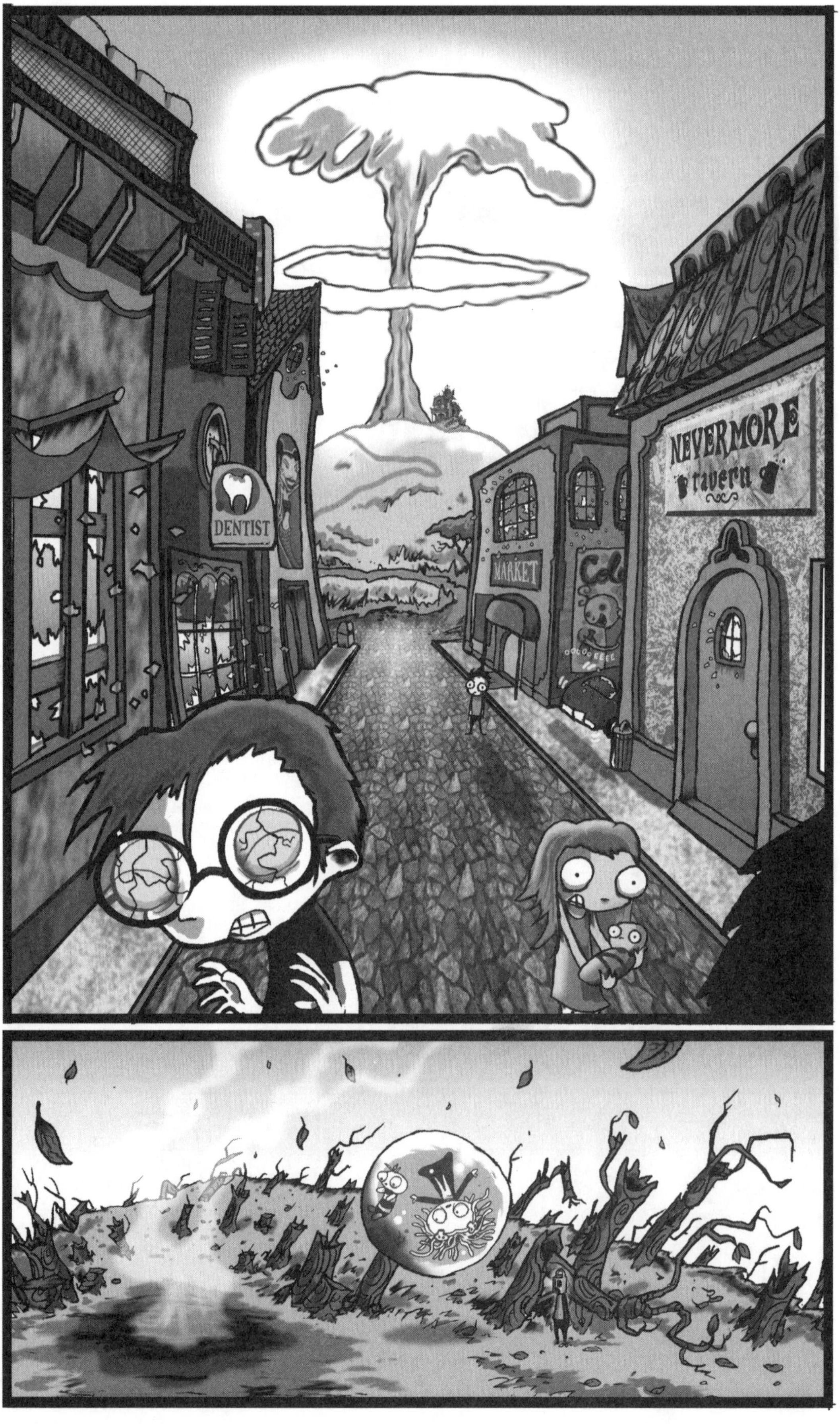
DENTIST
MARKET
NEVERMORE
tavern

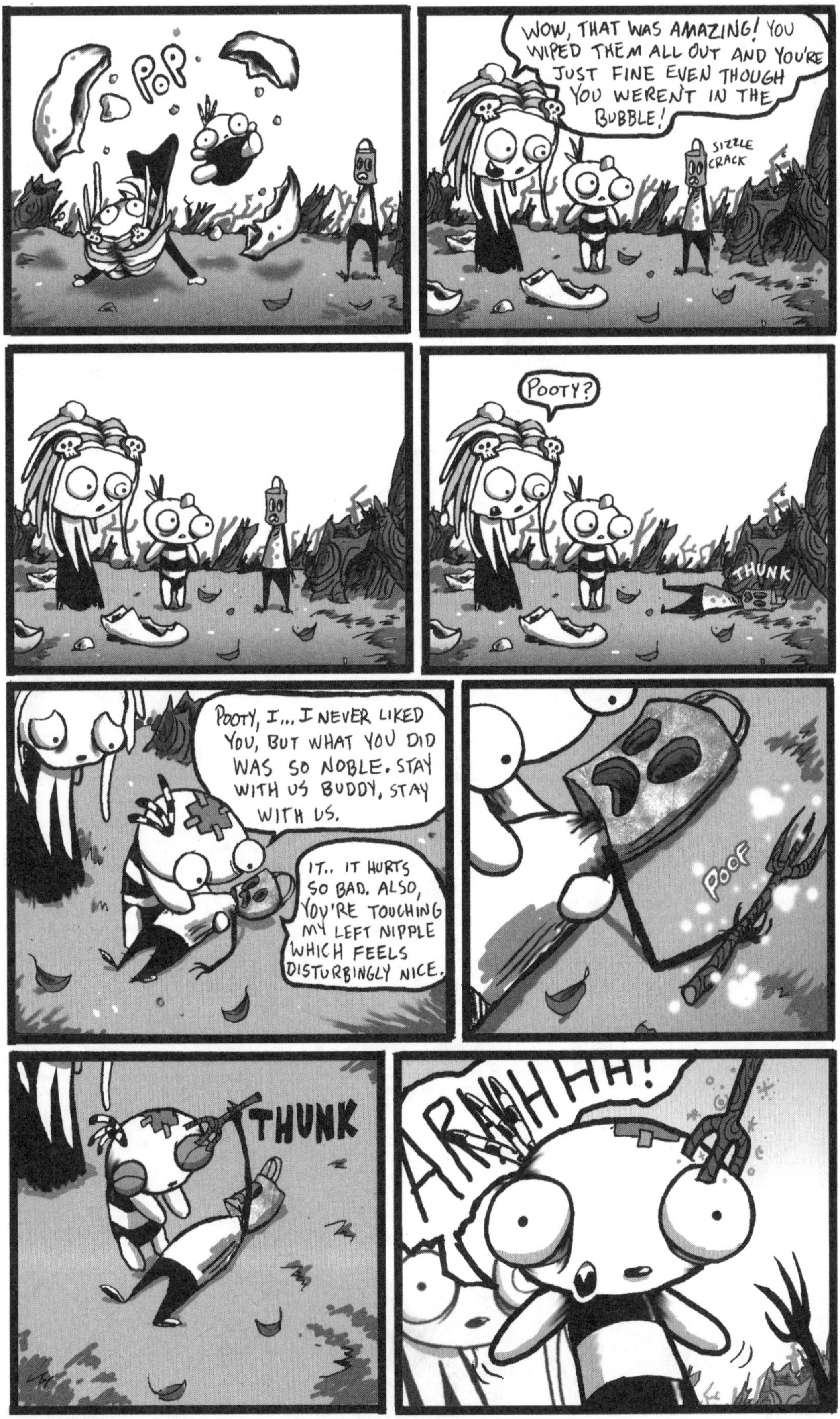
POP
WOW, THAT WAS AMAZING! YOU WIPED THEM ALL OUT AND YOU'RE JUST FINE EVEN THOUGH YOU WEREN'T IN THE BUBBLE!
SIZZLE CRACK
POOTY?
THUNK
POOTY, I... I NEVER LIKED YOU, BUT WHAT YOU DID WAS SO NOBLE. STAY WITH US BUDDY, STAY WITH US.
IT.. IT HURTS SO BAD. ALSO, YOU'RE TOUCHING MY LEFT NIPPLE WHICH FEELS DISTURBINGLY NICE.
POOF
THUNK
ARAAHHH!

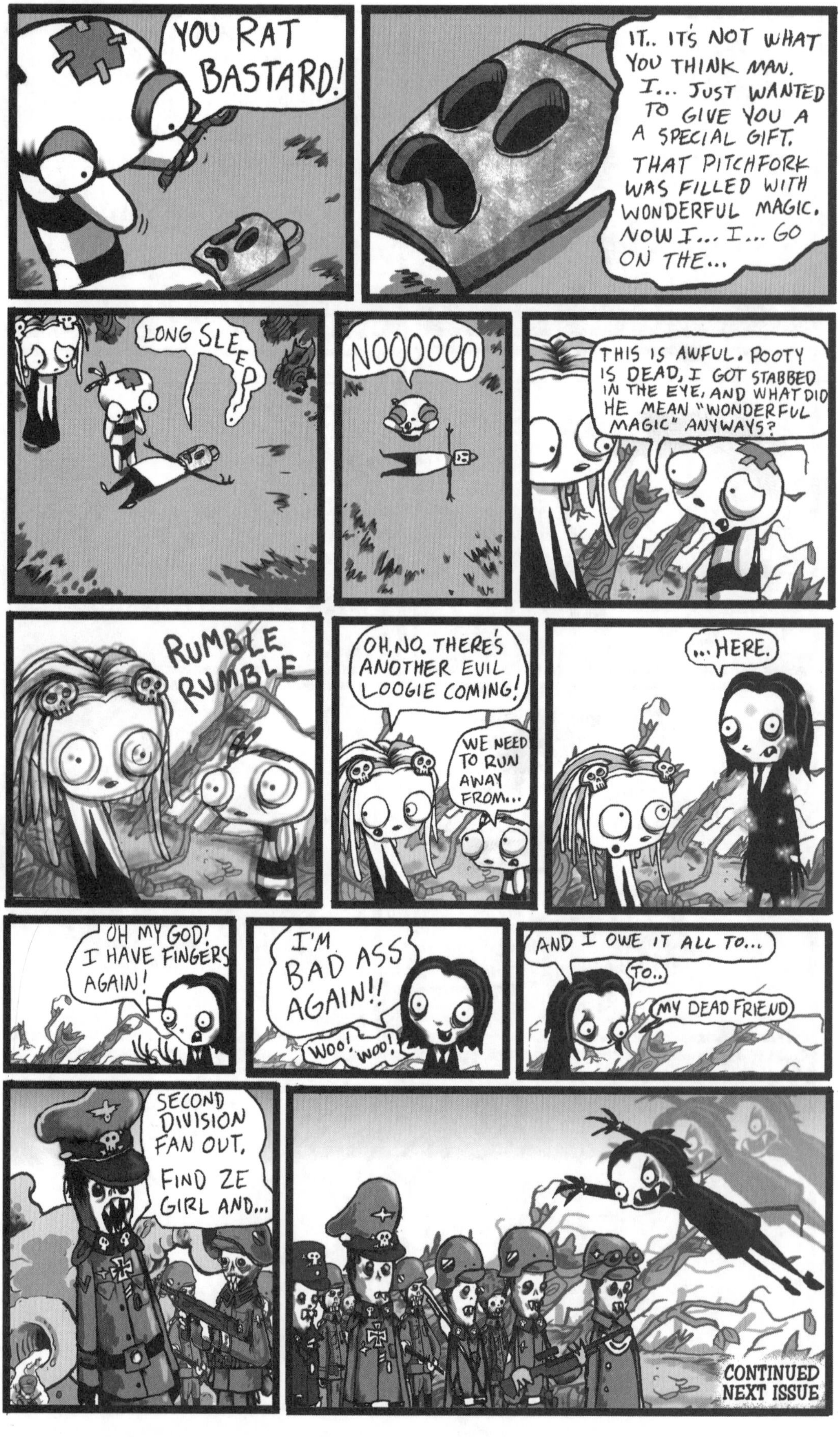
YOU RAT BASTARD!
IT.. IT'S NOT WHAT YOU THINK MAN. I... JUST WANTED TO GIVE YOU A A SPECIAL GIFT. THAT PITCHFORK WAS FILLED WITH WONDERFUL MAGIC. NOW I... I... GO ON THE...
LONG SLEEP
NOOOOOO
THIS IS AWFUL. POOTY IS DEAD, I GOT STABBED IN THE EYE, AND WHAT DID HE MEAN "WONDERFUL MAGIC" ANYWAYS?
RUMBLE RUMBLE
OH, NO. THERE'S ANOTHER EVIL LOOGIE COMING!
WE NEED TO RUN AWAY FROM...
...HERE.
OH MY GOD! I HAVE FINGERS AGAIN!
I'M BAD ASS AGAIN!!
WOO! WOO!
AND I OWE IT ALL TO...
TO..
MY DEAD FRIEND
SECOND DIVISION FAN OUT. FIND ZE GIRL AND...
CONTINUED NEXT ISSUE

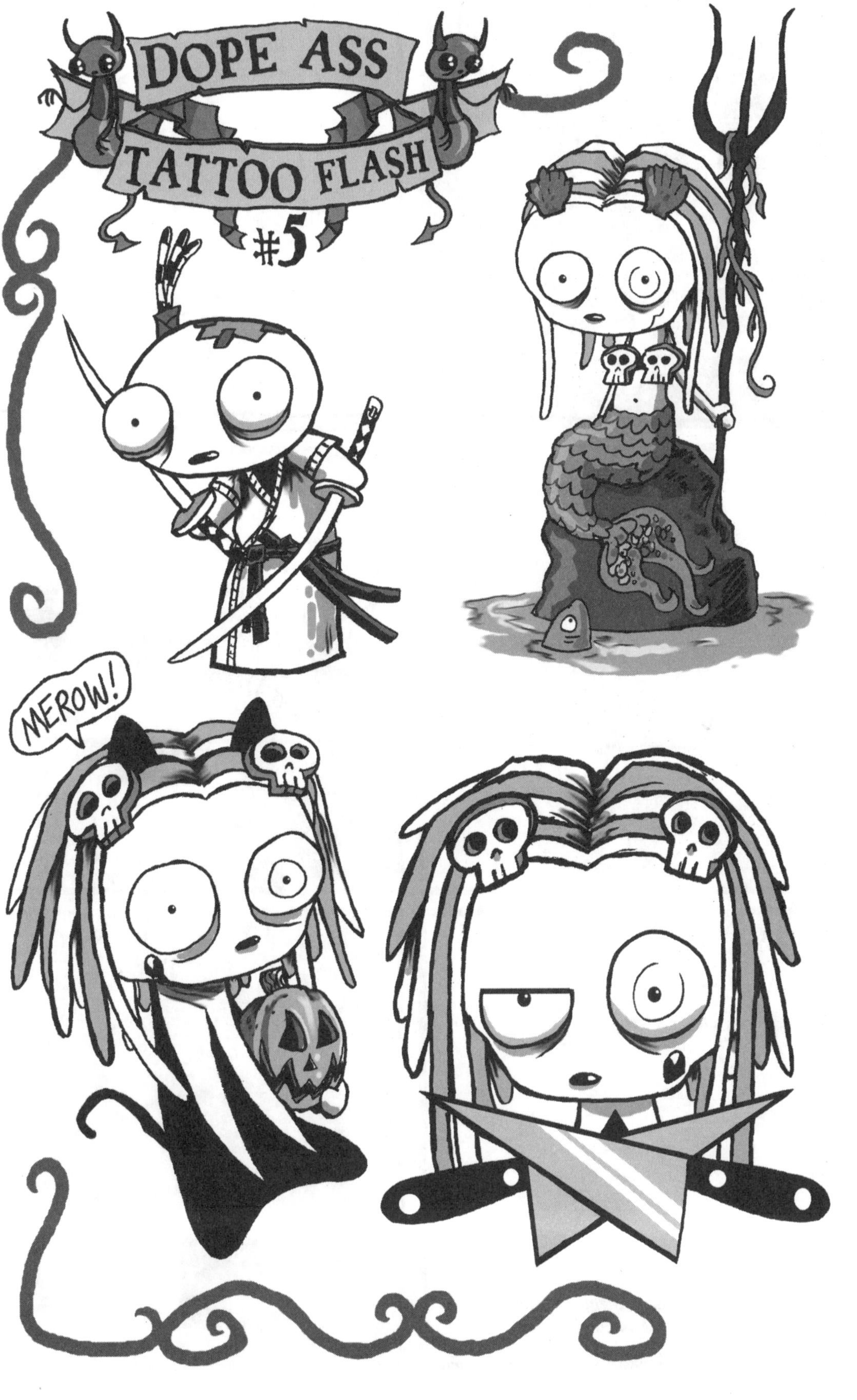
DOPE ASS
TATTOO FLASH
#5
MEROW!

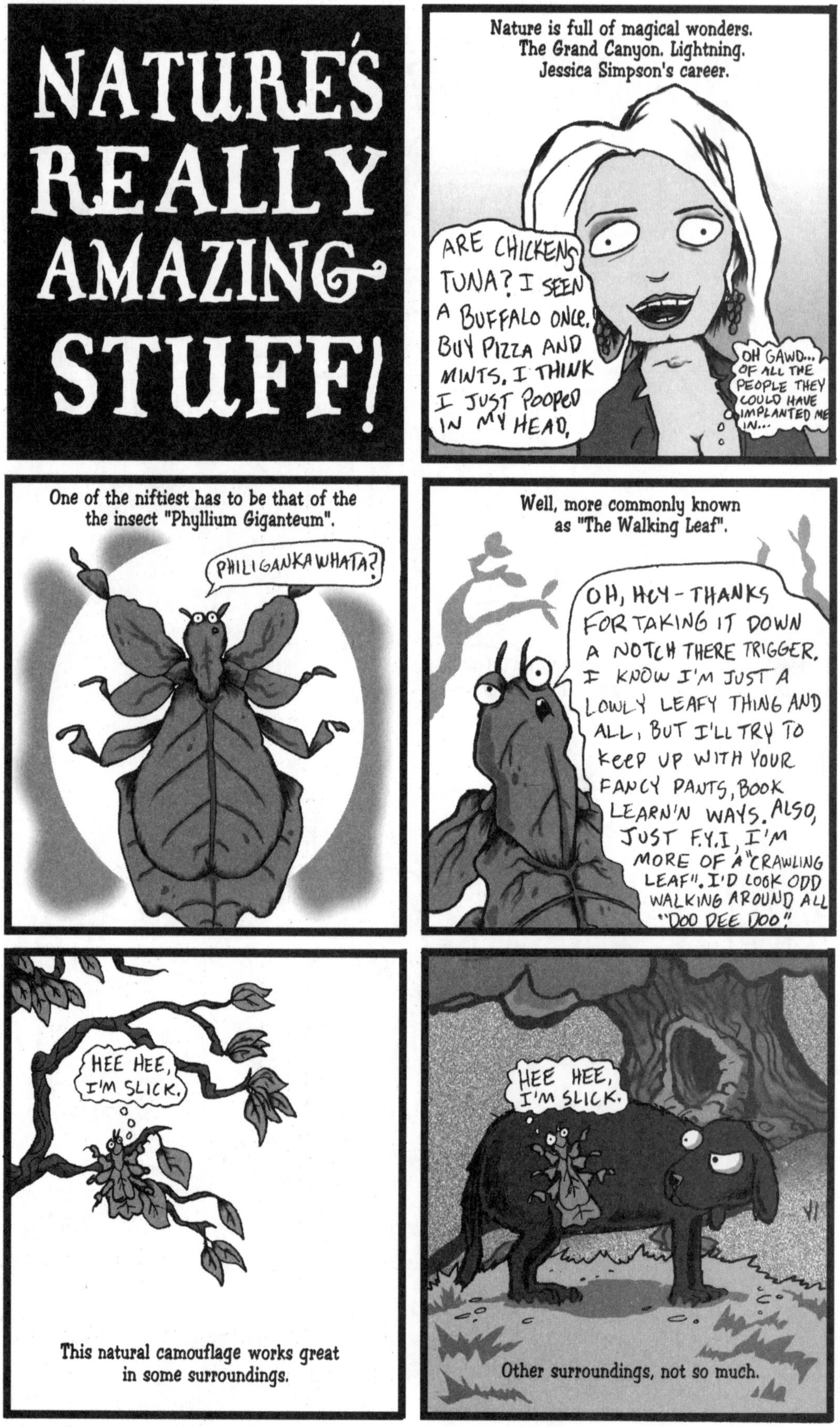
NATURE'S REALLY AMAZING STUFF!
Nature is full of magical wonders. The Grand Canyon. Lightning. Jessica Simpson's career.
ARE CHICKENS TUNA? I SEEN A BUFFALO ONCE. BUY PIZZA AND MINTS. I THINK I JUST POOPED IN MY HEAD.
OH GAWD... OF ALL THE PEOPLE THEY COULD HAVE IMPLANTED ME IN...
One of the niftiest has to be that of the the insect "Phyllium Giganteum".
PHILIGANKAWHATA?
Well, more commonly known as "The Walking Leaf".
OH, HEY - THANKS FOR TAKING IT DOWN A NOTCH THERE TRIGGER. I KNOW I'M JUST A LOWLY LEAFY THING AND ALL, BUT I'LL TRY TO KEEP UP WITH YOUR FANCY PANTS, BOOK LEARN'N WAYS. ALSO, JUST F.Y.I, I'M MORE OF A "CRAWLING LEAF". I'D LOOK ODD WALKING AROUND ALL "DOO DEE DOO"
HEE HEE, I'M SLICK.
This natural camouflage works great in some surroundings.
HEE HEE, I'M SLICK.
Other surroundings, not so much.

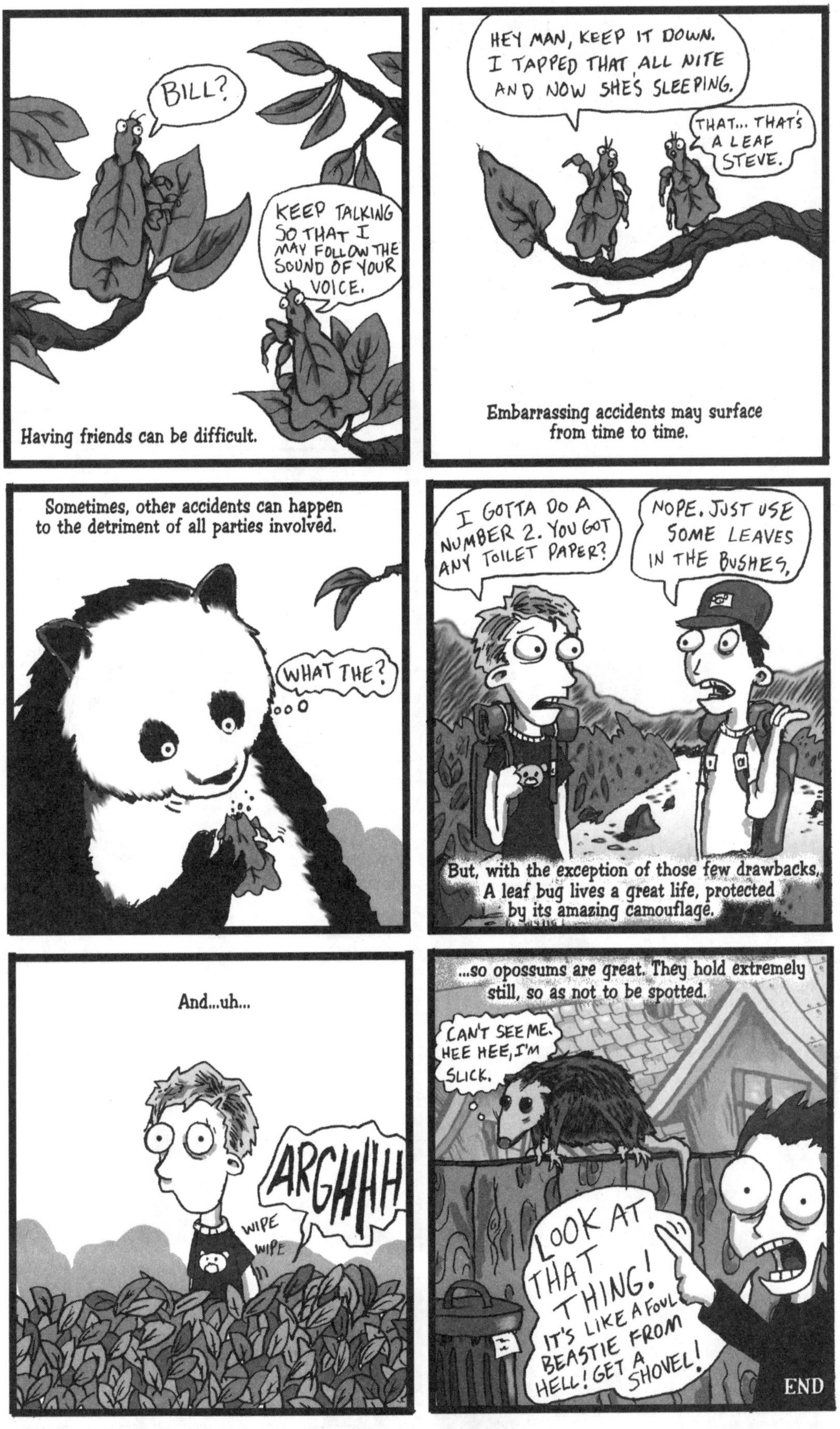
BILL?
KEEP TALKING SO THAT I MAY FOLLOW THE SOUND OF YOUR VOICE.
Having friends can be difficult.
HEY MAN, KEEP IT DOWN. I TAPPED THAT ALL NITE AND NOW SHE'S SLEEPING.
THAT... THAT'S A LEAF STEVE.
Embarrassing accidents may surface from time to time.
Sometimes, other accidents can happen to the detriment of all parties involved.
WHAT THE?
I GOTTA DO A NUMBER 2. YOU GOT ANY TOILET PAPER?
NOPE. JUST USE SOME LEAVES IN THE BUSHES.
But, with the exception of those few drawbacks, A leaf bug lives a great life, protected by its amazing camouflage.
And...uh...
WIPE
WIPE
ARGHHH
...so opossums are great. They hold extremely still, so as not to be spotted.
CAN'T SEE ME. HEE HEE, I'M SLICK.
LOOK AT THAT THING! IT'S LIKE A FOUL BEASTIE FROM HELL! GET A SHOVEL!
END

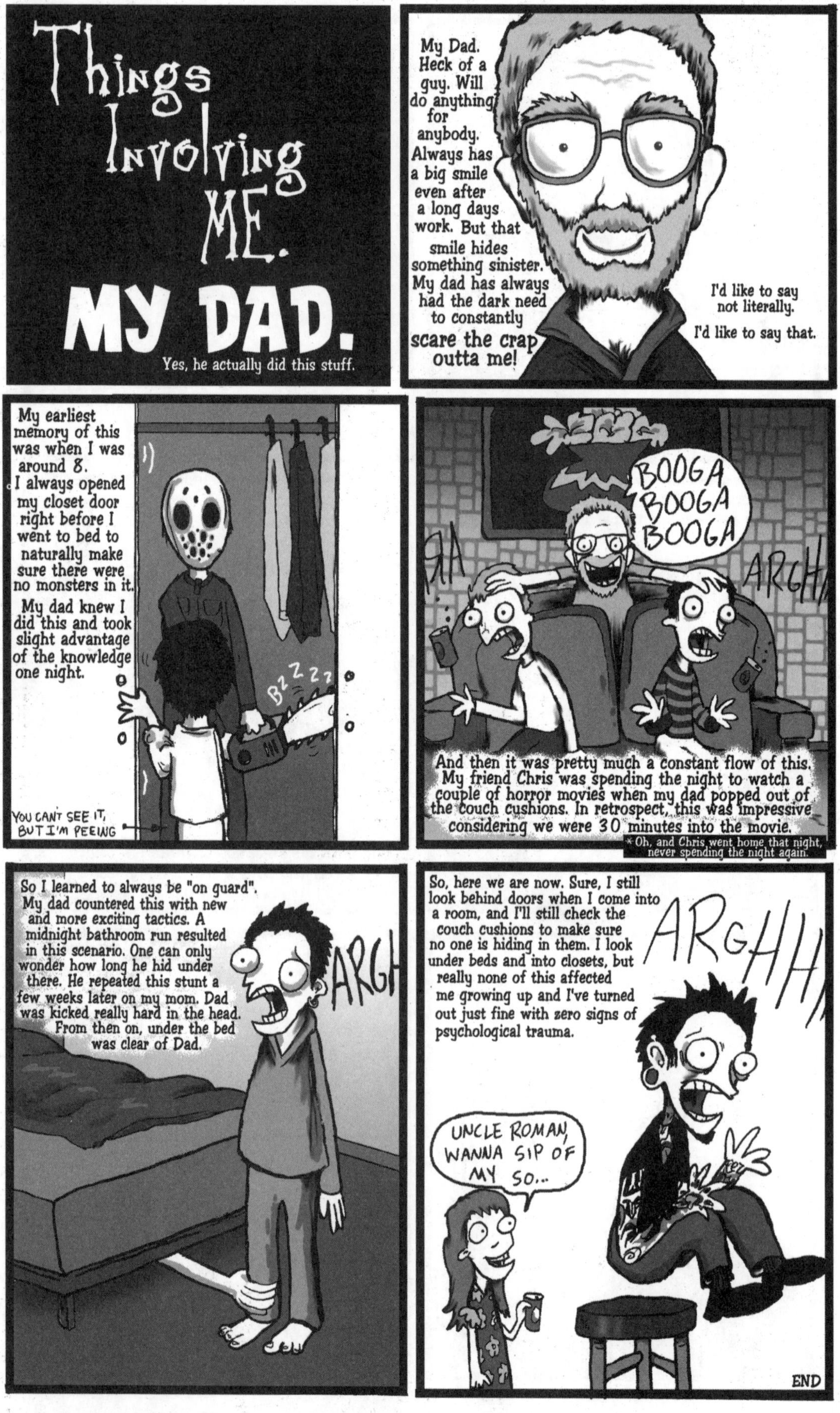
Things Involving ME.
MY DAD.
Yes, he actually did this stuff.
My Dad. Heck of a guy. Will do anything for anybody. Always has a big smile even after a long days work. But that smile hides something sinister. My dad has always had the dark need to constantly scare the crap outta me!
I'd like to say not literally.
I'd like to say that.
My earliest memory of this was when I was around 8. I always opened my closet door right before I went to bed to naturally make sure there were no monsters in it. My dad knew I did this and took slight advantage of the knowledge one night.
BZZZZ
YOU CAN'T SEE IT, BUT I'M PEEING
BOOGA BOOGA BOOGA
ARGH
And then it was pretty much a constant flow of this. My friend Chris was spending the night to watch a couple of horror movies when my dad popped out of the couch cushions. In retrospect, this was impressive considering we were 30 minutes into the movie.
* Oh, and Chris went home that night, never spending the night again.
So I learned to always be "on guard". My dad countered this with new and more exciting tactics. A midnight bathroom run resulted in this scenario. One can only wonder how long he hid under there. He repeated this stunt a few weeks later on my mom. Dad was kicked really hard in the head. From then on, under the bed was clear of Dad.
ARGH
So, here we are now. Sure, I still look behind doors when I come into a room, and I'll still check the couch cushions to make sure no one is hiding in them. I look under beds and into closets, but really none of this affected me growing up and I've turned out just fine with zero signs of psychological trauma.
ARGHH
UNCLE ROMAN, WANNA SIP OF MY SO...
END

#12
Lenore
the cute little dead girl.
by
Roman Dirge

Issue #12

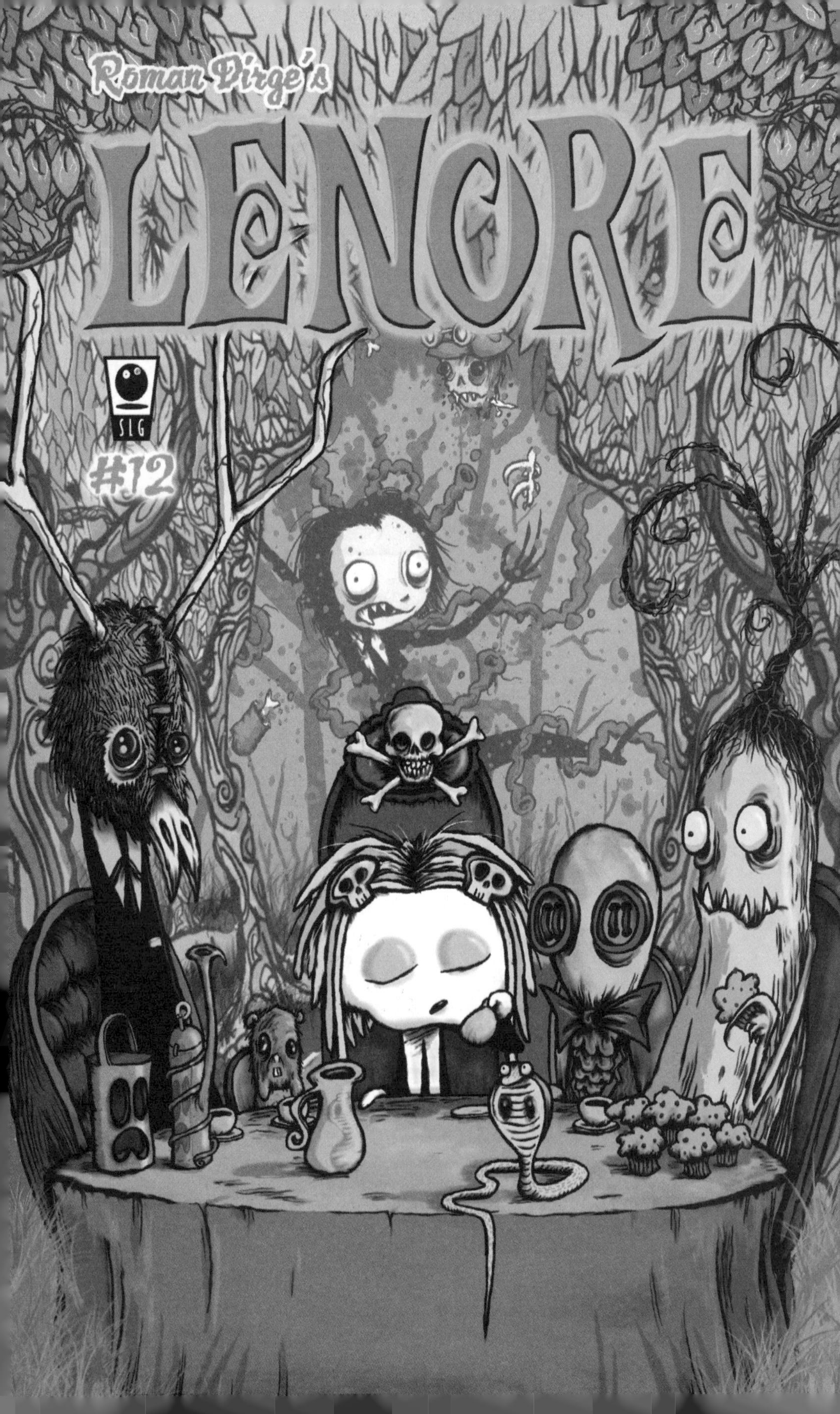

Roman Dirge's
LENORE
SLG
#12

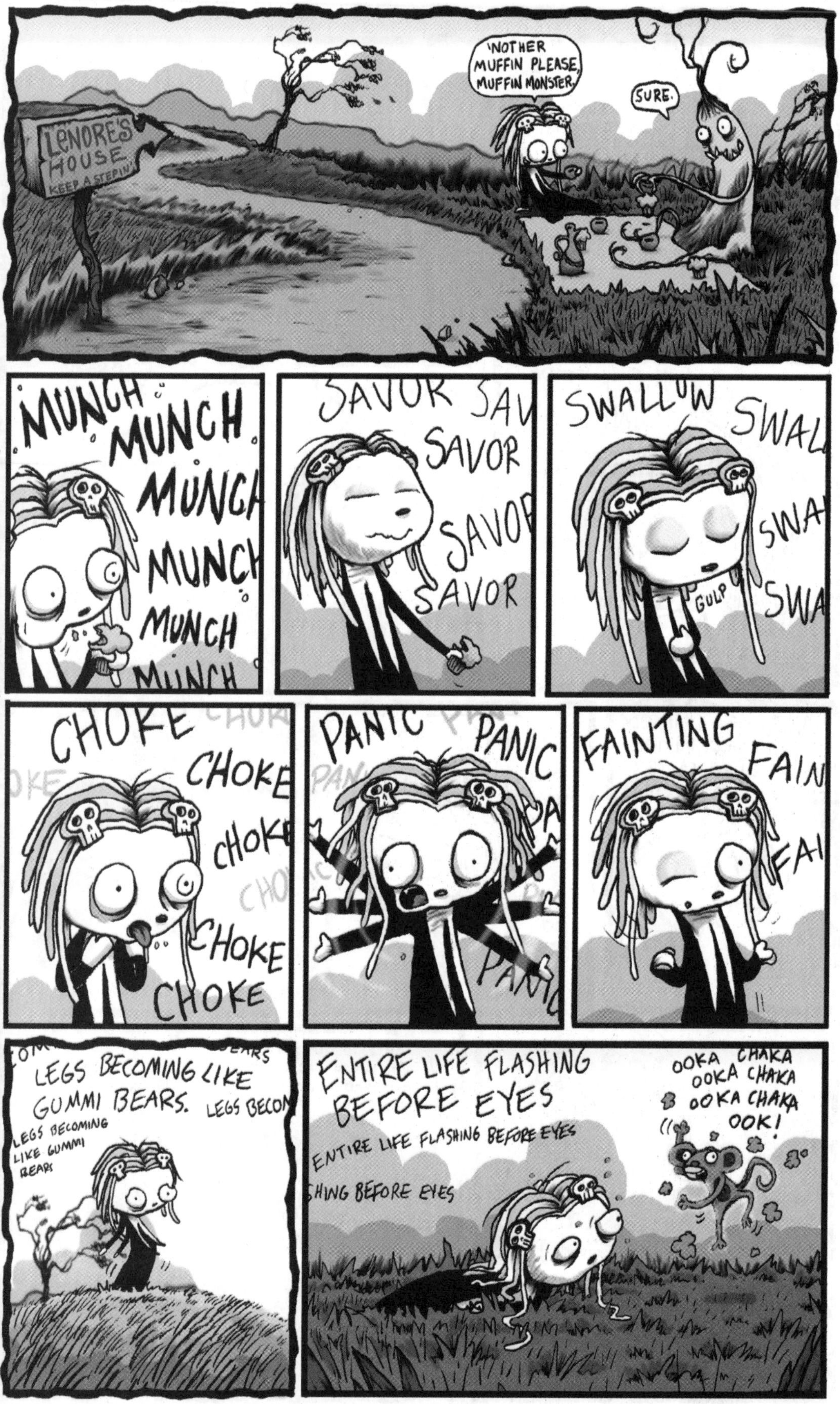
LENORE'S HOUSE
KEEP A STEPIN'
'NOTHER MUFFIN PLEASE, MUFFIN MONSTER.
SURE.
MUNCH MUNCH MUNCH MUNCH MUNCH
SAVOR SAVOR SAVOR SAVOR
SWALLOW
GULP
CHOKE CHOKE CHOKE CHOKE CHOKE
PANIC PANIC
FAINTING
LEGS BECOMING LIKE GUMMI BEARS.
LEGS BECOMING LIKE GUMMI BEARS
ENTIRE LIFE FLASHING BEFORE EYES
ENTIRE LIFE FLASHING BEFORE EYES
OOKA CHAKA OOKA CHAKA OOKA CHAKA OOK!

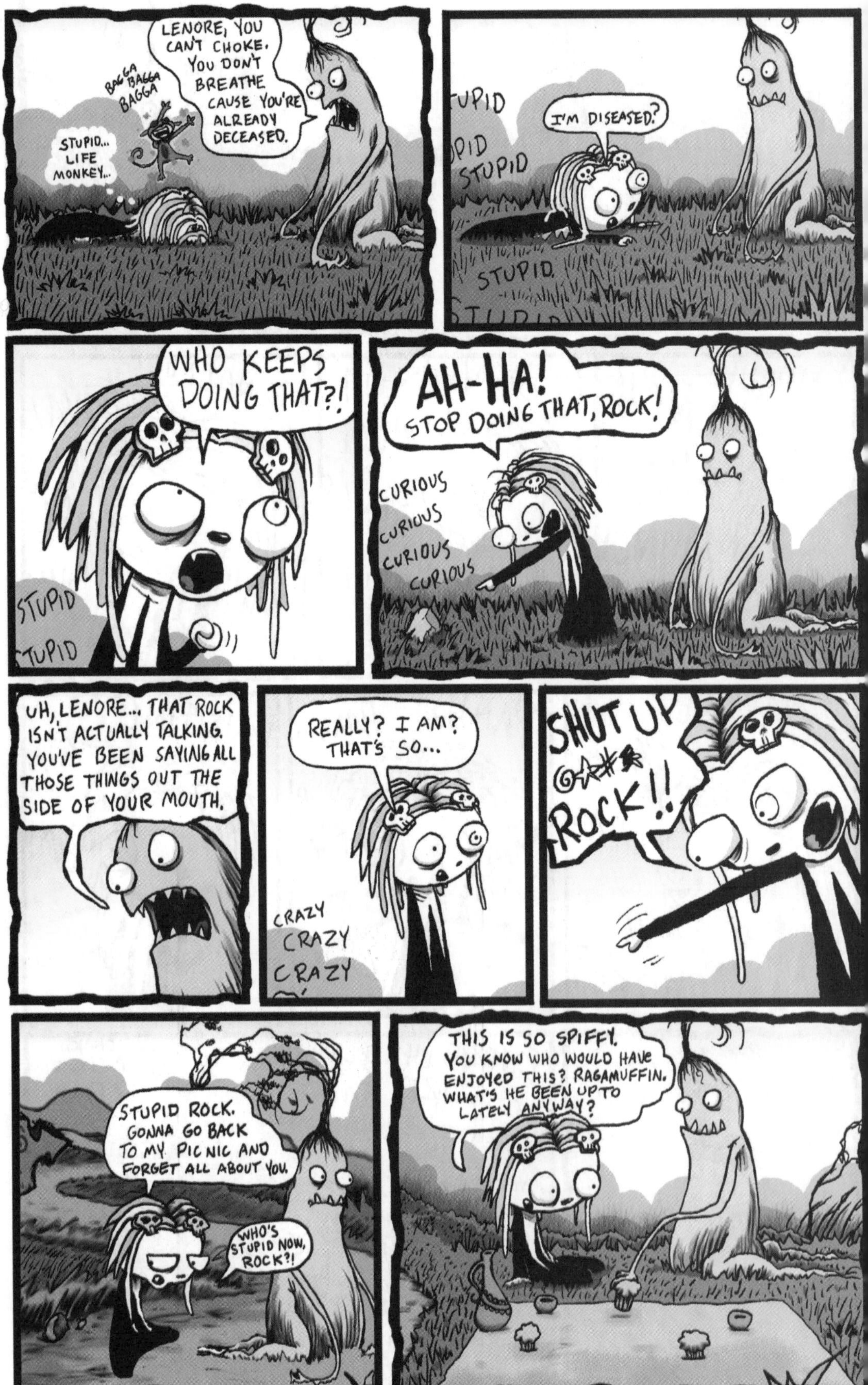
LENORE, YOU CAN'T CHOKE. YOU DON'T BREATHE CAUSE YOU'RE ALREADY DECEASED.
BAGGA BAGGA BAGGA
STUPID... LIFE MONKEY...
STUPID
PID
STUPID
I'M DISEASED?
STUPID
WHO KEEPS DOING THAT?!
STUPID
TUPID
AH-HA! STOP DOING THAT, ROCK!
CURIOUS
CURIOUS
CURIOUS
CURIOUS
UH, LENORE... THAT ROCK ISN'T ACTUALLY TALKING. YOU'VE BEEN SAYING ALL THOSE THINGS OUT THE SIDE OF YOUR MOUTH.
REALLY? I AM? THAT'S SO...
CRAZY
CRAZY
CRAZY
SHUT UP @*#* ROCK!!
STUPID ROCK. GONNA GO BACK TO MY PICNIC AND FORGET ALL ABOUT YOU.
WHO'S STUPID NOW, ROCK?!
THIS IS SO SPIFFY. YOU KNOW WHO WOULD HAVE ENJOYED THIS? RAGAMUFFIN. WHAT'S HE BEEN UP TO LATELY ANYWAY?

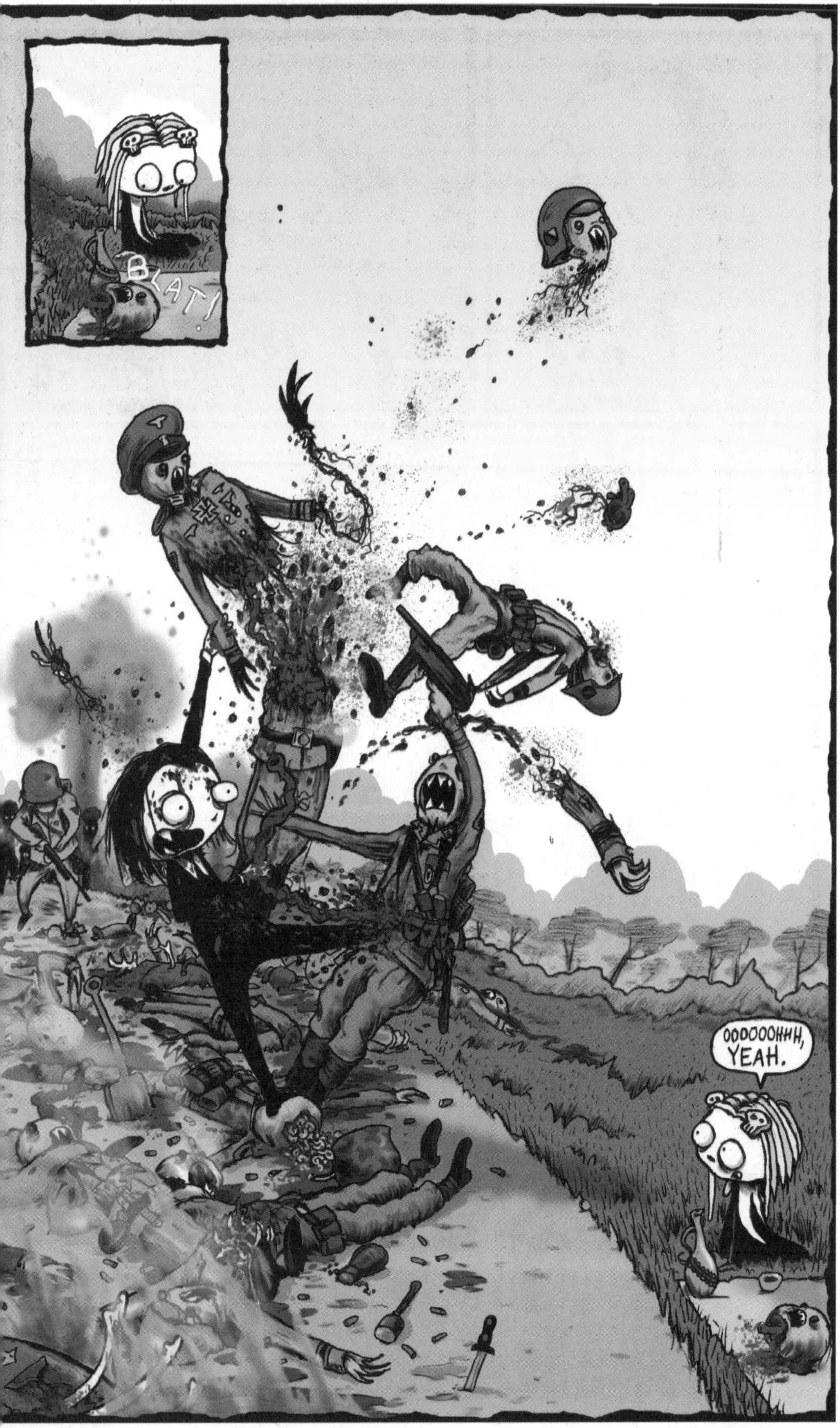
BLAT!
OOOOOOHHH, YEAH.

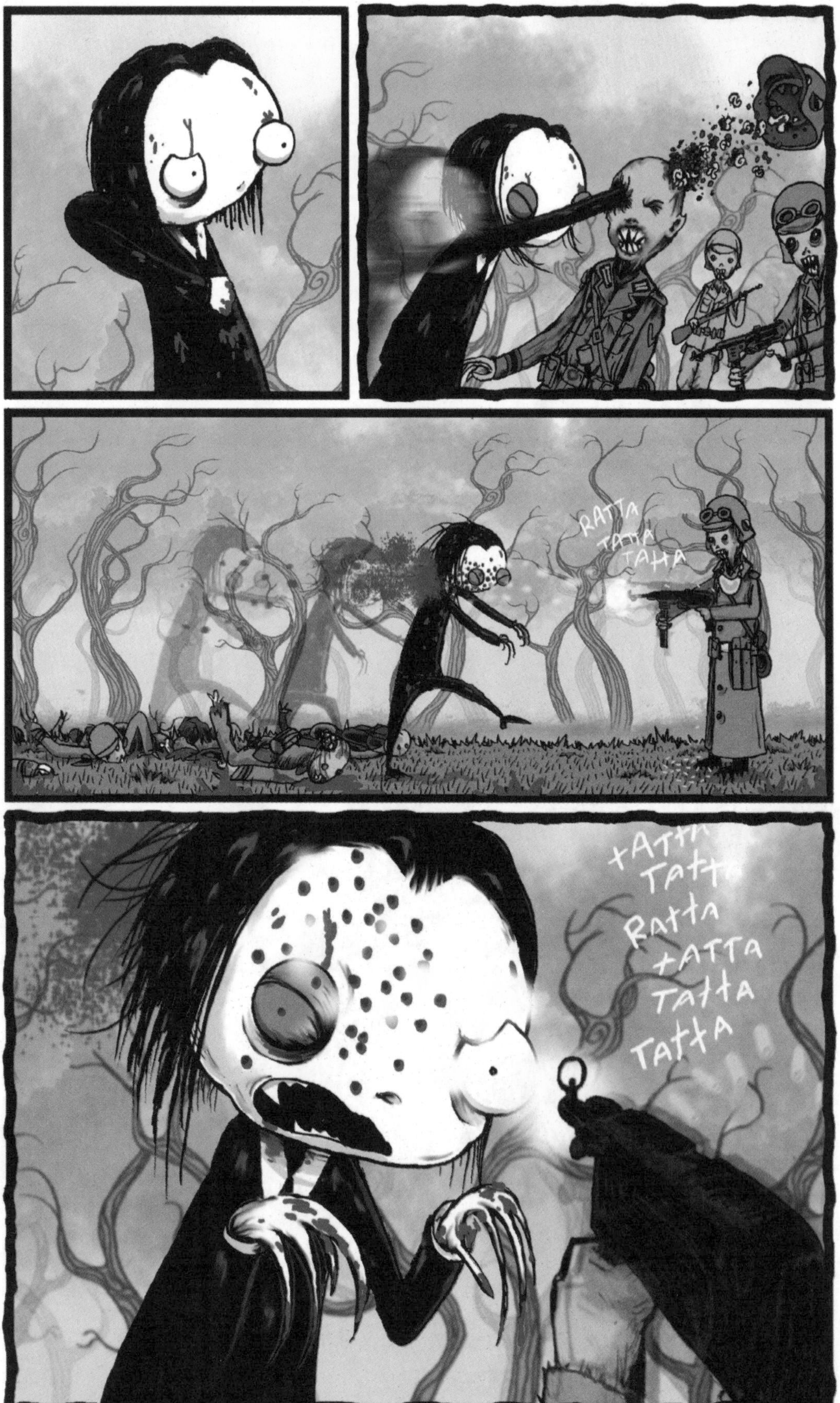

RATTA
TATTA
TAHA
tATTA
Tatta
Ratta
tATTa
TAtta
Tatta

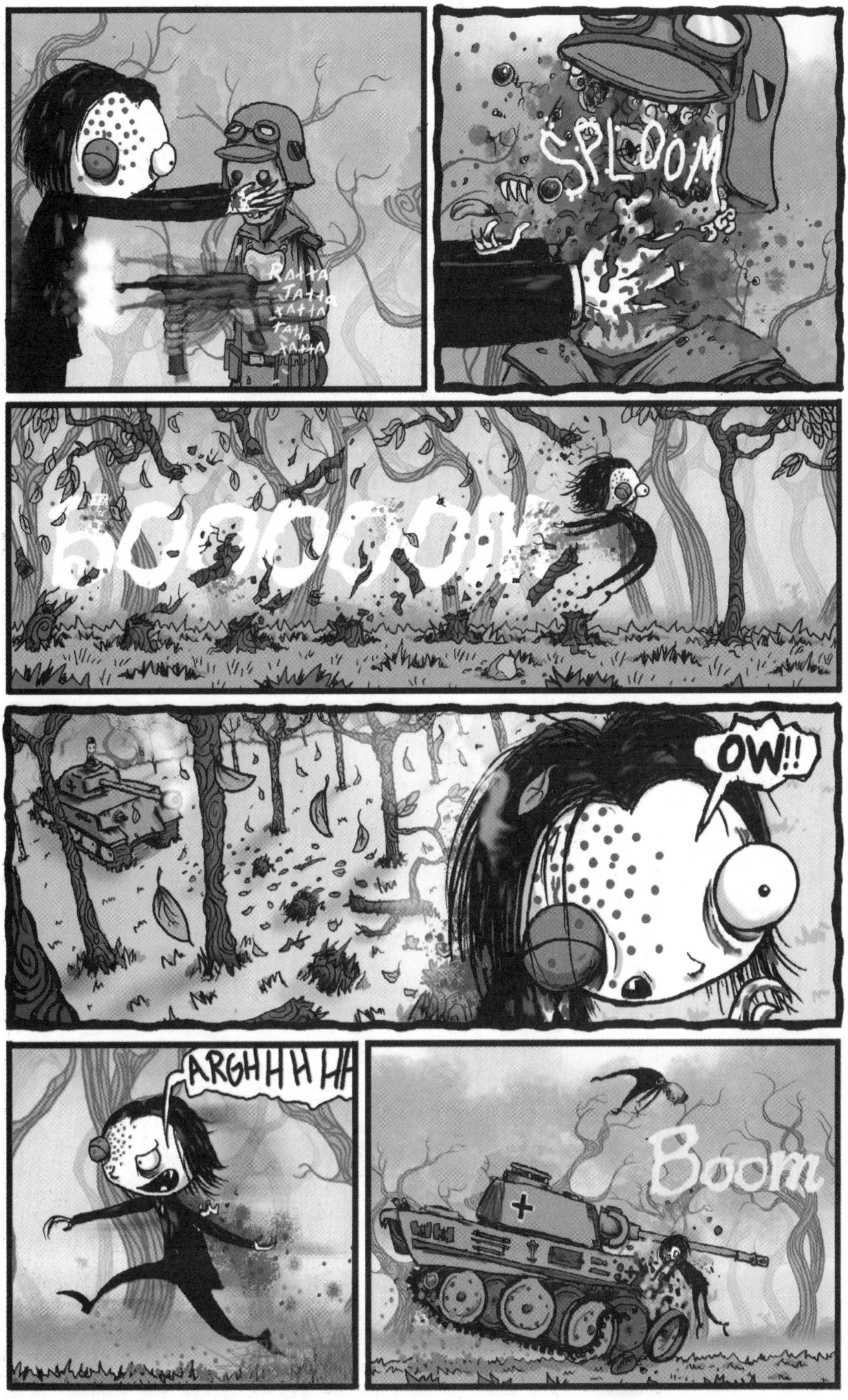
Ratta
Tatta
tatta
tatta
tatta
SPLOOM
BOOOOOM
OW!!
ARGHHHHH
Boom

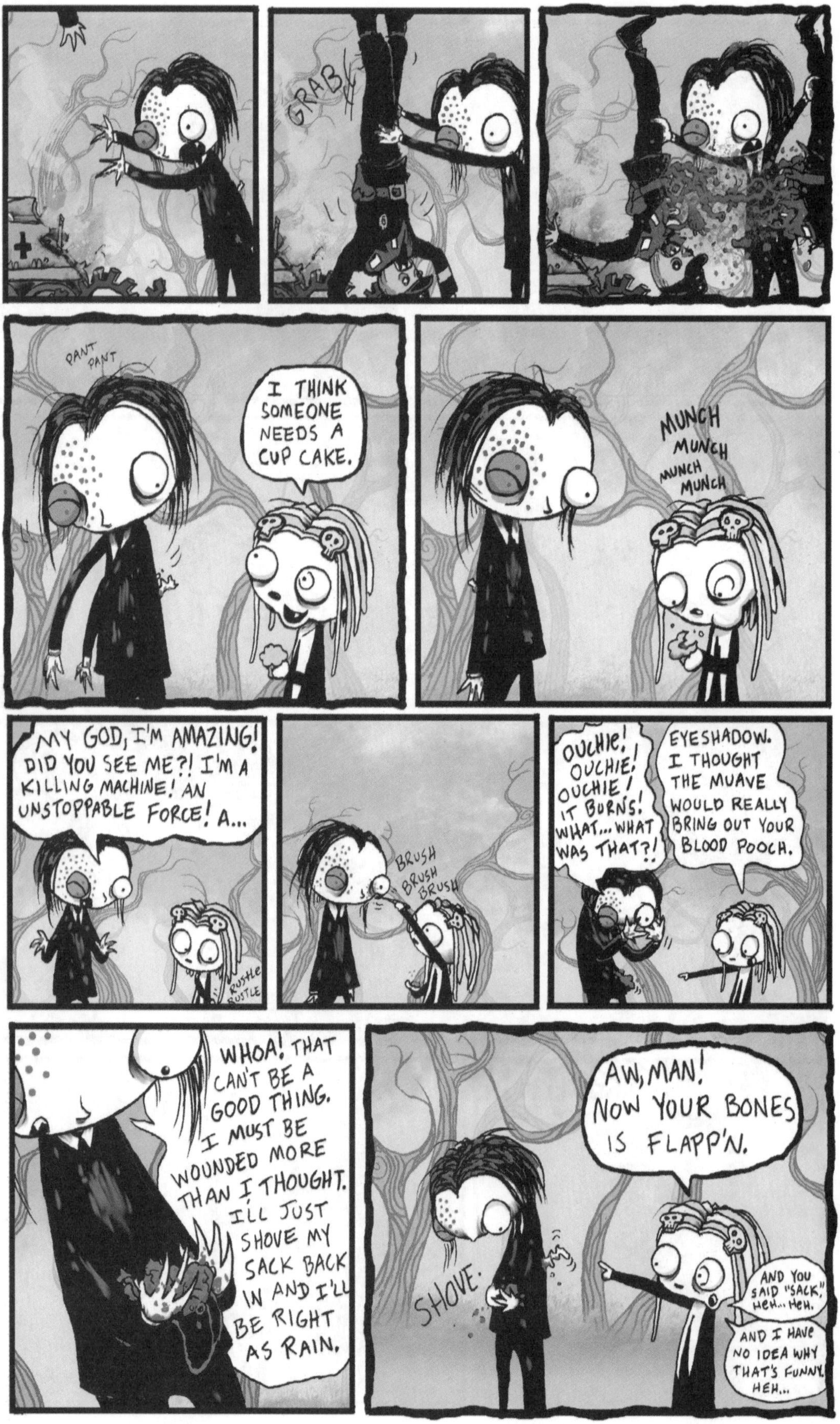
GRAB
PANT PANT
I THINK SOMEONE NEEDS A CUP CAKE.
MUNCH MUNCH MUNCH MUNCH
MY GOD, I'M AMAZING! DID YOU SEE ME?! I'M A KILLING MACHINE! AN UNSTOPPABLE FORCE! A...
RUSTLE RUSTLE
BRUSH BRUSH BRUSH
OUCHIE! OUCHIE! OUCHIE! IT BURNS! WHAT... WHAT WAS THAT?!
EYESHADOW. I THOUGHT THE MUAVE WOULD REALLY BRING OUT YOUR BLOOD POOCH.
WHOA! THAT CAN'T BE A GOOD THING. I MUST BE WOUNDED MORE THAN I THOUGHT. I'LL JUST SHOVE MY SACK BACK IN AND I'LL BE RIGHT AS RAIN.
AW, MAN! NOW YOUR BONES IS FLAPP'N.
SHOVE.
AND YOU SAID "SACK," HEH... HEH.
AND I HAVE NO IDEA WHY THAT'S FUNNY. HEH...

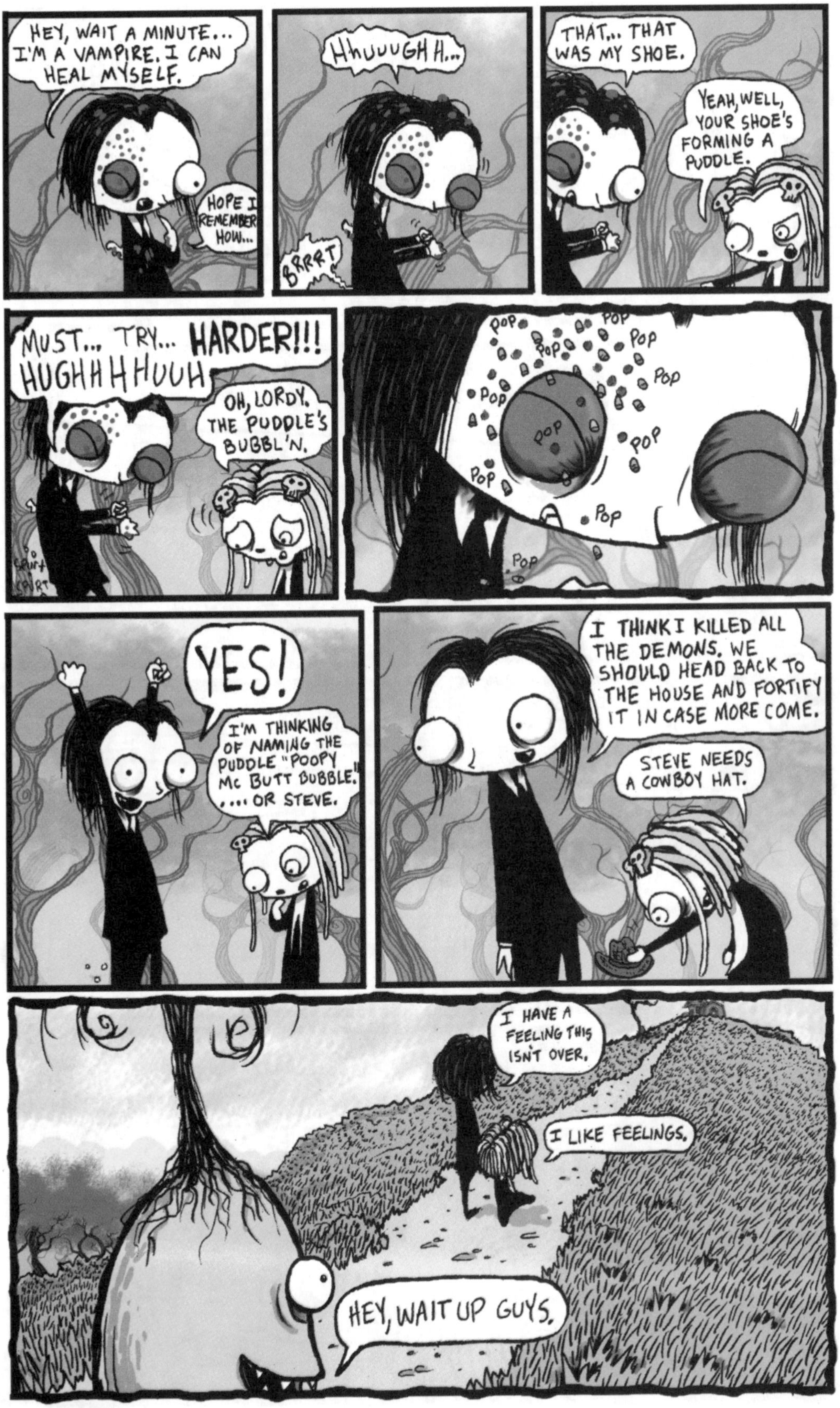
HEY, WAIT A MINUTE... I'M A VAMPIRE. I CAN HEAL MYSELF.
HOPE I REMEMBER HOW...
HHUUUGHH...
BRRRT
THAT... THAT WAS MY SHOE.
YEAH, WELL, YOUR SHOE'S FORMING A PUDDLE.
MUST... TRY... HARDER!!! HUGHHHHUUH
OH, LORDY. THE PUDDLE'S BUBBL'N.
POP POP POP POP POP POP POP POP POP POP POP
YES!
I'M THINKING OF NAMING THE PUDDLE "POOPY MC BUTT BUBBLE." ....OR STEVE.
I THINK I KILLED ALL THE DEMONS. WE SHOULD HEAD BACK TO THE HOUSE AND FORTIFY IT IN CASE MORE COME.
STEVE NEEDS A COWBOY HAT.
I HAVE A FEELING THIS ISN'T OVER.
I LIKE FEELINGS.
HEY, WAIT UP GUYS.

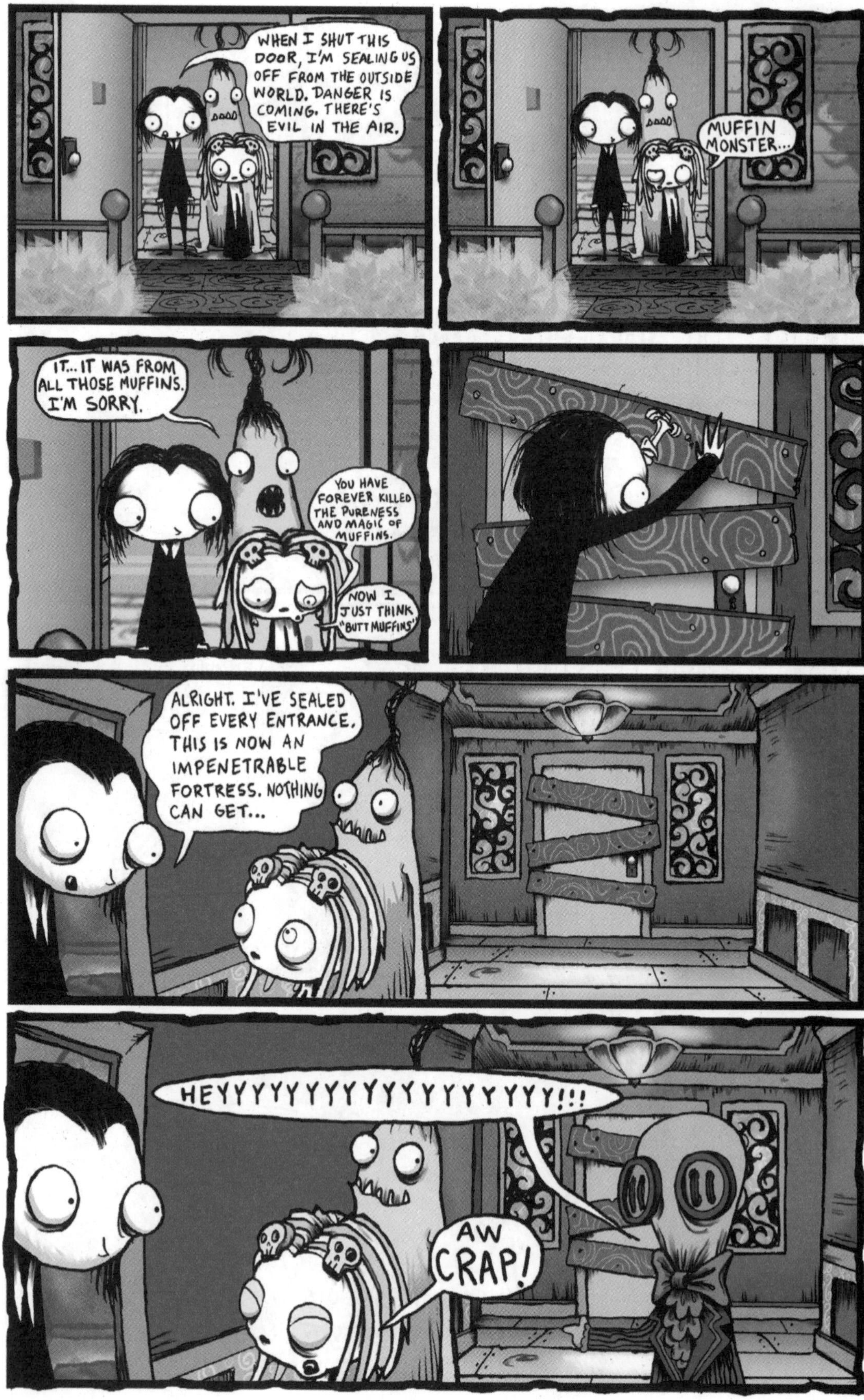

WHEN I SHUT THIS DOOR, I'M SEALING US OFF FROM THE OUTSIDE WORLD. DANGER IS COMING. THERE'S EVIL IN THE AIR.
MUFFIN MONSTER...
IT... IT WAS FROM ALL THOSE MUFFINS. I'M SORRY.
YOU HAVE FOREVER KILLED THE PURENESS AND MAGIC OF MUFFINS.
NOW I JUST THINK "BUTT MUFFINS"
ALRIGHT. I'VE SEALED OFF EVERY ENTRANCE. THIS IS NOW AN IMPENETRABLE FORTRESS. NOTHING CAN GET...
HEYYYYYYYYYYYYYYYYYYYY!!!
AW CRAP!

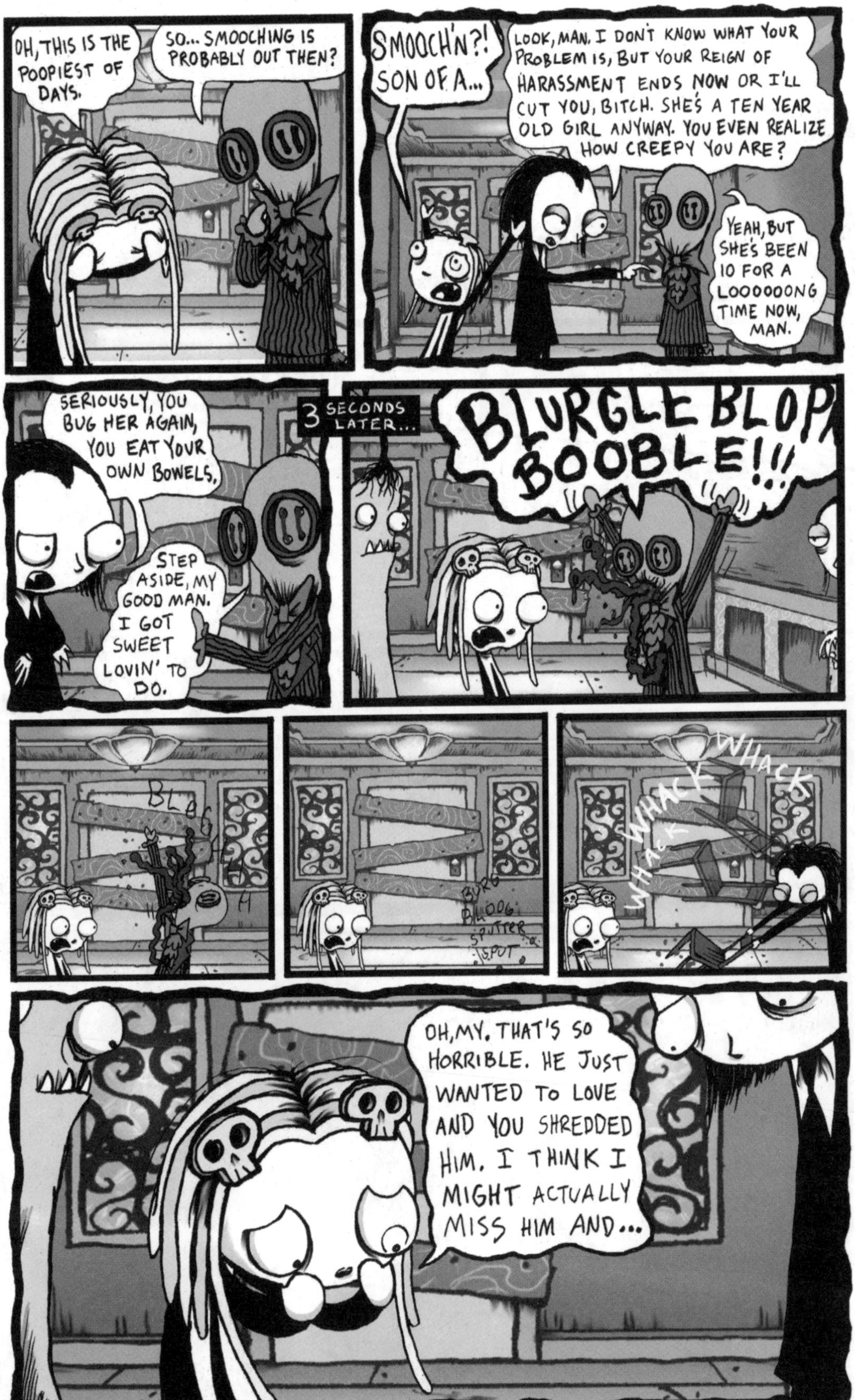
OH, THIS IS THE POOPIEST OF DAYS.
SO... SMOOCHING IS PROBABLY OUT THEN?
SMOOCH'N?! SON OF A...
LOOK, MAN. I DON'T KNOW WHAT YOUR PROBLEM IS, BUT YOUR REIGN OF HARASSMENT ENDS NOW OR I'LL CUT YOU, BITCH. SHE'S A TEN YEAR OLD GIRL ANYWAY. YOU EVEN REALIZE HOW CREEPY YOU ARE?
YEAH, BUT SHE'S BEEN 10 FOR A LOOOOOONG TIME NOW, MAN.
SERIOUSLY, YOU BUG HER AGAIN, YOU EAT YOUR OWN BOWELS.
STEP ASIDE, MY GOOD MAN. I GOT SWEET LOVIN' TO DO.
3 SECONDS LATER...
BLURGLE BLOP BOOBLE!!!
WHACK WHACK WHACK
OH, MY. THAT'S SO HORRIBLE. HE JUST WANTED TO LOVE AND YOU SHREDDED HIM. I THINK I MIGHT ACTUALLY MISS HIM AND...

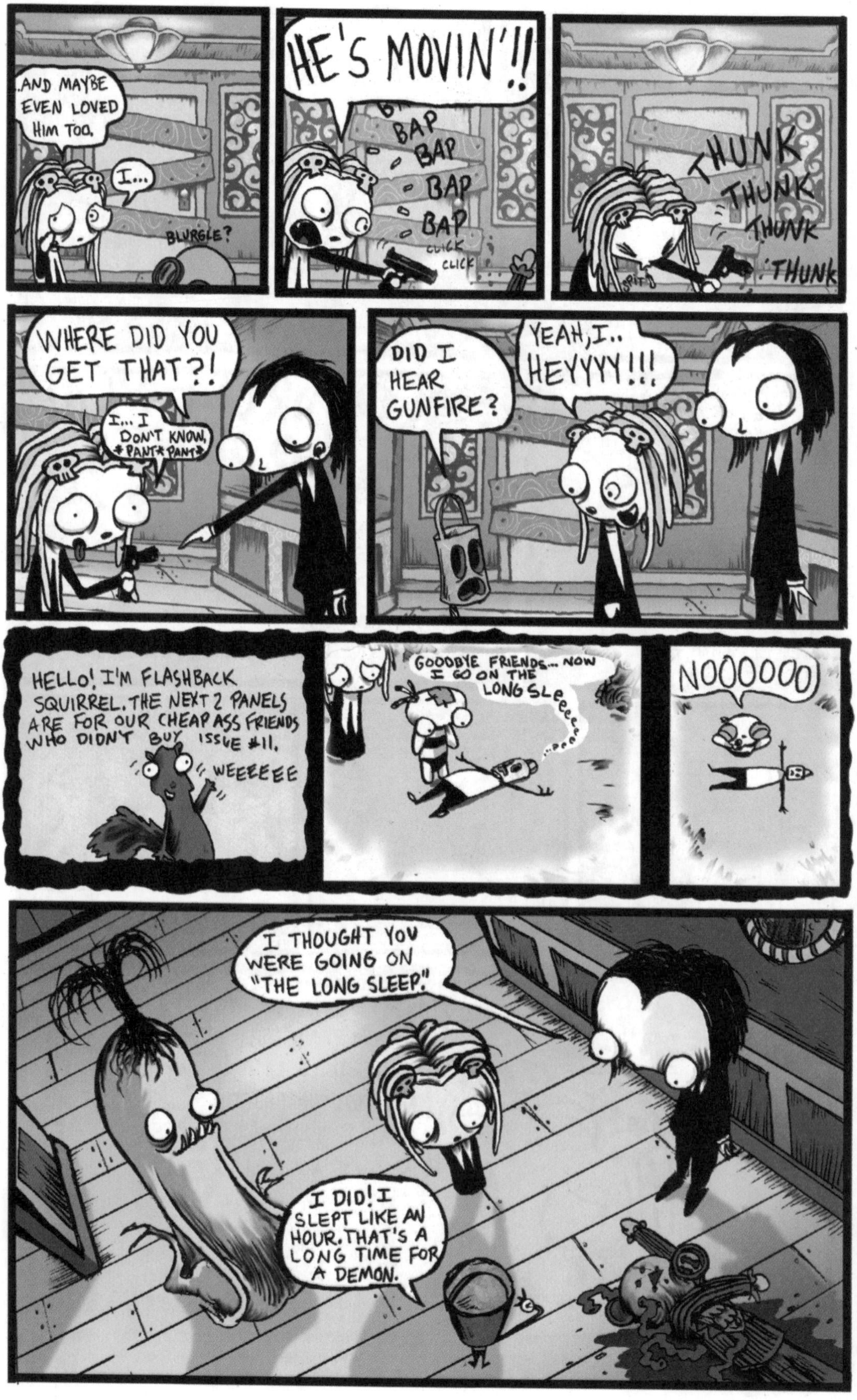

...AND MAYBE EVEN LOVED HIM TOO.
I...
BLURGLE?
HE'S MOVIN'!!
BAP BAP BAP BAP
CLICK CLICK
THUNK THUNK THUNK THUNK
SPIT
WHERE DID YOU GET THAT?!
I... I DON'T KNOW. *PANT* PANT*
DID I HEAR GUNFIRE?
YEAH, I.. HEYYYY!!!
HELLO! I'M FLASHBACK SQUIRREL. THE NEXT 2 PANELS ARE FOR OUR CHEAP ASS FRIENDS WHO DIDN'T BUY ISSUE #11.
WEEEEEE
GOODBYE FRIENDS... NOW I GO ON THE LONG SLEeeee...
NOOOOOO
I THOUGHT YOU WERE GOING ON "THE LONG SLEEP."
I DID! I SLEPT LIKE AN HOUR. THAT'S A LONG TIME FOR A DEMON.

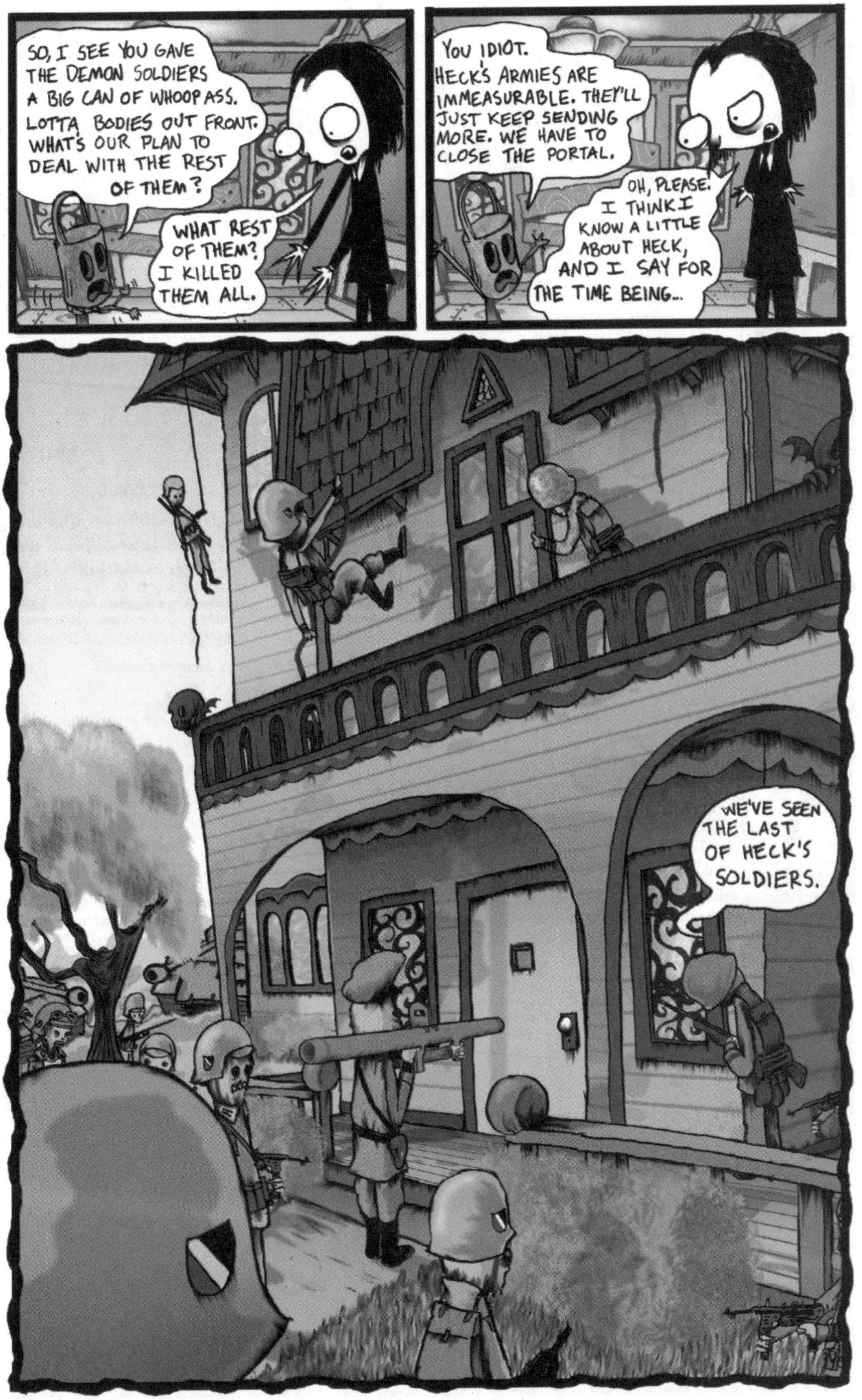
SO, I SEE YOU GAVE THE DEMON SOLDIERS A BIG CAN OF WHOOP ASS. LOTTA BODIES OUT FRONT. WHAT'S OUR PLAN TO DEAL WITH THE REST OF THEM?
WHAT REST OF THEM? I KILLED THEM ALL.
YOU IDIOT. HECK'S ARMIES ARE IMMEASURABLE. THEY'LL JUST KEEP SENDING MORE. WE HAVE TO CLOSE THE PORTAL.
OH, PLEASE. I THINK I KNOW A LITTLE ABOUT HECK, AND I SAY FOR THE TIME BEING...
WE'VE SEEN THE LAST OF HECK'S SOLDIERS.

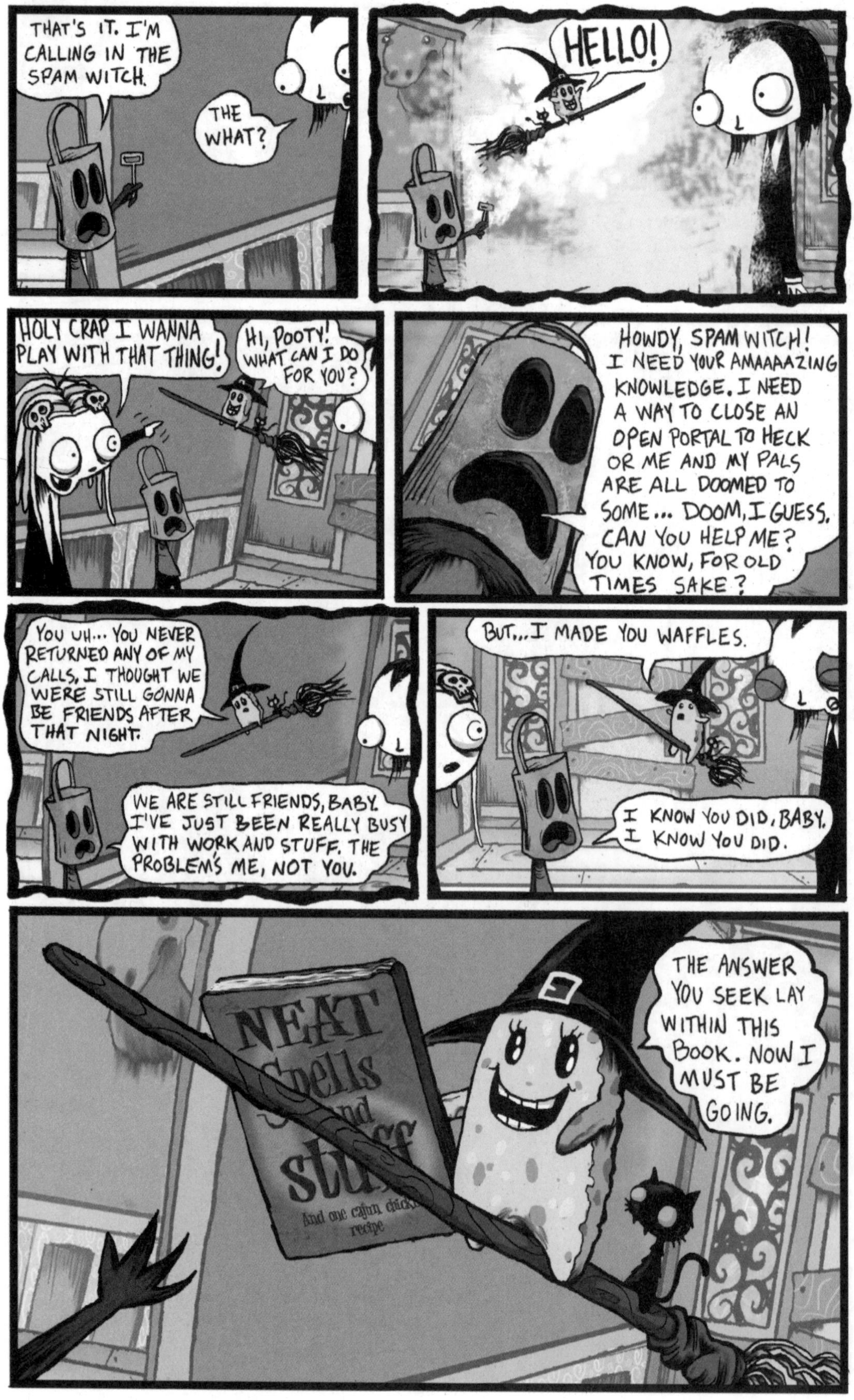
THAT'S IT. I'M CALLING IN THE SPAM WITCH.
THE WHAT?
HELLO!
HOLY CRAP I WANNA PLAY WITH THAT THING!
HI, POOTY! WHAT CAN I DO FOR YOU?
HOWDY, SPAM WITCH! I NEED YOUR AMAAAAZING KNOWLEDGE. I NEED A WAY TO CLOSE AN OPEN PORTAL TO HECK OR ME AND MY PALS ARE ALL DOOMED TO SOME... DOOM, I GUESS. CAN YOU HELP ME? YOU KNOW, FOR OLD TIMES SAKE?
YOU UH... YOU NEVER RETURNED ANY OF MY CALLS. I THOUGHT WE WERE STILL GONNA BE FRIENDS AFTER THAT NIGHT.
WE ARE STILL FRIENDS, BABY. I'VE JUST BEEN REALLY BUSY WITH WORK AND STUFF. THE PROBLEM'S ME, NOT YOU.
BUT... I MADE YOU WAFFLES.
I KNOW YOU DID, BABY. I KNOW YOU DID.
THE ANSWER YOU SEEK LAY WITHIN THIS BOOK. NOW I MUST BE GOING.
NEAT Spells and stuff
And one cajun chick recipe

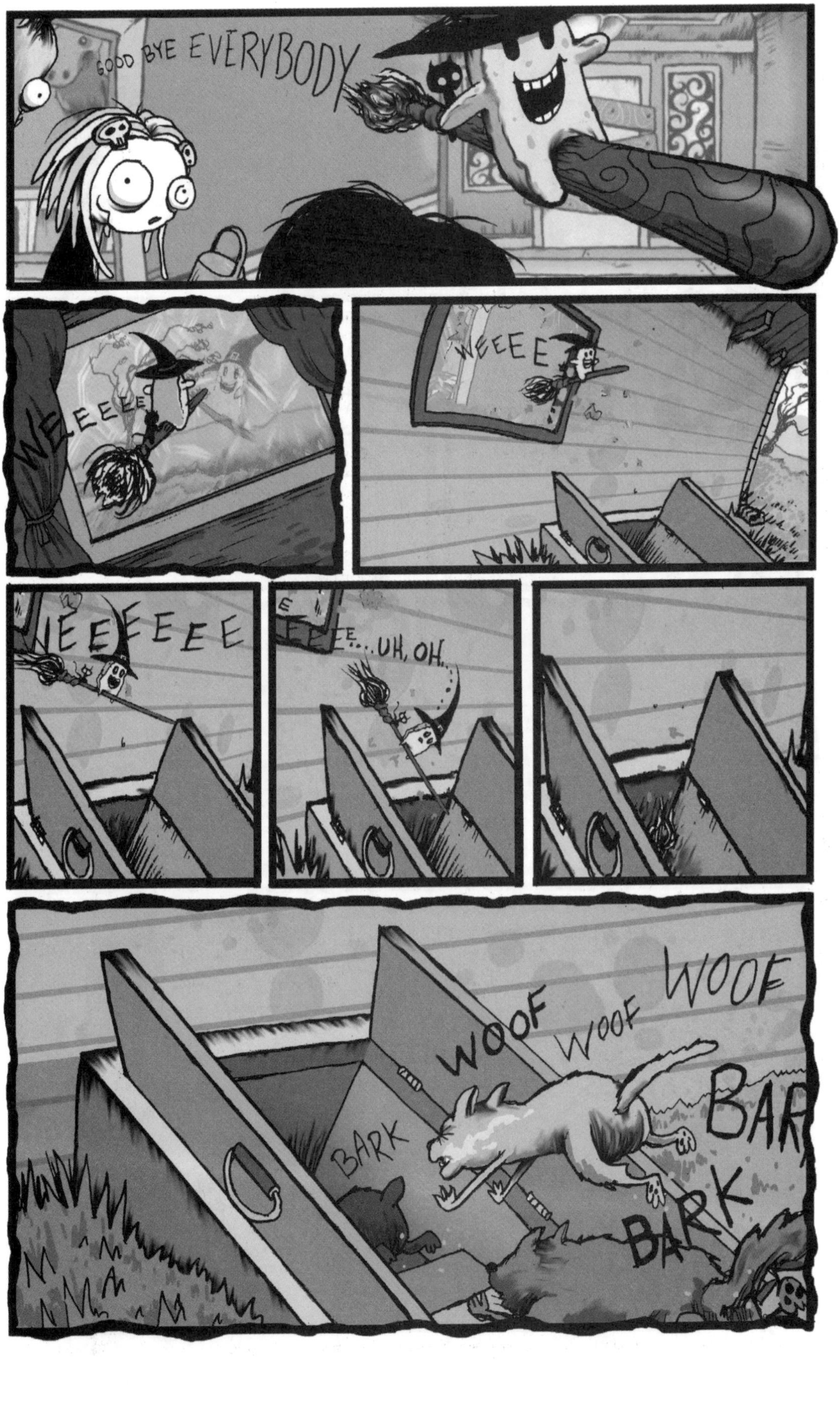
GOOD BYE EVERYBODY
WEEEEEE
WEEEE
WEEEEEEE
EEEE...UH, OH.
WOOF
WOOF
WOOF
BARK
BAR
BARK
BARK

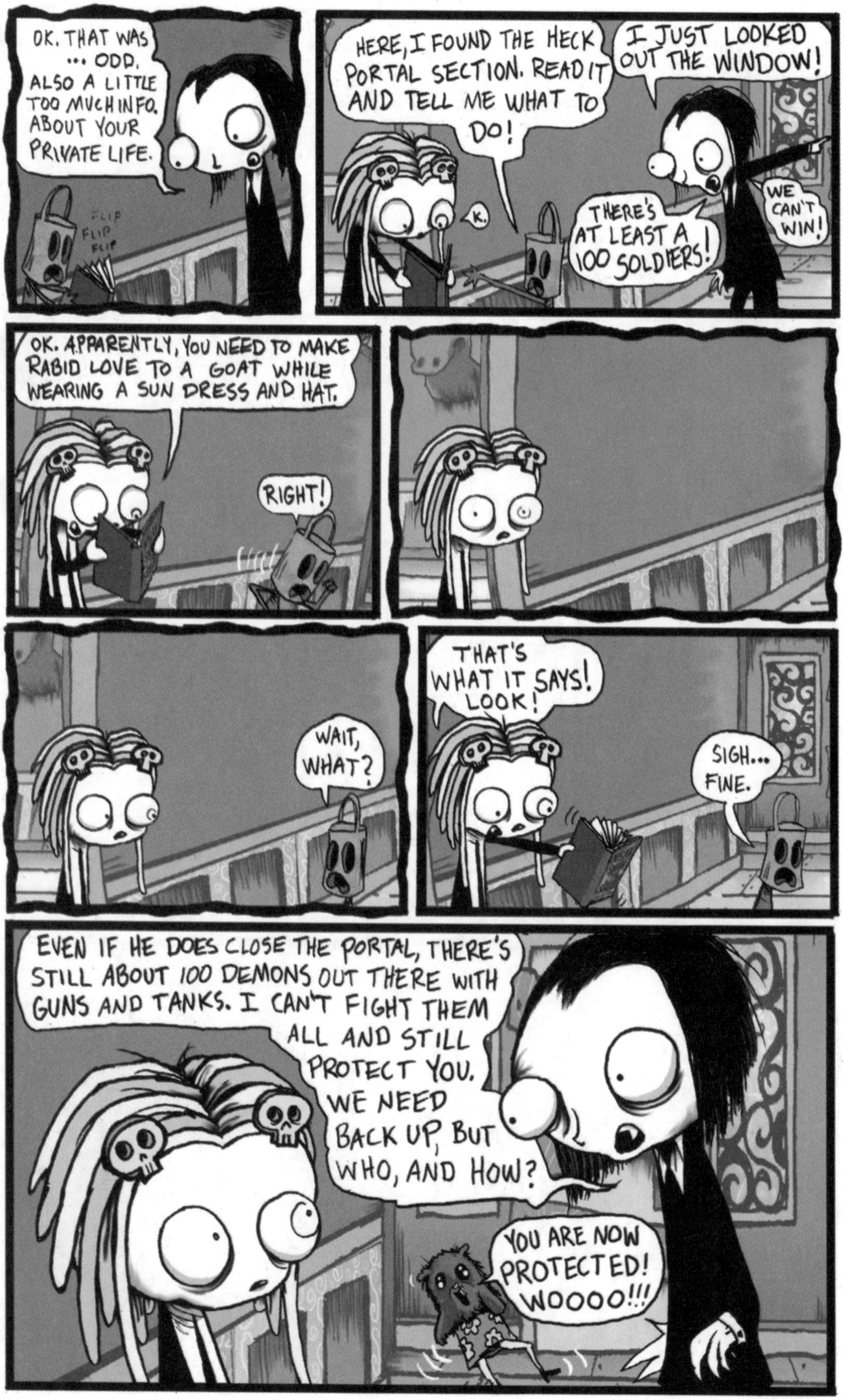
OK. THAT WAS ... ODD. ALSO A LITTLE TOO MUCH INFO. ABOUT YOUR PRIVATE LIFE.
FLIP FLIP FLIP
HERE, I FOUND THE HECK PORTAL SECTION. READ IT AND TELL ME WHAT TO DO!
K.
I JUST LOOKED OUT THE WINDOW!
THERE'S AT LEAST A 100 SOLDIERS!
WE CAN'T WIN!
OK. APPARENTLY, YOU NEED TO MAKE RABID LOVE TO A GOAT WHILE WEARING A SUN DRESS AND HAT.
RIGHT!
WAIT, WHAT?
THAT'S WHAT IT SAYS! LOOK!
SIGH... FINE.
EVEN IF HE DOES CLOSE THE PORTAL, THERE'S STILL ABOUT 100 DEMONS OUT THERE WITH GUNS AND TANKS. I CAN'T FIGHT THEM ALL AND STILL PROTECT YOU. WE NEED BACK UP, BUT WHO, AND HOW?
YOU ARE NOW PROTECTED! WOOOO!!!

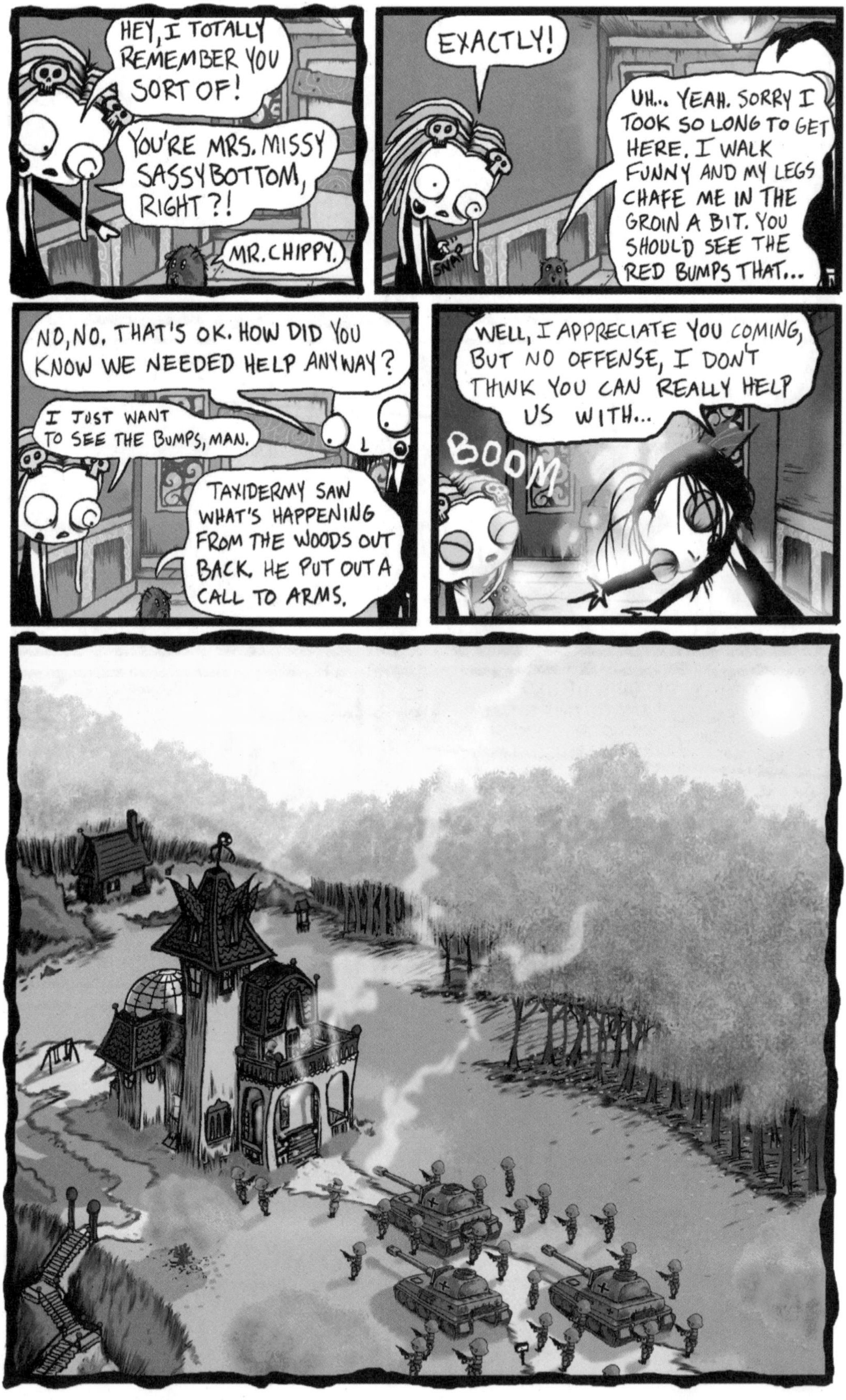
HEY, I TOTALLY REMEMBER YOU SORT OF!
YOU'RE MRS. MISSY SASSYBOTTOM, RIGHT?!
MR. CHIPPY.
EXACTLY!
SNAP
UH... YEAH. SORRY I TOOK SO LONG TO GET HERE. I WALK FUNNY AND MY LEGS CHAFE ME IN THE GROIN A BIT. YOU SHOULD SEE THE RED BUMPS THAT...
NO, NO. THAT'S OK. HOW DID YOU KNOW WE NEEDED HELP ANYWAY?
I JUST WANT TO SEE THE BUMPS, MAN.
TAXIDERMY SAW WHAT'S HAPPENING FROM THE WOODS OUT BACK. HE PUT OUT A CALL TO ARMS.
WELL, I APPRECIATE YOU COMING, BUT NO OFFENSE, I DON'T THINK YOU CAN REALLY HELP US WITH...
BOOM

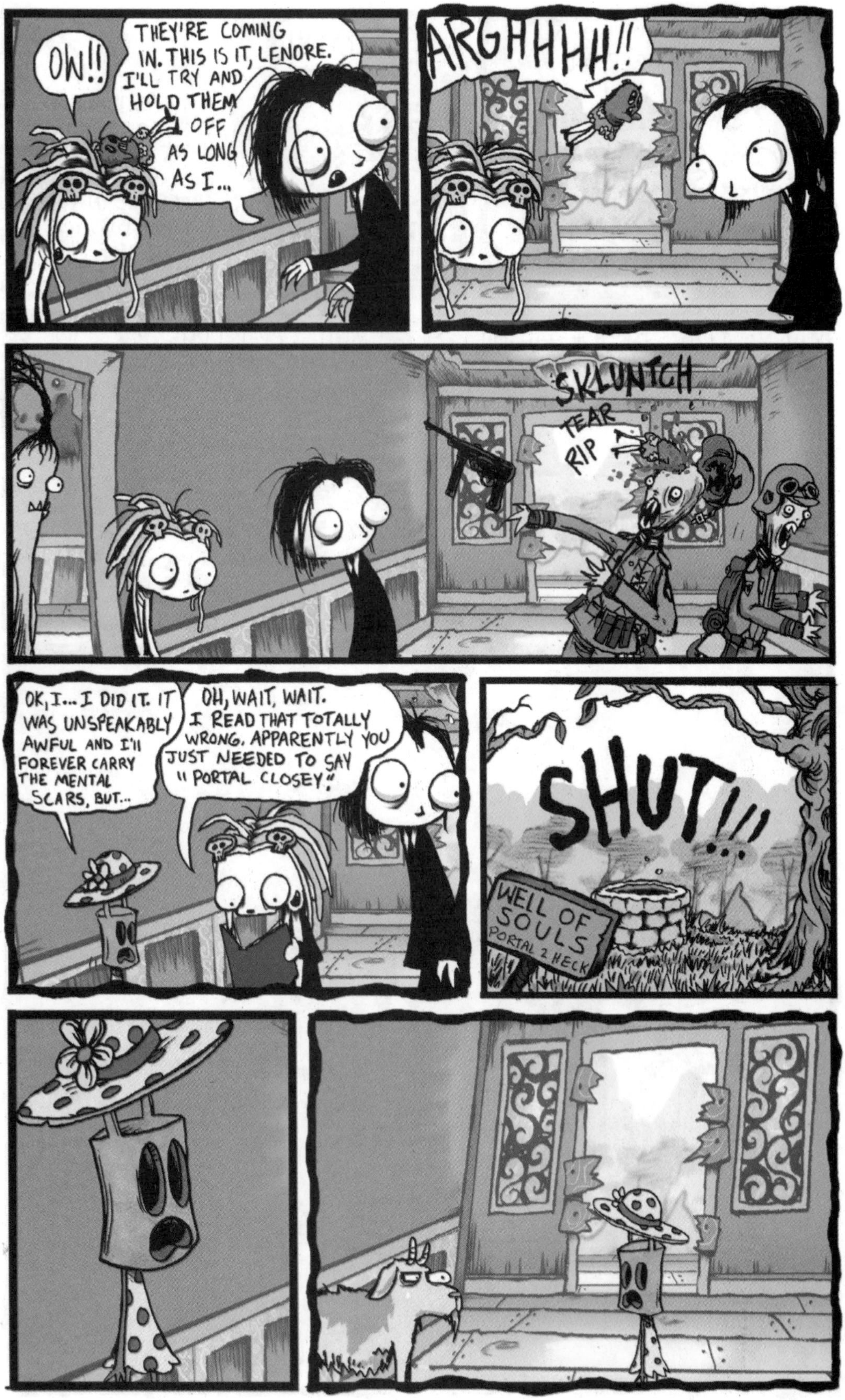

OW!!
THEY'RE COMING IN. THIS IS IT, LENORE. I'LL TRY AND HOLD THEM OFF AS LONG AS I...
ARGHHHH!!
SKLUNTCH
TEAR
RIP
OK, I... I DID IT. IT WAS UNSPEAKABLY AWFUL AND I'LL FOREVER CARRY THE MENTAL SCARS, BUT...
OH, WAIT, WAIT. I READ THAT TOTALLY WRONG. APPARENTLY YOU JUST NEEDED TO SAY "PORTAL CLOSEY."
SHUT!!!
WELL OF SOULS
PORTAL 2 HECK

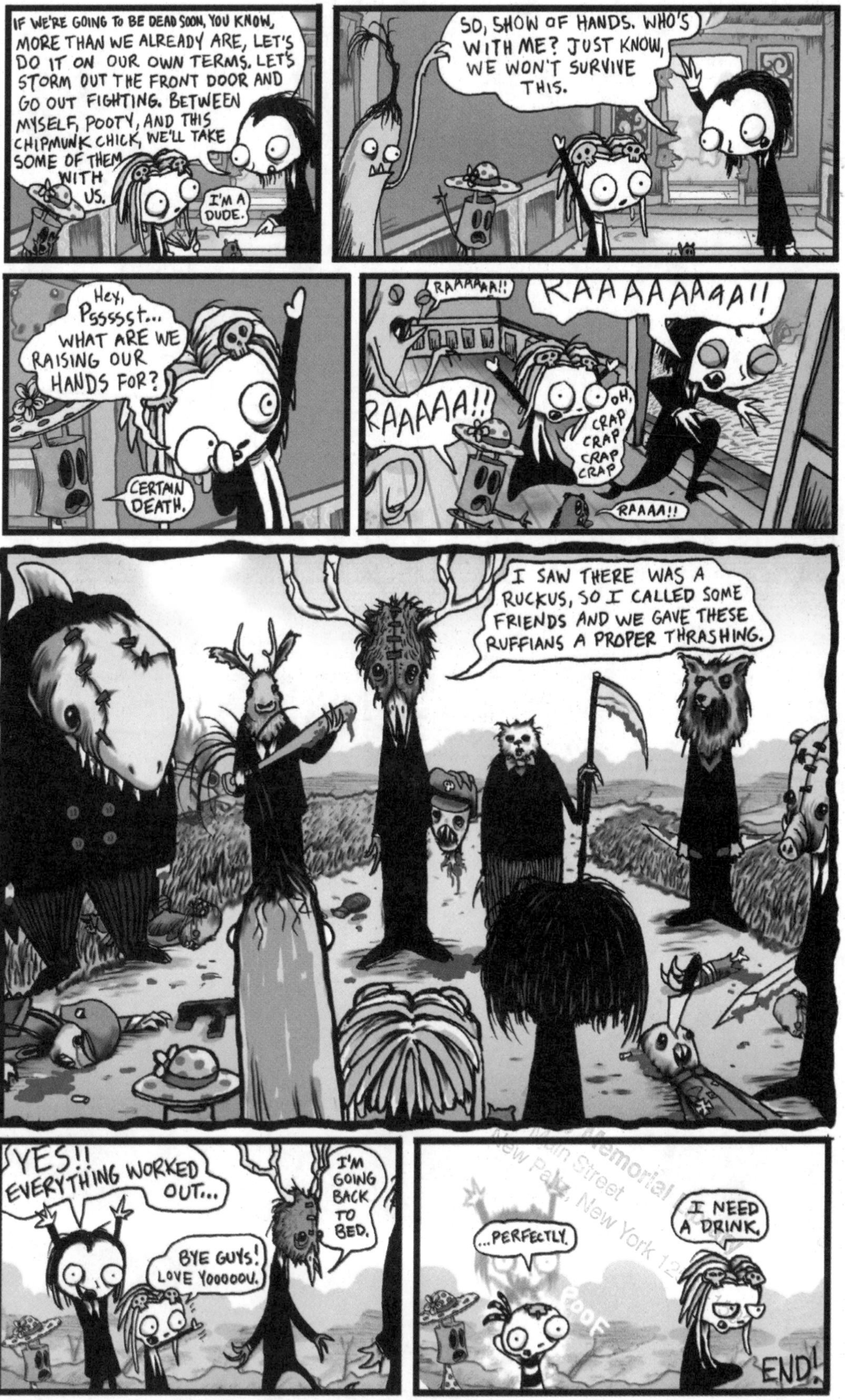

IF WE'RE GOING TO BE DEAD SOON, YOU KNOW, MORE THAN WE ALREADY ARE, LET'S DO IT ON OUR OWN TERMS. LET'S STORM OUT THE FRONT DOOR AND GO OUT FIGHTING. BETWEEN MYSELF, POOTY, AND THIS CHIPMUNK CHICK, WE'LL TAKE SOME OF THEM WITH US.
I'M A DUDE.
SO, SHOW OF HANDS. WHO'S WITH ME? JUST KNOW, WE WON'T SURVIVE THIS.
Hey, Psssst... WHAT ARE WE RAISING OUR HANDS FOR?
CERTAIN DEATH.
RAAAAAA!!
RAAAAAAAAA!!
RAAAAA!!
OH, CRAP CRAP CRAP CRAP
RAAAA!!
I SAW THERE WAS A RUCKUS, SO I CALLED SOME FRIENDS AND WE GAVE THESE RUFFIANS A PROPER THRASHING.
YES!! EVERYTHING WORKED OUT...
I'M GOING BACK TO BED.
BYE GUYS! LOVE YOOOOOU.
...PERFECTLY.
POOF
I NEED A DRINK.
END!

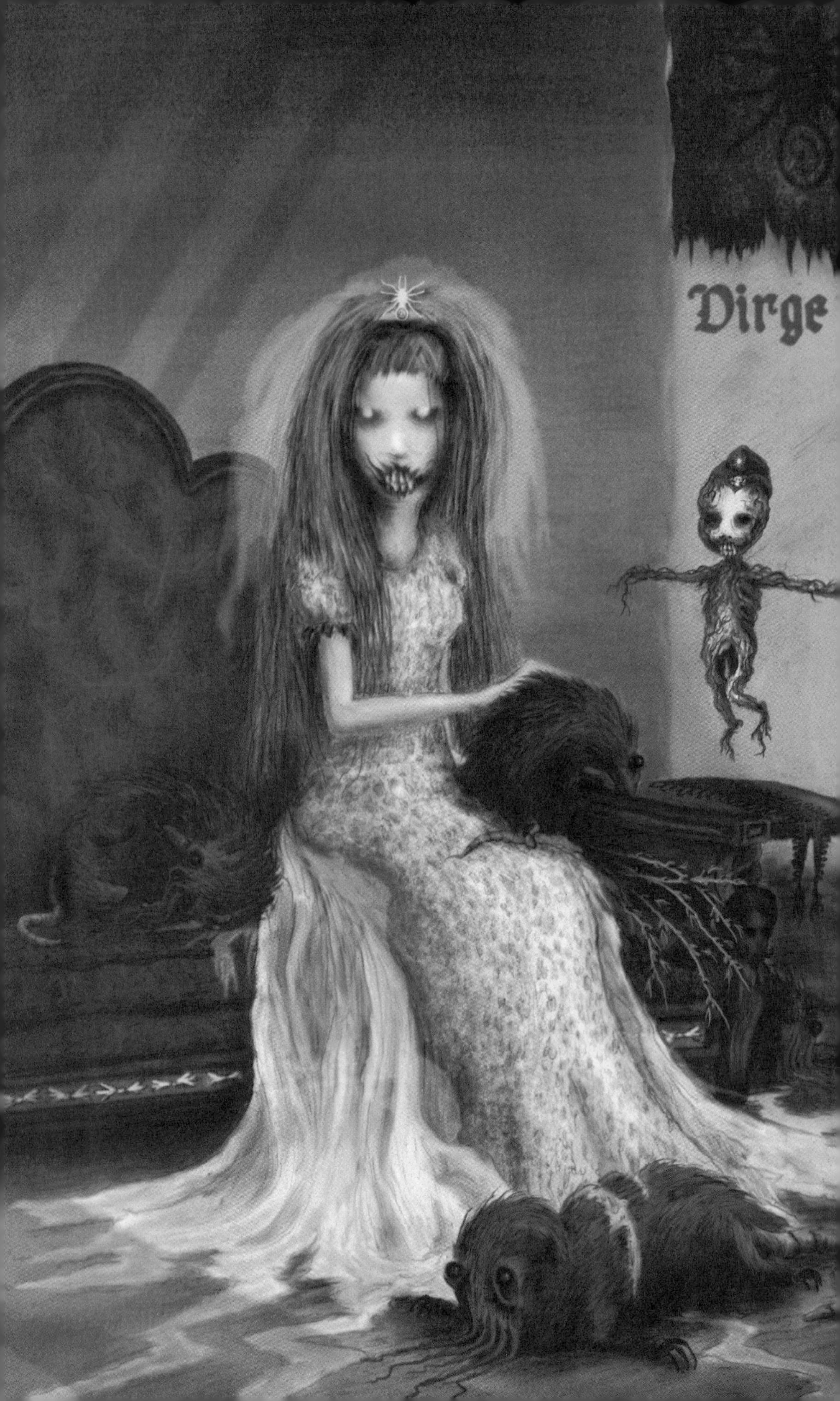
Dirge

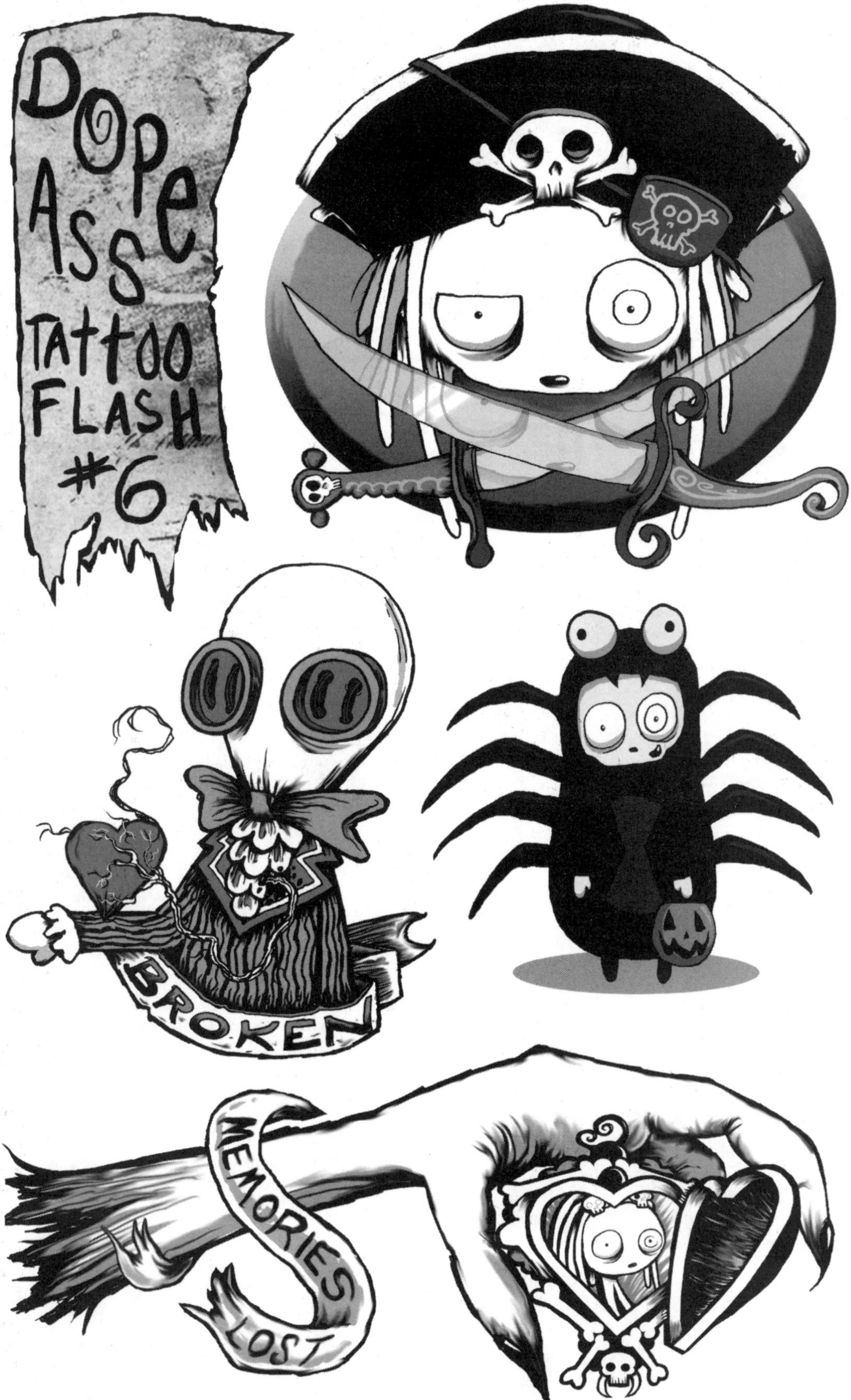

Dope Asse
Tattoo Flash
#6
BROKEN
MEMORIES
LOST

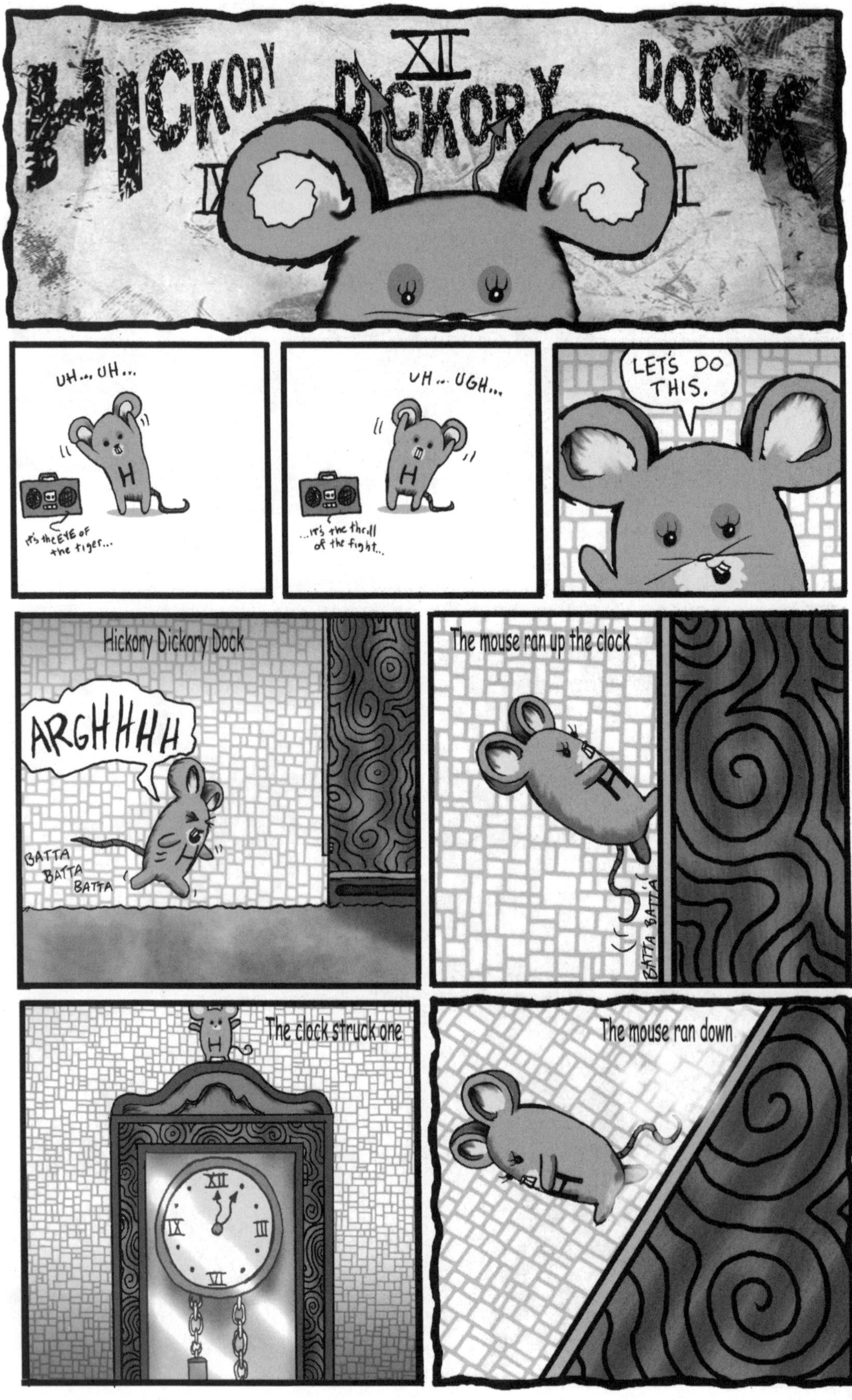
HICKORY DICKORY DOCK
XII
IX
III
UH... UH...
it's the EYE of the tiger...
UH... UGH...
...it's the thrill of the fight...
LET'S DO THIS.
Hickory Dickory Dock
ARGHHHH
BATTA BATTA BATTA
The mouse ran up the clock
BATTA BATTA
The clock struck one
XII
IX
III
VI
The mouse ran down

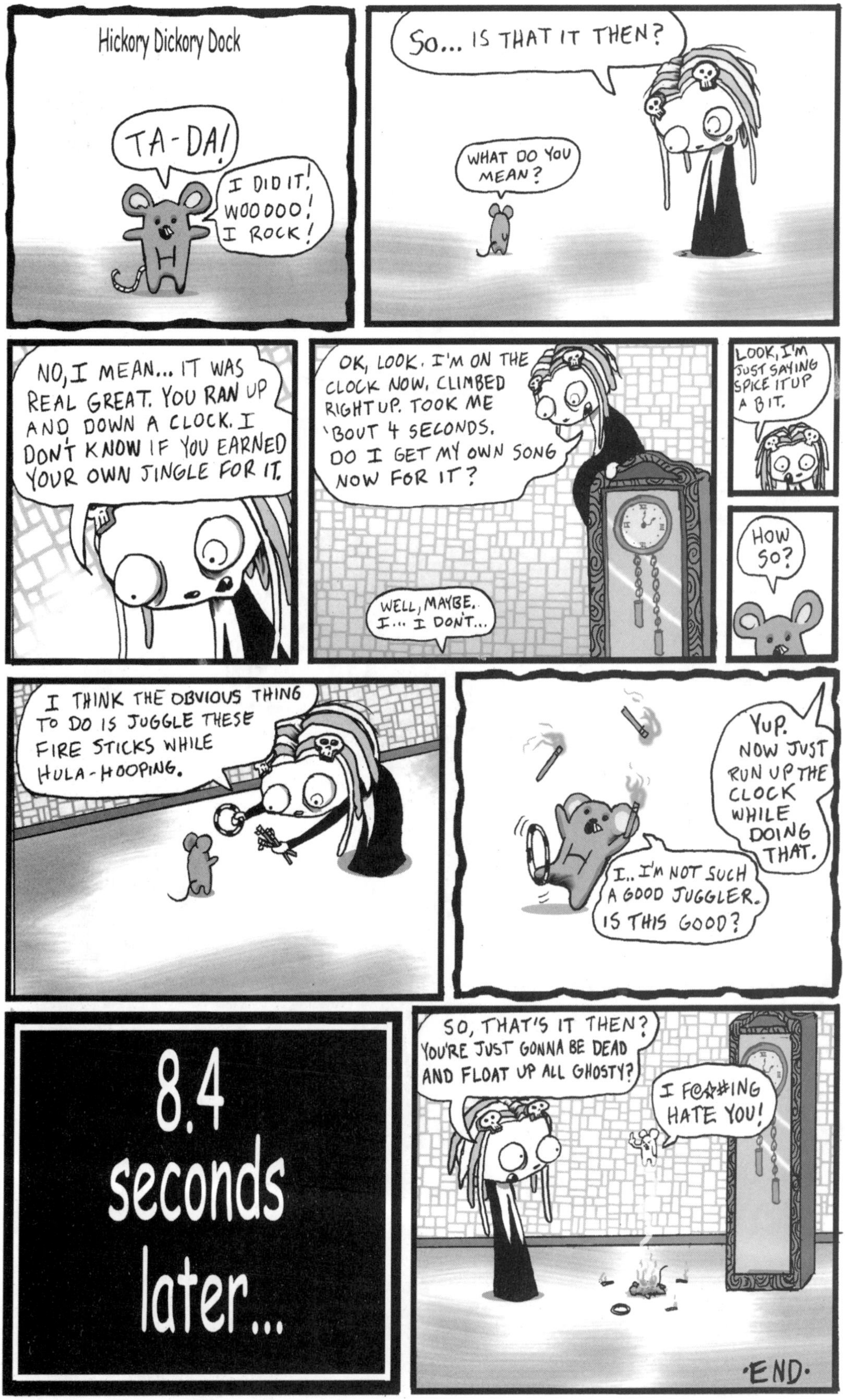
Hickory Dickory Dock
TA-DA!
I DID IT! WOODOO! I ROCK!
SO... IS THAT IT THEN?
WHAT DO YOU MEAN?
NO, I MEAN... IT WAS REAL GREAT. YOU RAN UP AND DOWN A CLOCK. I DON'T KNOW IF YOU EARNED YOUR OWN JINGLE FOR IT.
OK, LOOK. I'M ON THE CLOCK NOW. CLIMBED RIGHT UP. TOOK ME 'BOUT 4 SECONDS. DO I GET MY OWN SONG NOW FOR IT?
WELL, MAYBE. I... I DON'T...
LOOK, I'M JUST SAYING SPICE IT UP A BIT.
HOW SO?
I THINK THE OBVIOUS THING TO DO IS JUGGLE THESE FIRE STICKS WHILE HULA-HOOPING.
YUP. NOW JUST RUN UP THE CLOCK WHILE DOING THAT.
I.. I'M NOT SUCH A GOOD JUGGLER. IS THIS GOOD?
8.4 seconds later...
SO, THAT'S IT THEN? YOU'RE JUST GONNA BE DEAD AND FLOAT UP ALL GHOSTY?
I F@*#ING HATE YOU!
·END·

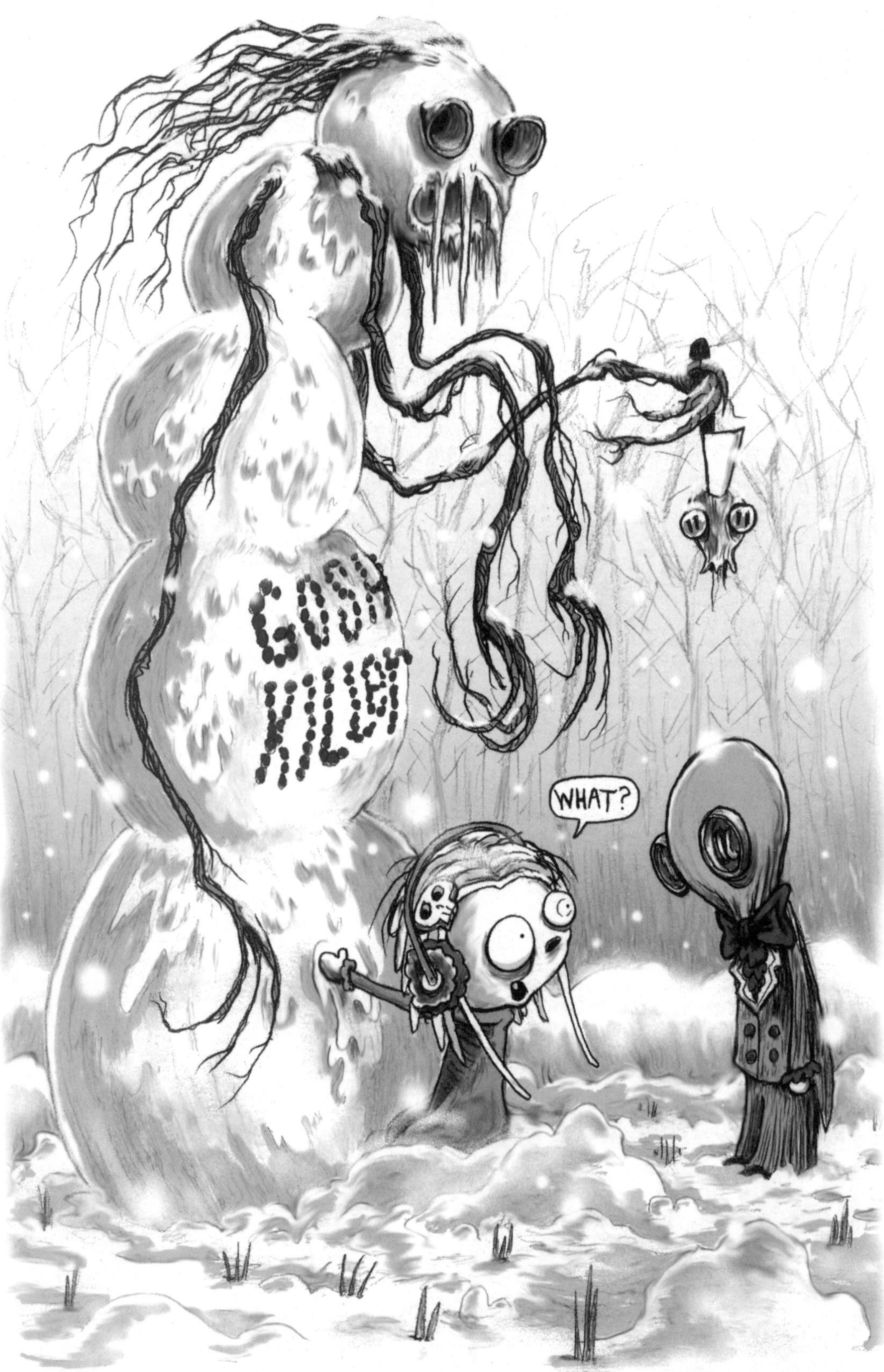
GOSH KILLER
WHAT?

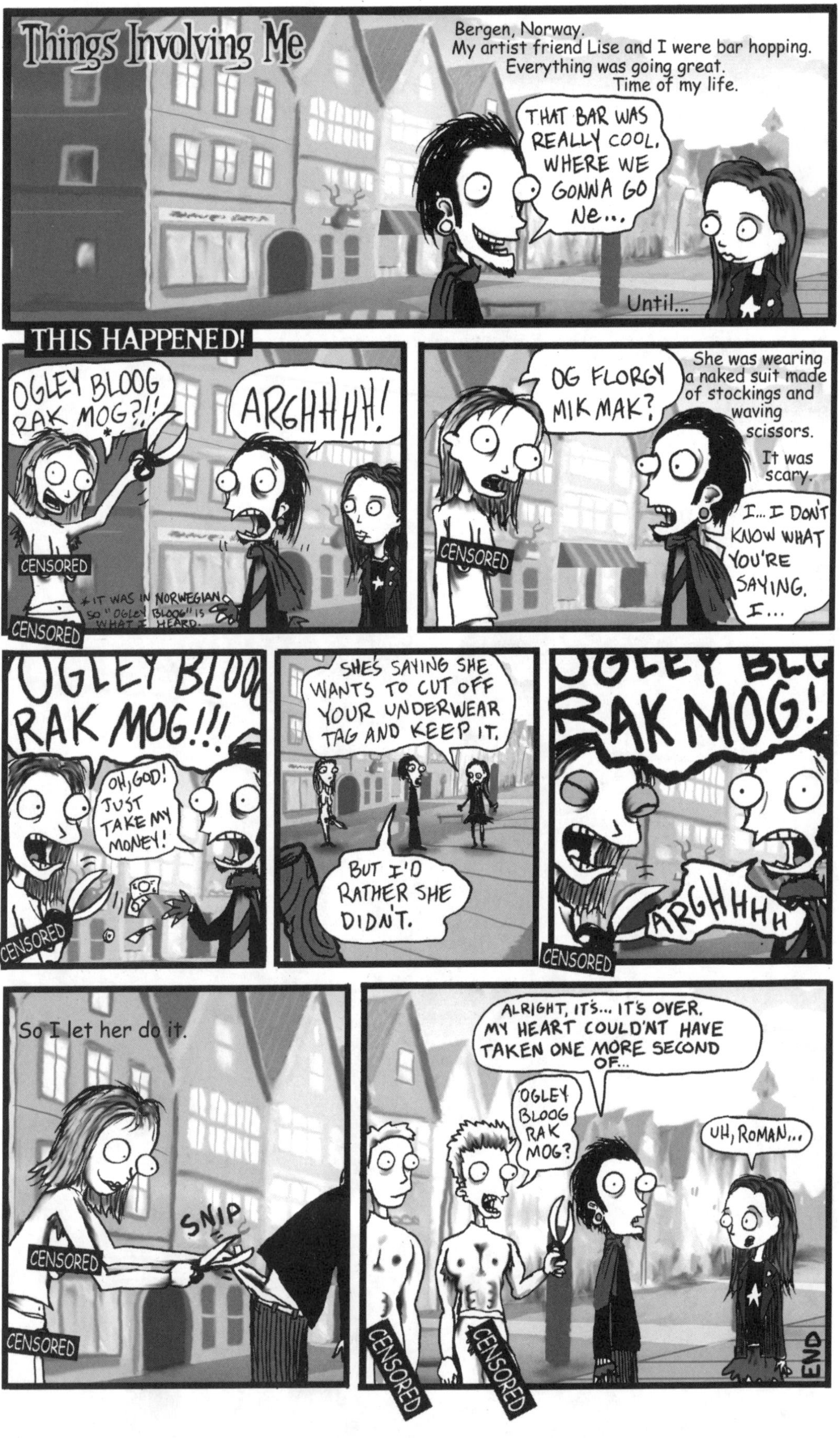
Things Involving Me
Bergen, Norway.
My artist friend Lise and I were bar hopping.
Everything was going great.
Time of my life.
THAT BAR WAS REALLY COOL. WHERE WE GONNA GO NE...
Until...
THIS HAPPENED!
OGLEY BLOOG RAK MOG?!!*
ARGHHHH!
CENSORED
CENSORED
* IT WAS IN NORWEGIAN, SO "OGLEY BLOOG" IS WHAT I HEARD.
OG FLORGY MIK MAK?
She was wearing a naked suit made of stockings and waving scissors.
It was scary.
CENSORED
I... I DON'T KNOW WHAT YOU'RE SAYING. I...
OGLEY BLOOG RAK MOG!!!
OH, GOD! JUST TAKE MY MONEY!
CENSORED
SHE'S SAYING SHE WANTS TO CUT OFF YOUR UNDERWEAR TAG AND KEEP IT.
BUT I'D RATHER SHE DIDN'T.
OGLEY BLO RAK MOG!
ARGHHHHH
CENSORED
So I let her do it.
SNIP
CENSORED
CENSORED
ALRIGHT, IT'S... IT'S OVER. MY HEART COULD'NT HAVE TAKEN ONE MORE SECOND OF...
OGLEY BLOOG RAK MOG?
UH, ROMAN...
CENSORED
CENSORED
END

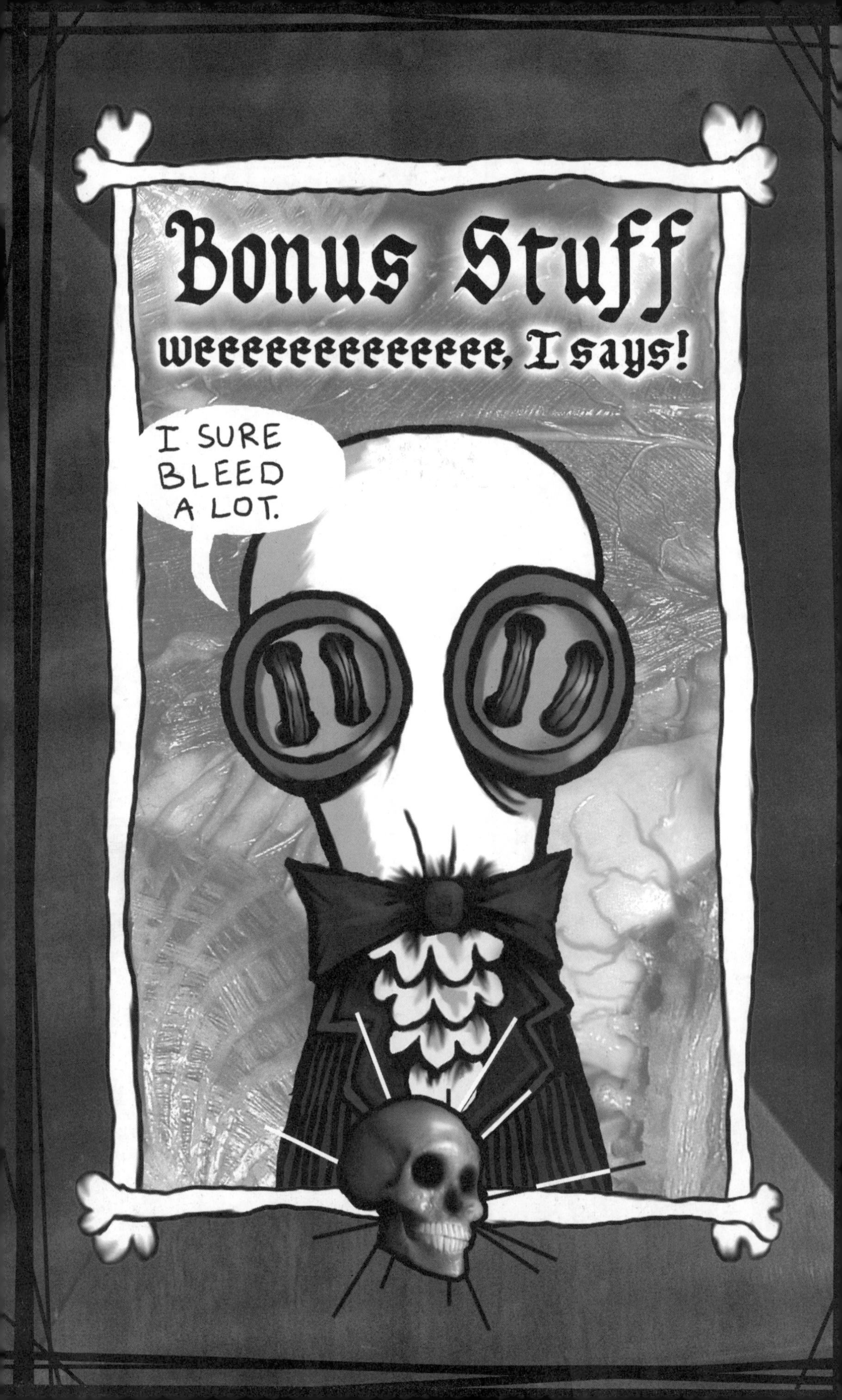

Bonus Stuff
weeeeeeeeeeeeee, I says!
I SURE BLEED A LOT.

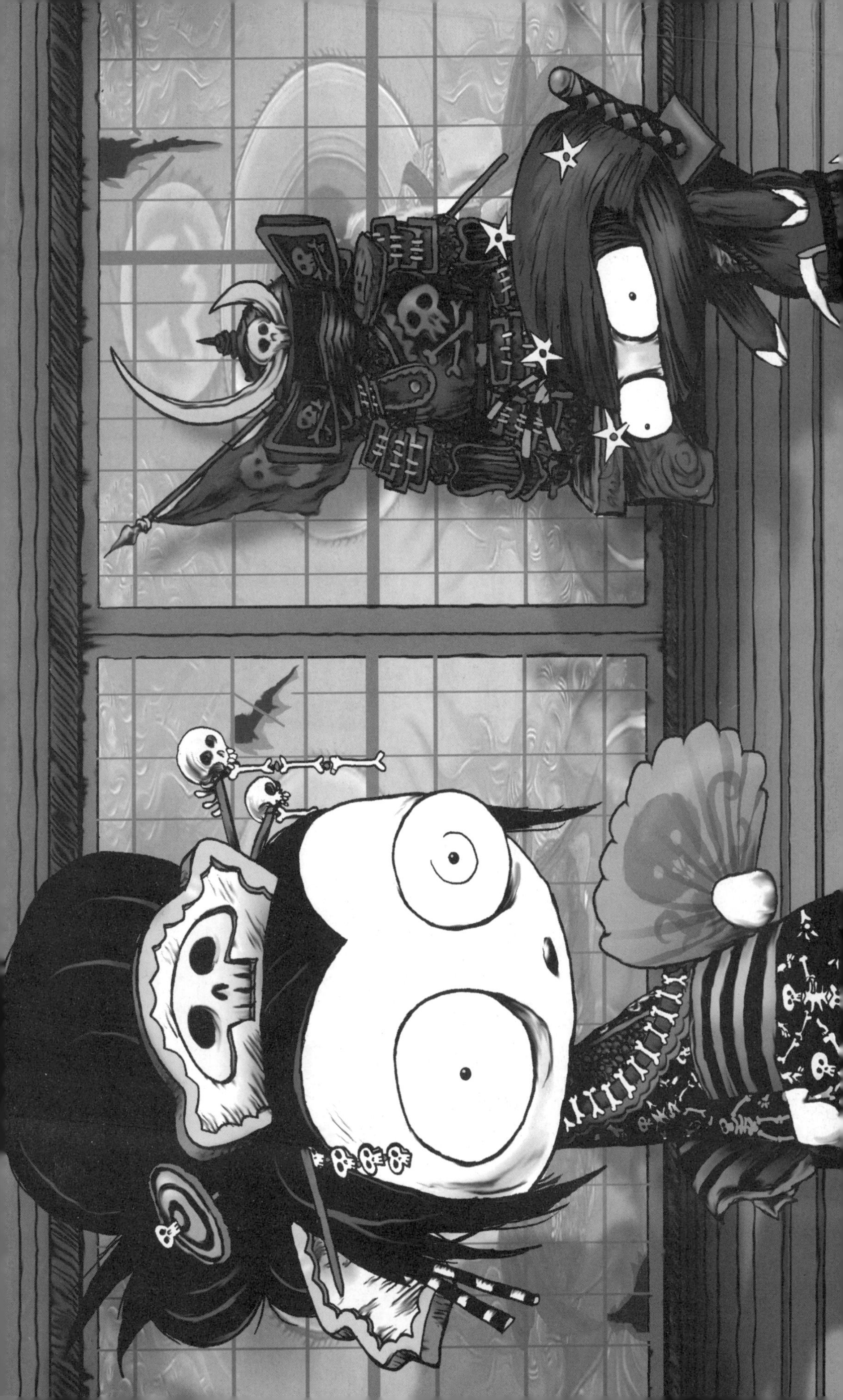

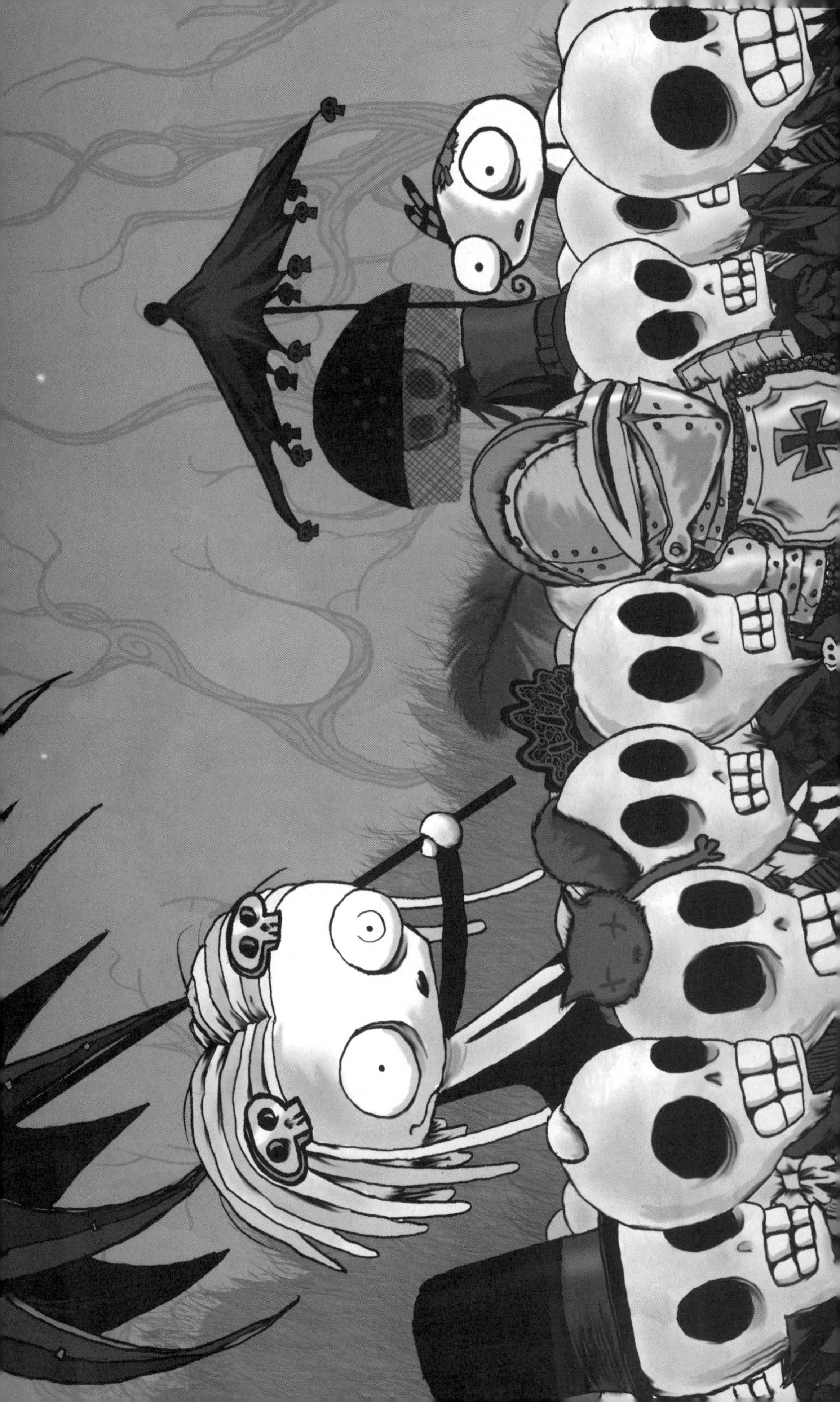

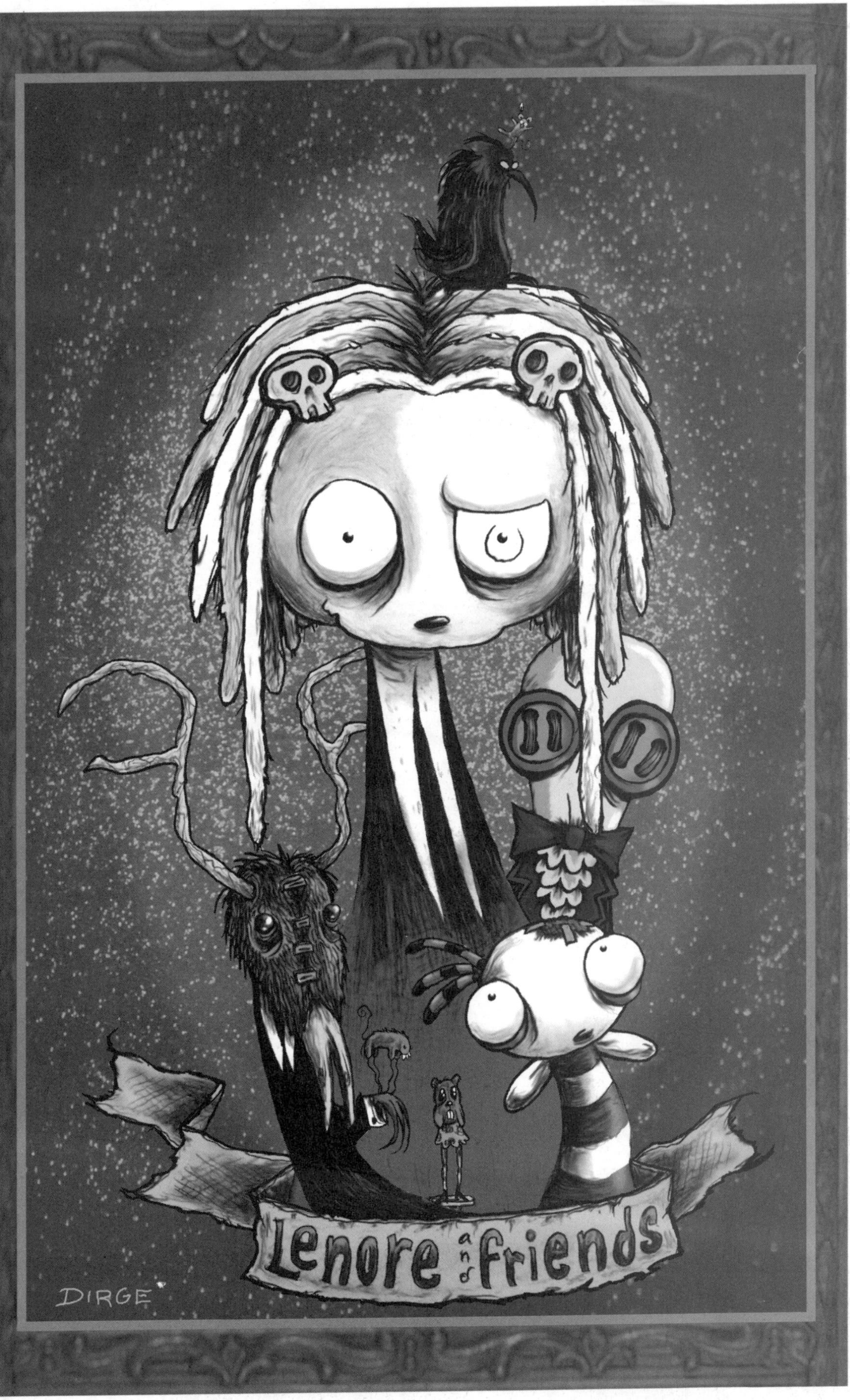

Lenore and Friends
DIRGE

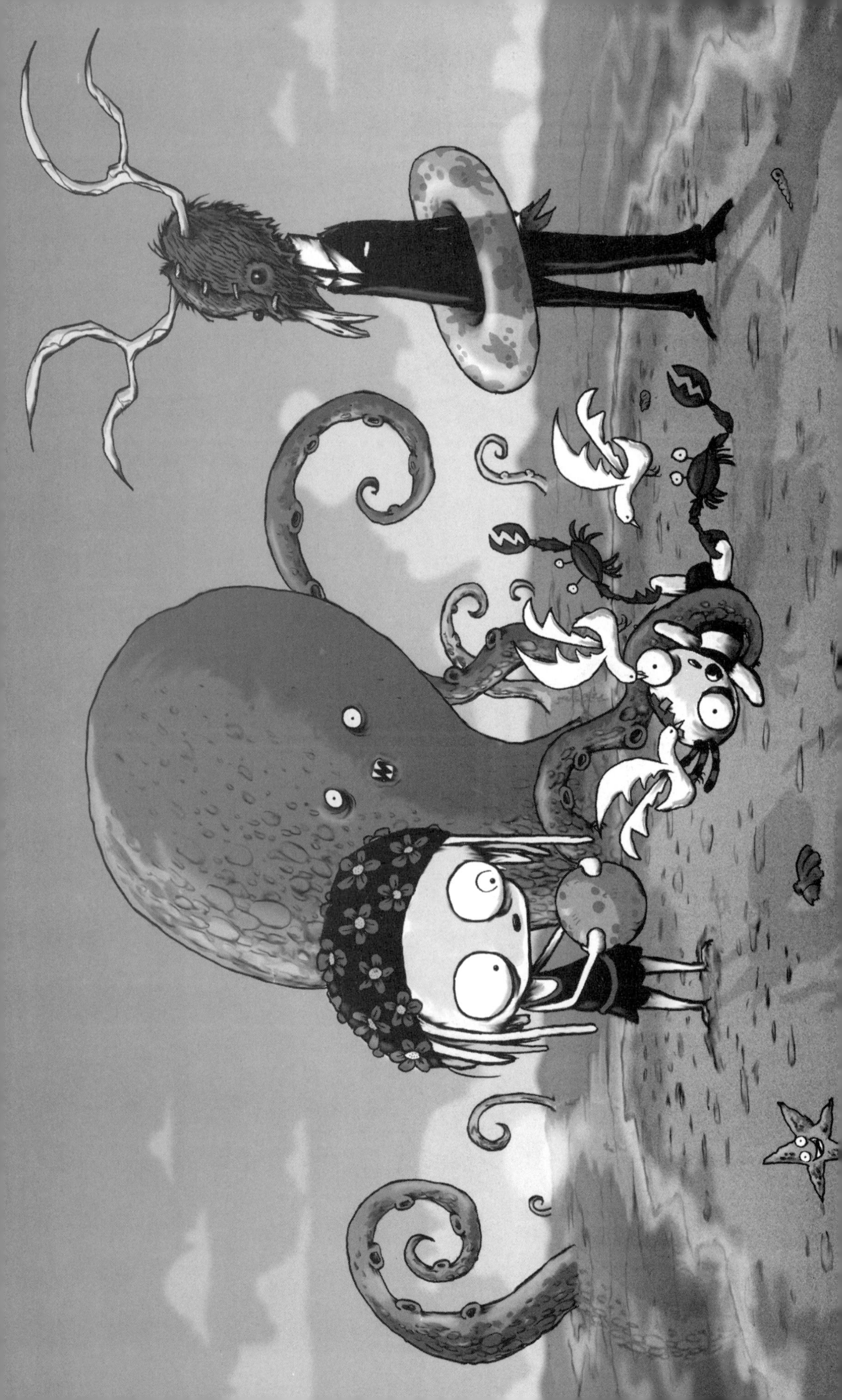

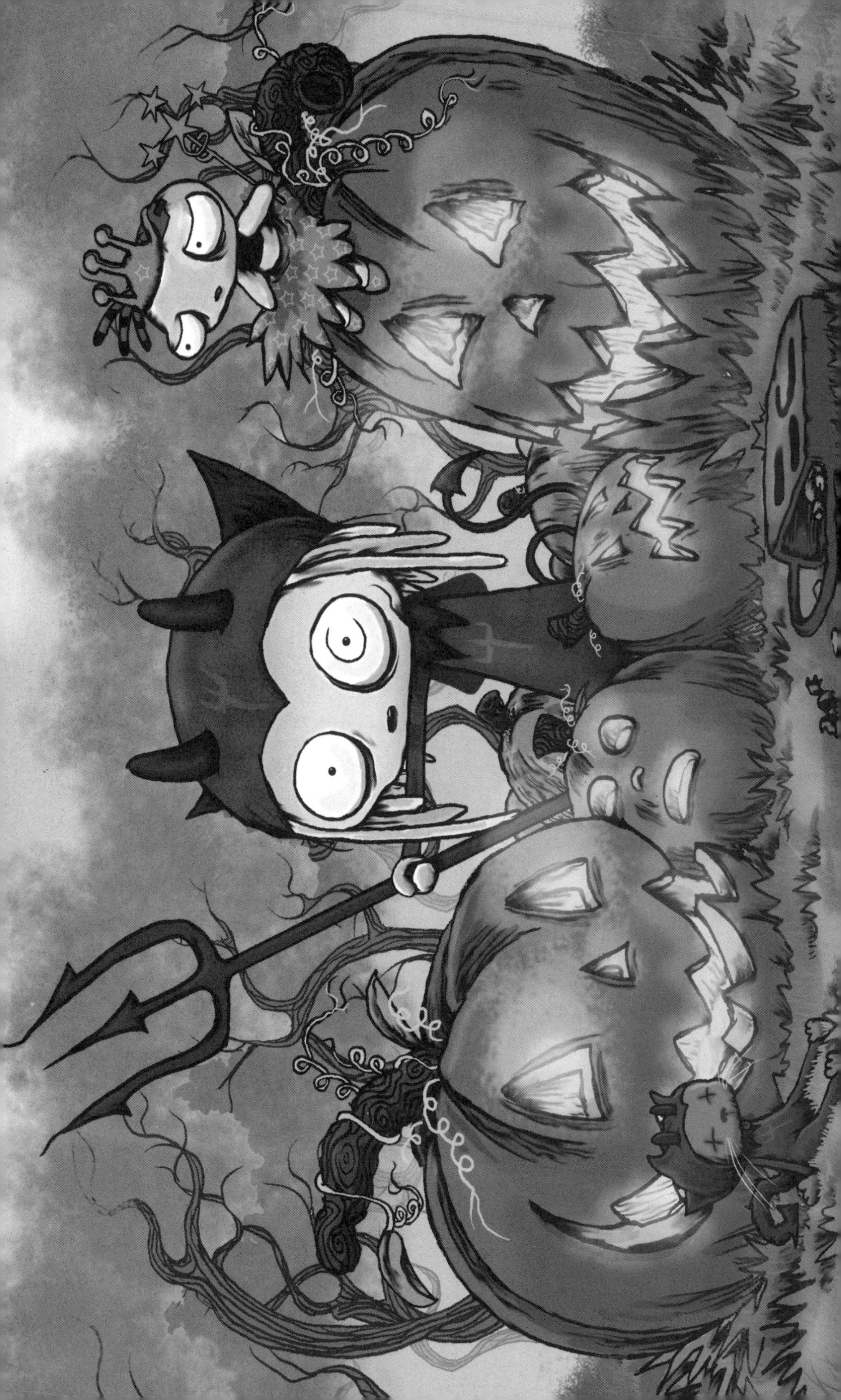

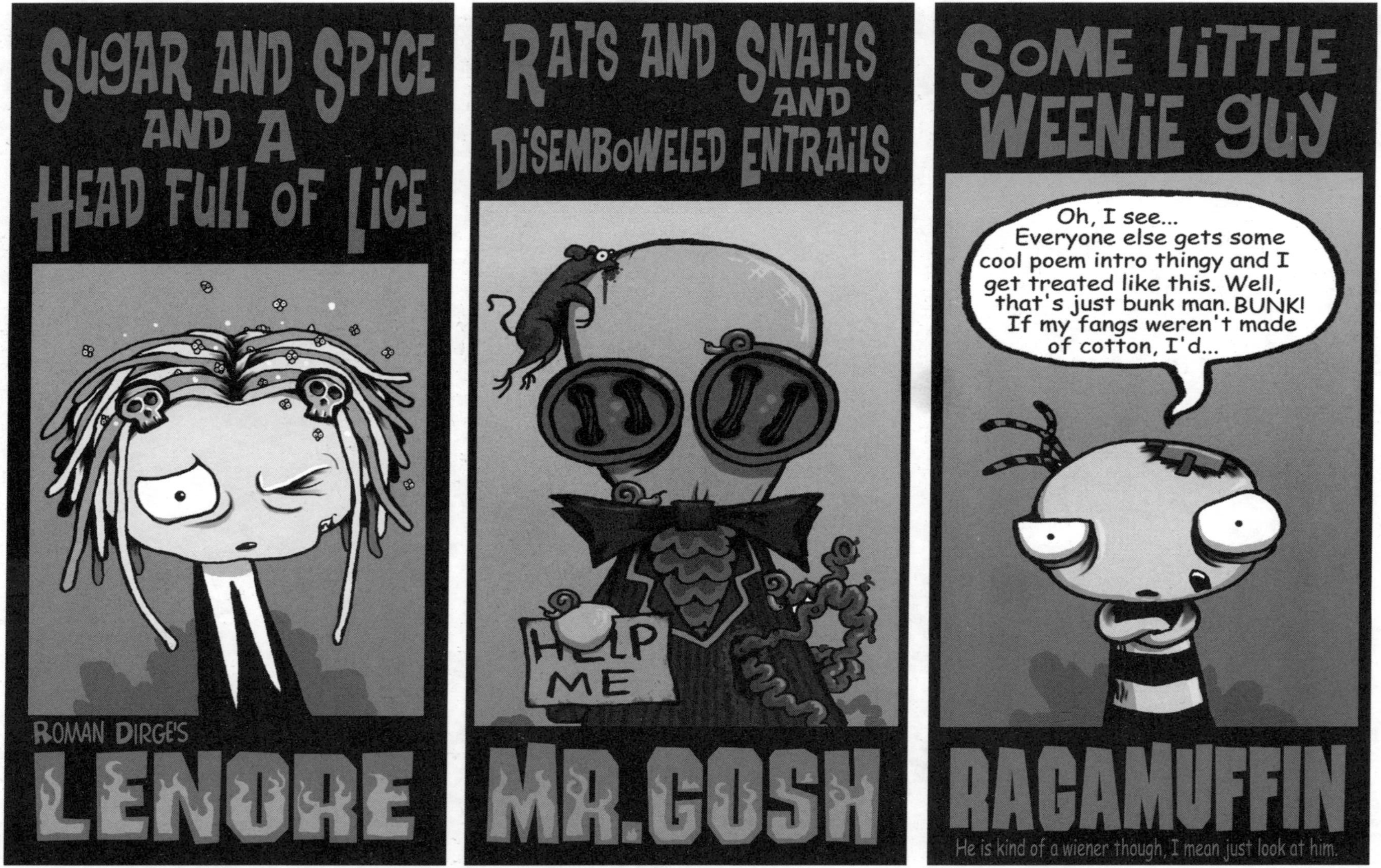
Sugar and Spice and a Head Full of Lice
Roman Dirge's
LENORE
Rats and Snails and Disemboweled Entrails
HELP ME
MR. GOSH
Some Little Weenie Guy
Oh, I see... Everyone else gets some cool poem intro thingy and I get treated like this. Well, that's just bunk man. BUNK! If my fangs weren't made of cotton, I'd...
RAGAMUFFIN
He is kind of a wiener though, I mean just look at him.

Originally appeared in Voltaire's Deady the Evil Teddy volume #3

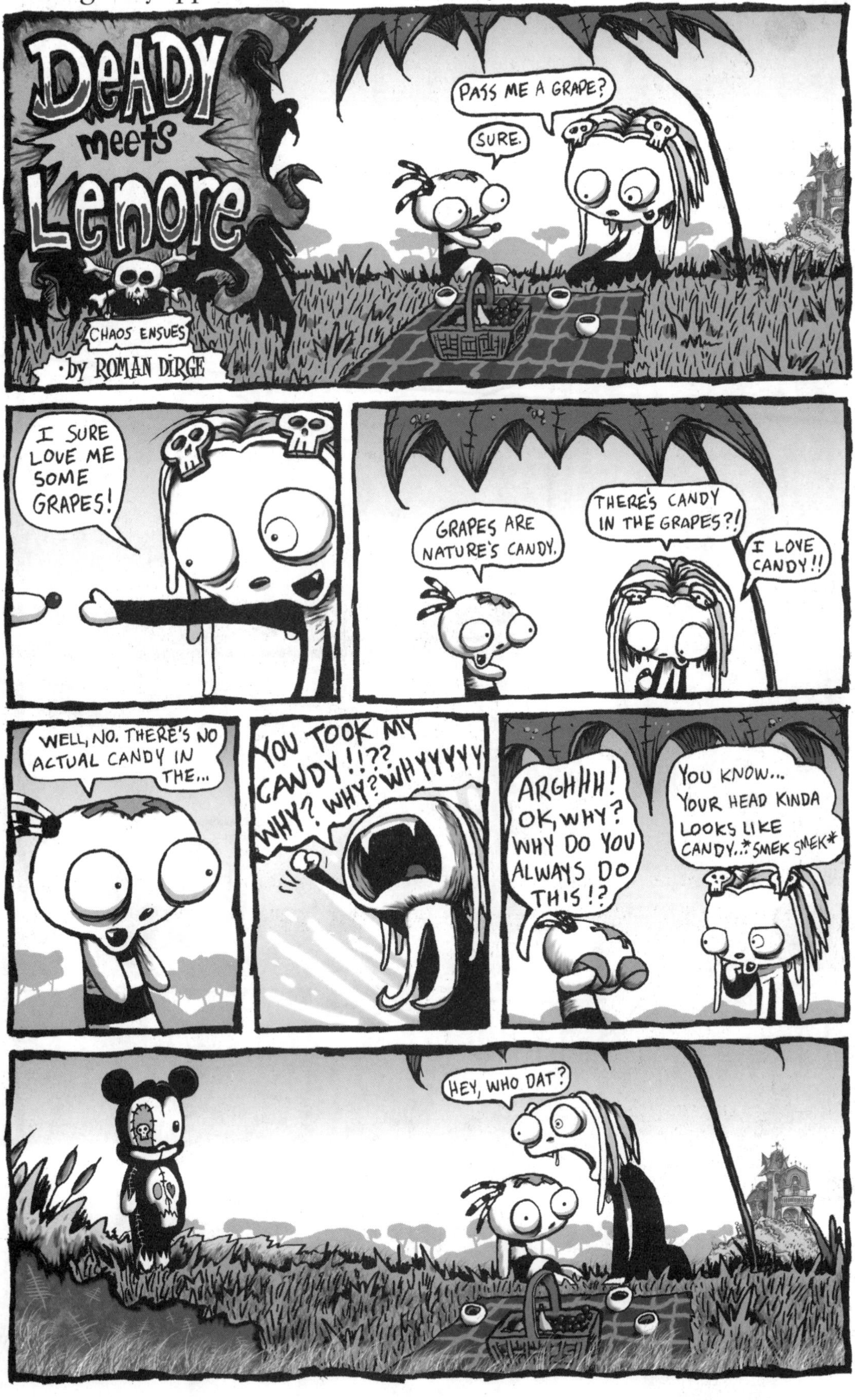
DeADY meets Lenore
CHAOS ENSUES
·by ROMAN DIRGE
PASS ME A GRAPE?
SURE.
I SURE LOVE ME SOME GRAPES!
GRAPES ARE NATURE'S CANDY.
THERE'S CANDY IN THE GRAPES?!
I LOVE CANDY!!
WELL, NO. THERE'S NO ACTUAL CANDY IN THE...
YOU TOOK MY CANDY!!?? WHY? WHY? WHYYYYY
ARGHHH! OK, WHY? WHY DO YOU ALWAYS DO THIS!?
YOU KNOW... YOUR HEAD KINDA LOOKS LIKE CANDY...*SMEK SMEK*
HEY, WHO DAT?

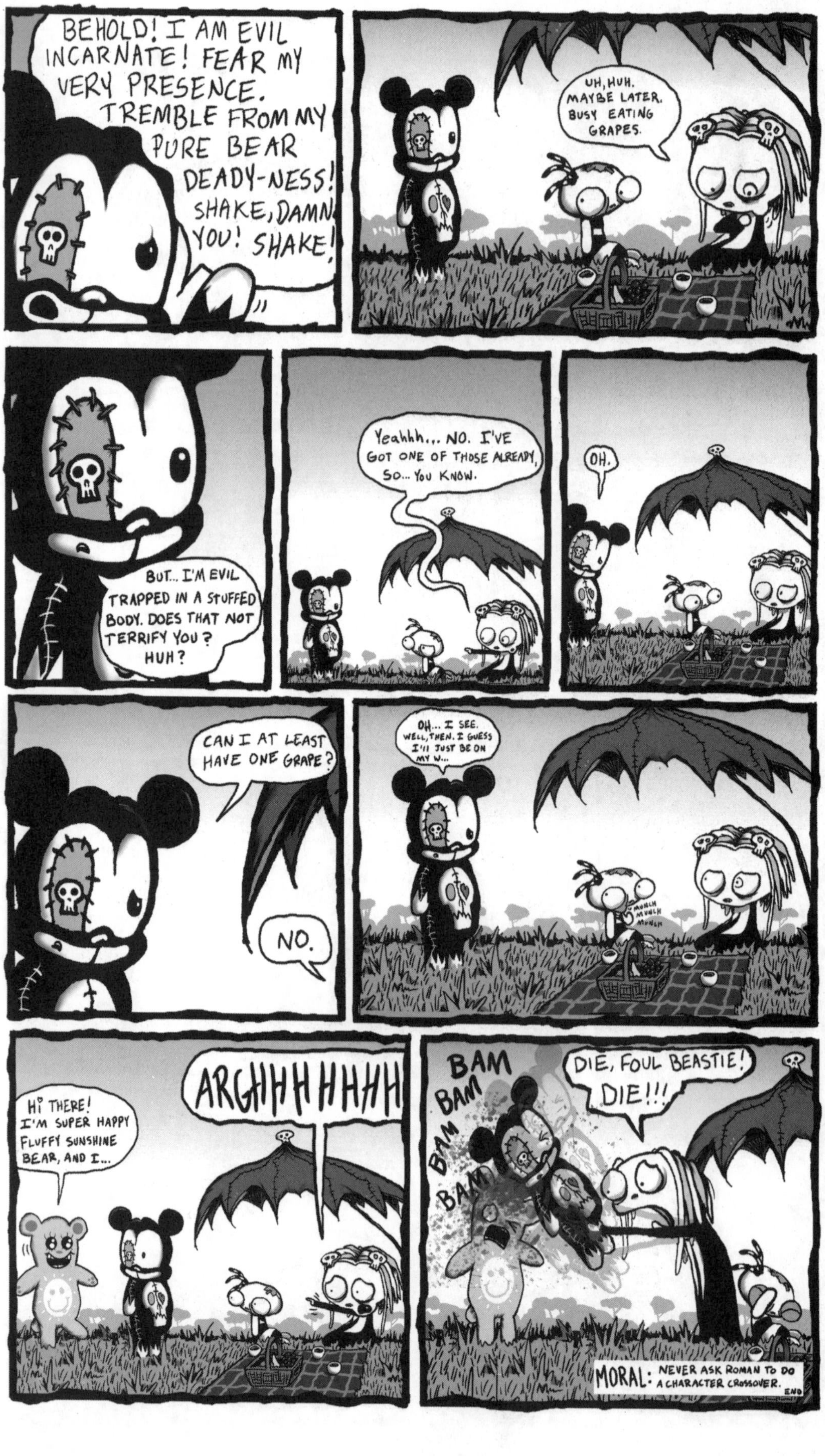
BEHOLD! I AM EVIL INCARNATE! FEAR MY VERY PRESENCE. TREMBLE FROM MY PURE BEAR DEADY-NESS! SHAKE, DAMN YOU! SHAKE!
UH, HUH. MAYBE LATER. BUSY EATING GRAPES.
BUT... I'M EVIL TRAPPED IN A STUFFED BODY. DOES THAT NOT TERRIFY YOU? HUH?
Yeahhh... NO. I'VE GOT ONE OF THOSE ALREADY, SO... YOU KNOW.
OH.
CAN I AT LEAST HAVE ONE GRAPE?
NO.
OH... I SEE. WELL, THEN. I GUESS I'LL JUST BE ON MY W...
MUNCH MUNCH MUNCH
Hi THERE! I'M SUPER HAPPY FLUFFY SUNSHINE BEAR, AND I...
ARGHHHHHH
BAM BAM BAM BAM
DIE, FOUL BEASTIE! DIE!!!
MORAL: NEVER ASK ROMAN TO DO A CHARACTER CROSSOVER.
END

Lenore

the cute little dead girl

Art by other peeps. . .

Eeeeeeeeeeeeeevil peeps

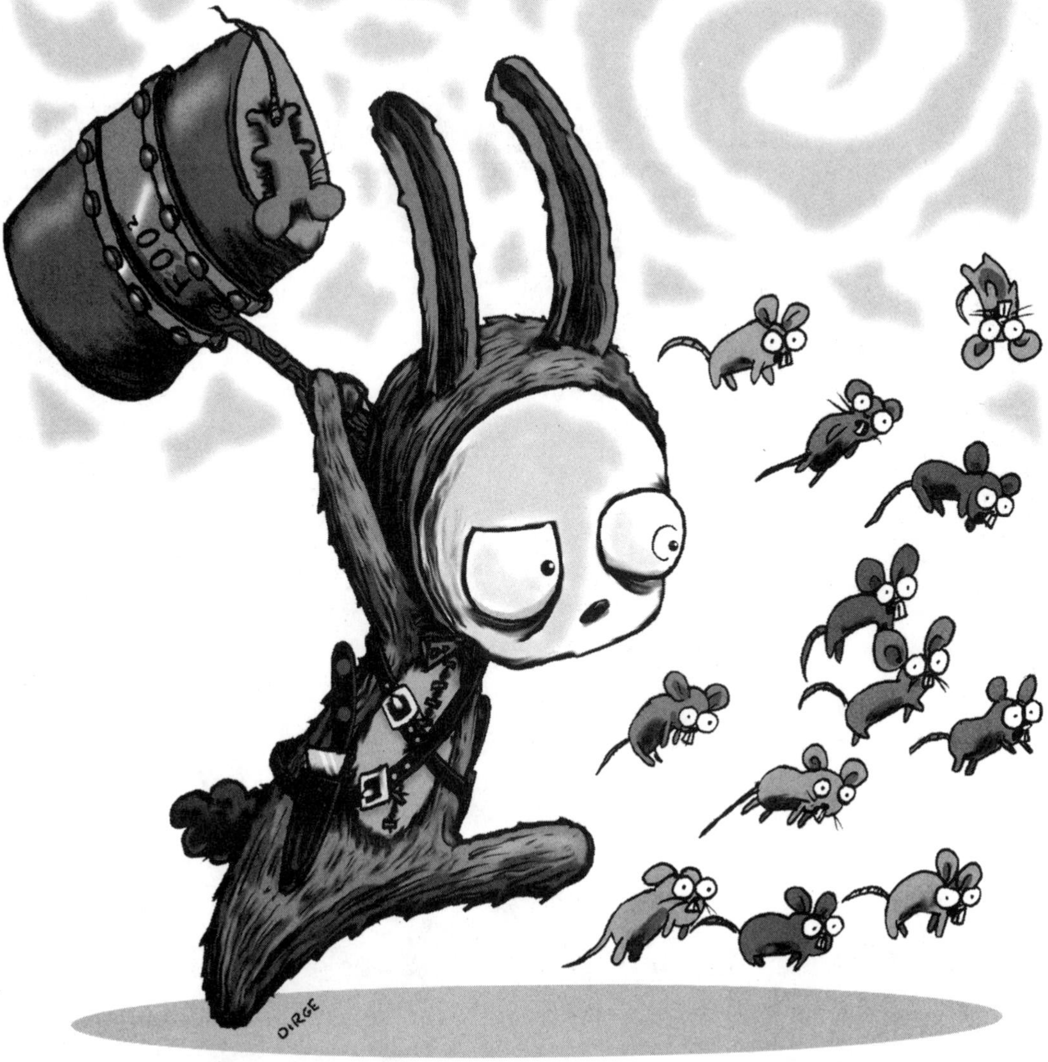
DIRGE

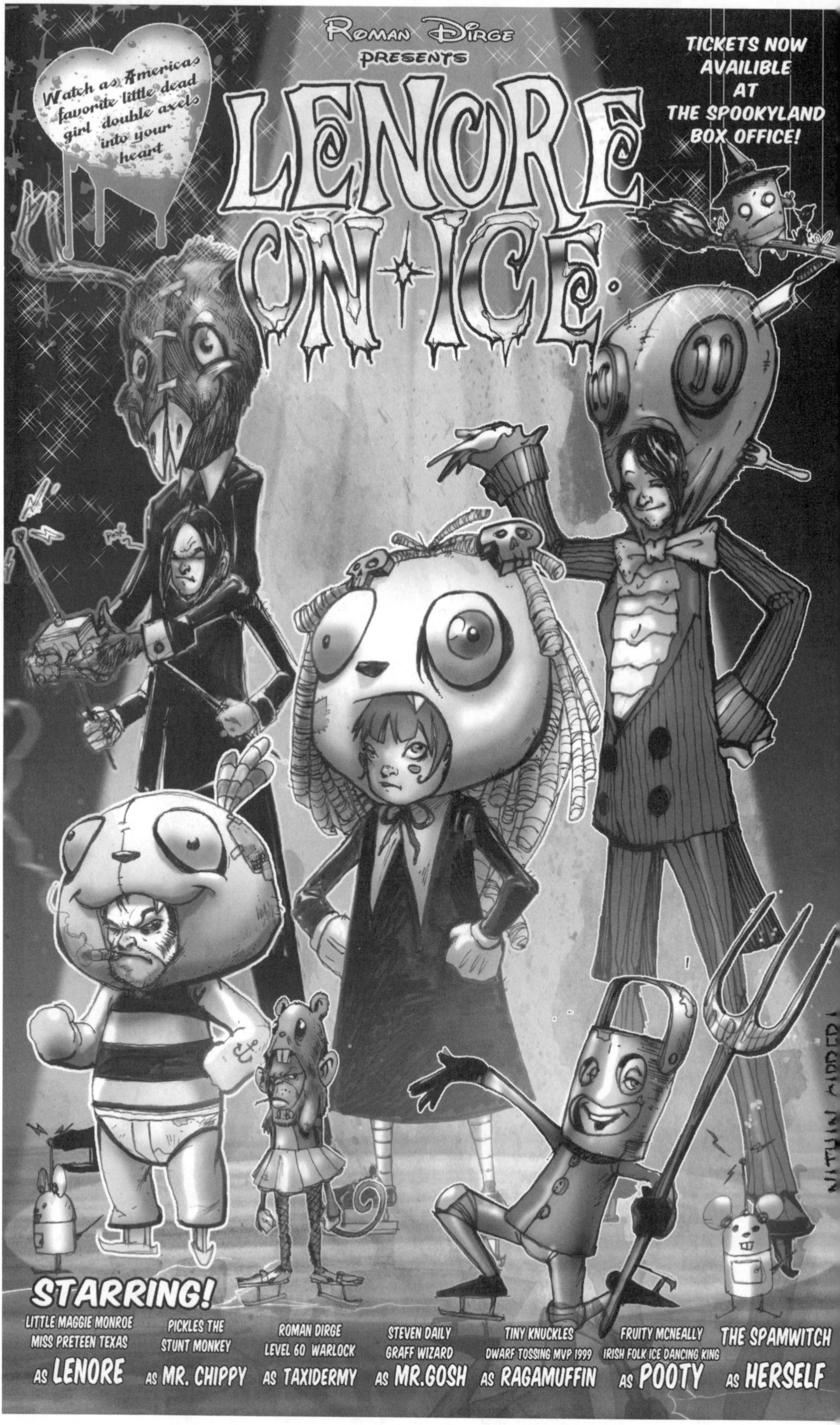

ROMAN DIRGE
PRESENTS
LENORE ON ICE
Watch as Americas favorite little dead girl double axels into your heart
TICKETS NOW AVAILIBLE AT THE SPOOKYLAND BOX OFFICE!
STARRING!
LITTLE MAGGIE MONROE MISS PRETEEN TEXAS AS LENORE
PICKLES THE STUNT MONKEY AS MR. CHIPPY
ROMAN DIRGE LEVEL 60 WARLOCK AS TAXIDERMY
STEVEN DAILY GRAFF WIZARD AS MR.GOSH
TINY KNUCKLES DWARF TOSSING MVP 1999 AS RAGAMUFFIN
FRUITY MCNEALLY IRISH FOLK ICE DANCING KING AS POOTY
THE SPAMWITCH AS HERSELF

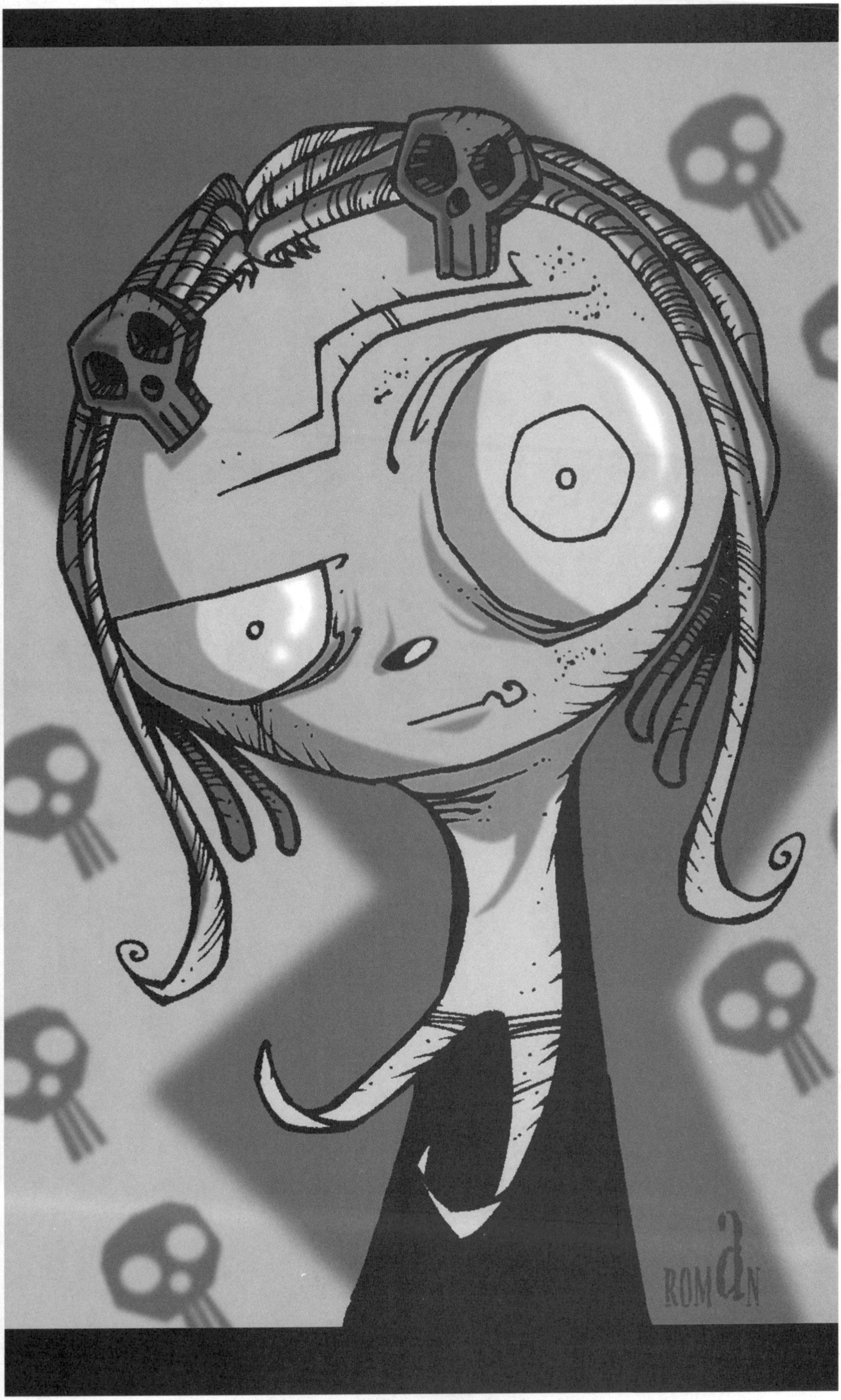
ROMaN

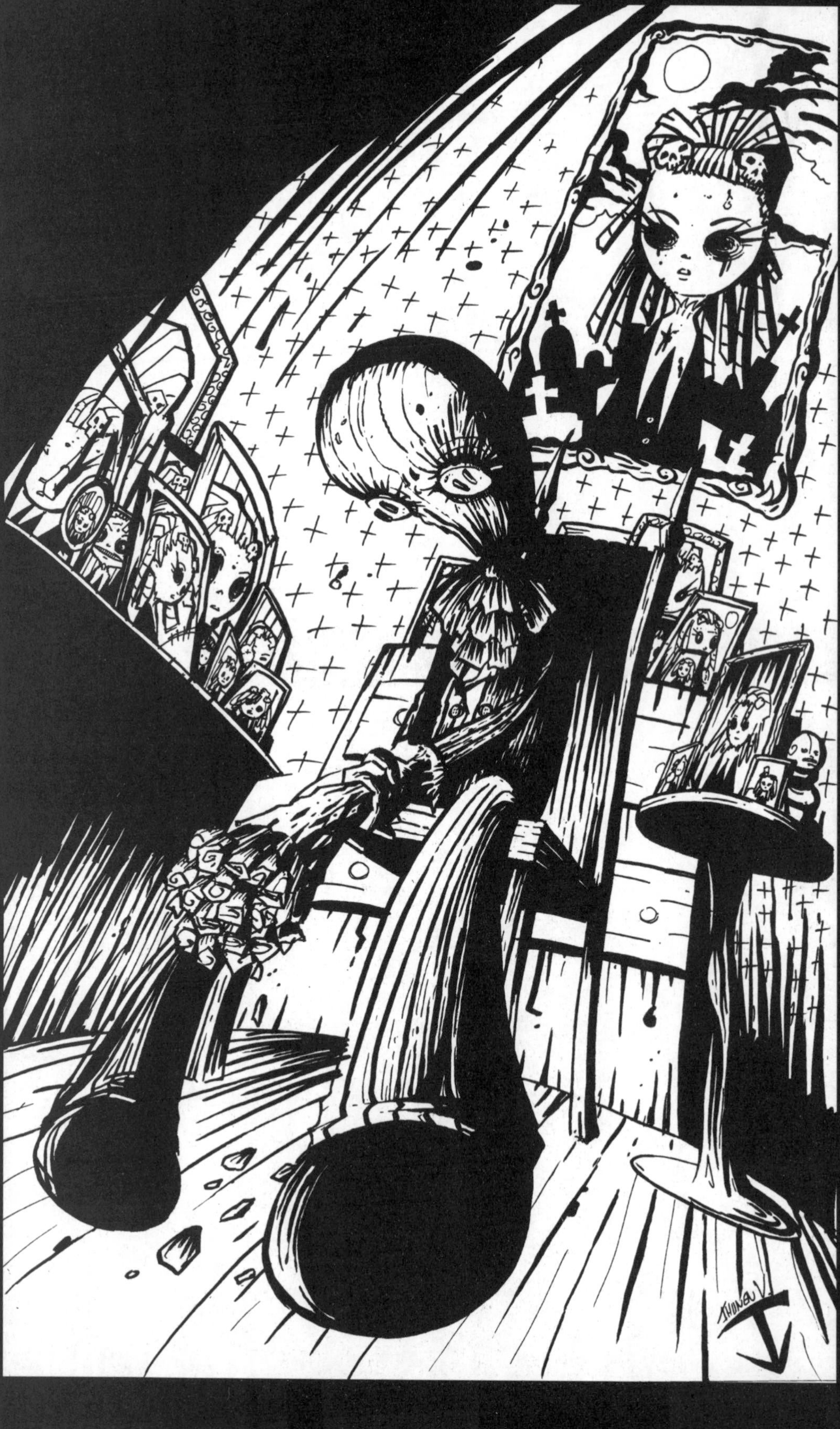

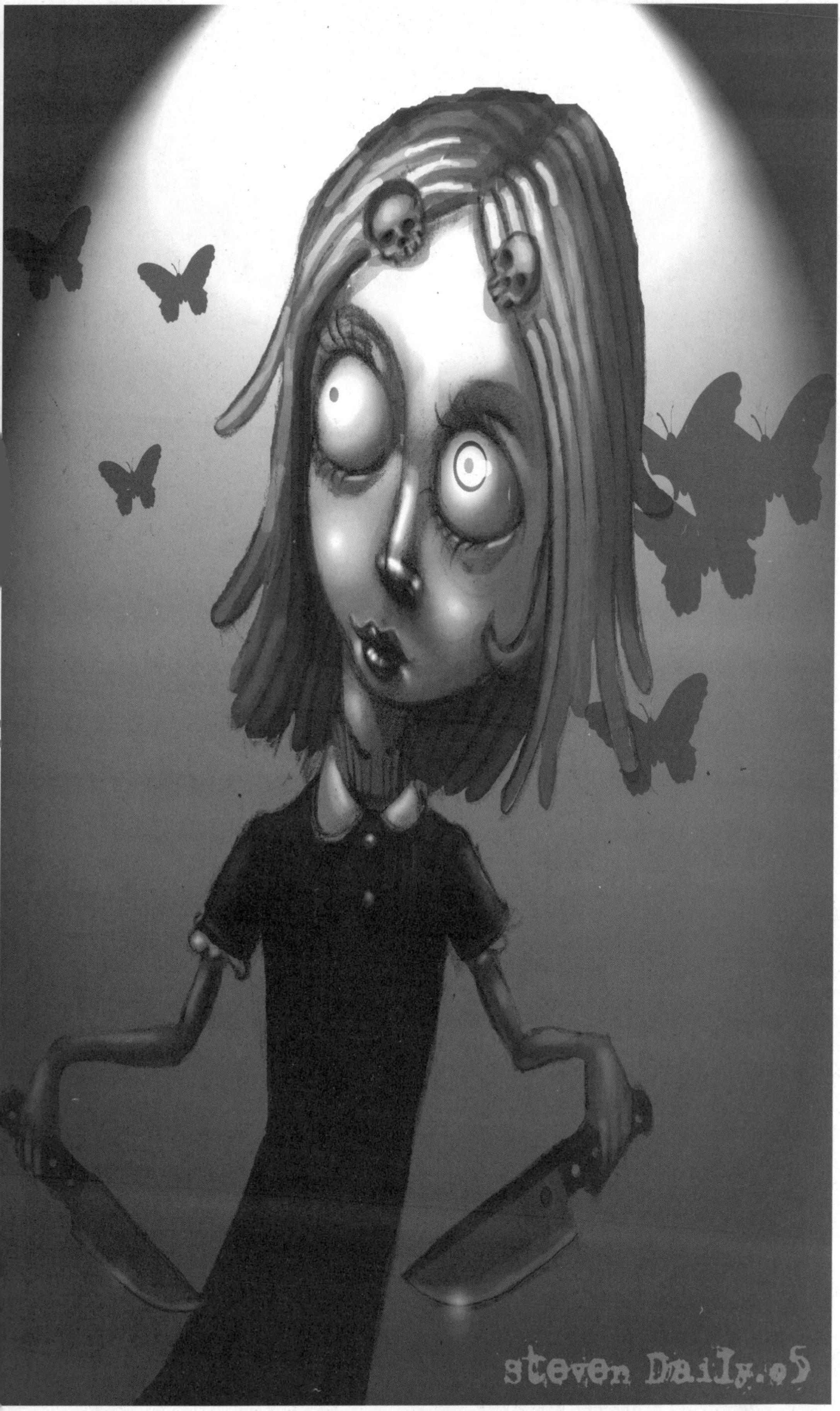
steven Daily.05

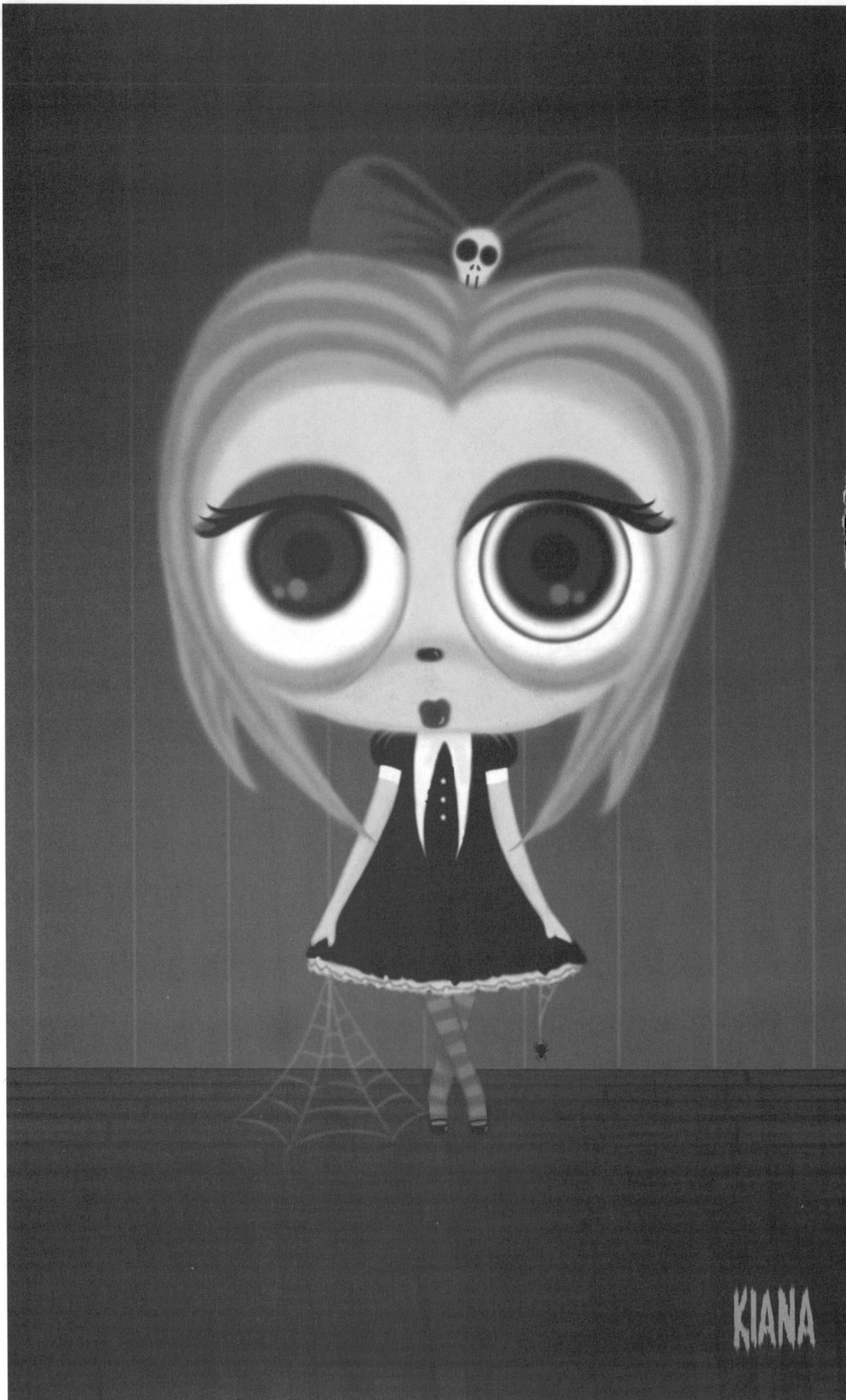
KIANA

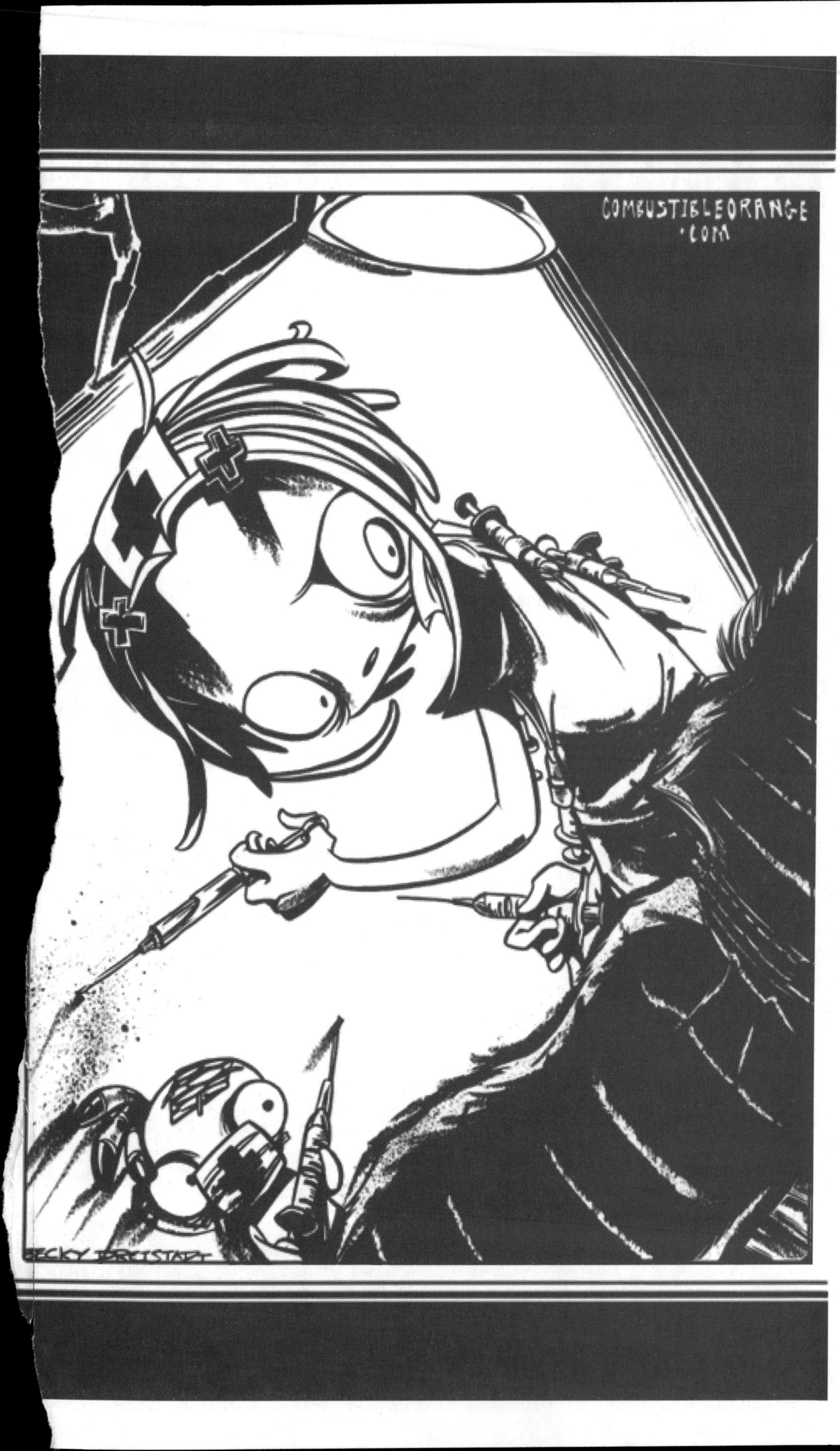
COMBUSTIBLEORANGE
.COM

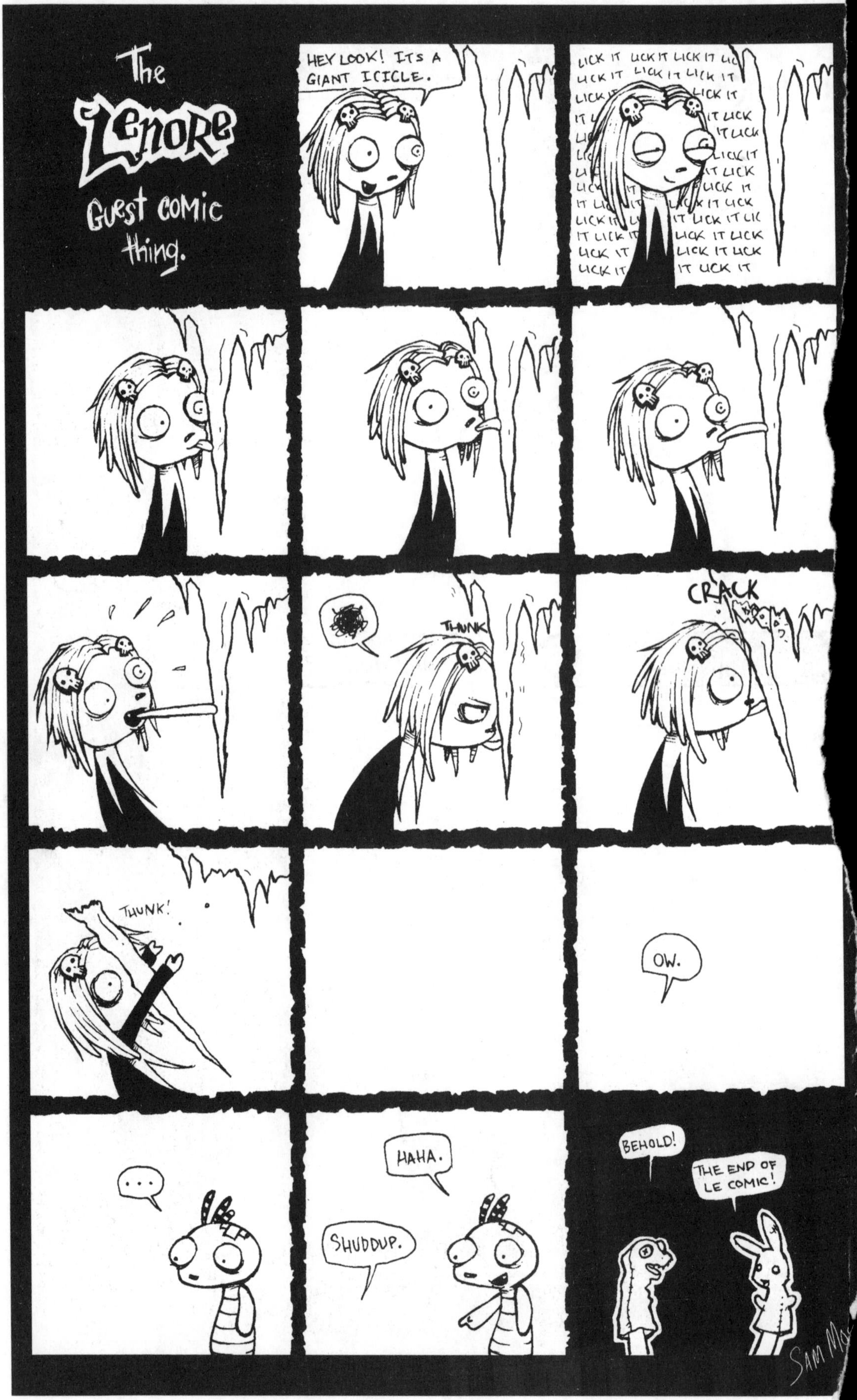
The Lenore Guest comic thing.
HEY LOOK! ITS A GIANT ICICLE.
LICK IT LICK IT LICK IT LIC
LICK IT LICK IT LICK IT
CRACK
THUNK
THUNK!
OW.
...
HAHA.
SHUDDUP.
BEHOLD!
THE END OF LE COMIC!

Continued from "Deady The Evil Teddy"...

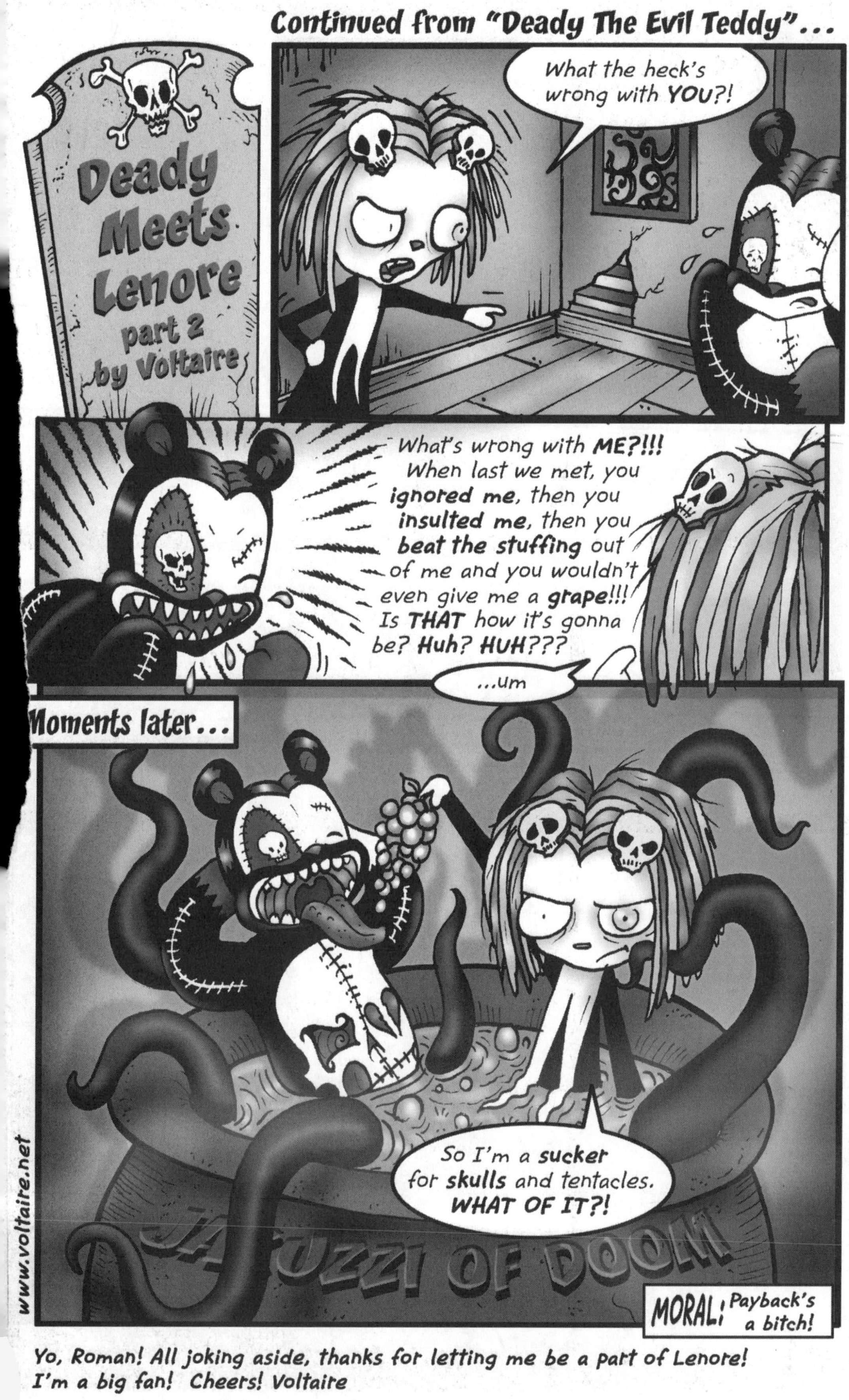
Deady Meets Lenore
part 2
by Voltaire
What the heck's wrong with YOU?!
What's wrong with ME?!!! When last we met, you ignored me, then you insulted me, then you beat the stuffing out of me and you wouldn't even give me a grape!!! Is THAT how it's gonna be? Huh? HUH???
...um
Moments later...
So I'm a sucker for skulls and tentacles. WHAT OF IT?!
JACUZZI OF DOOM
MORAL: Payback's a bitch!
www.voltaire.net

Yo, Roman! All joking aside, thanks for letting me be a part of Lenore!
I'm a big fan! Cheers! Voltaire

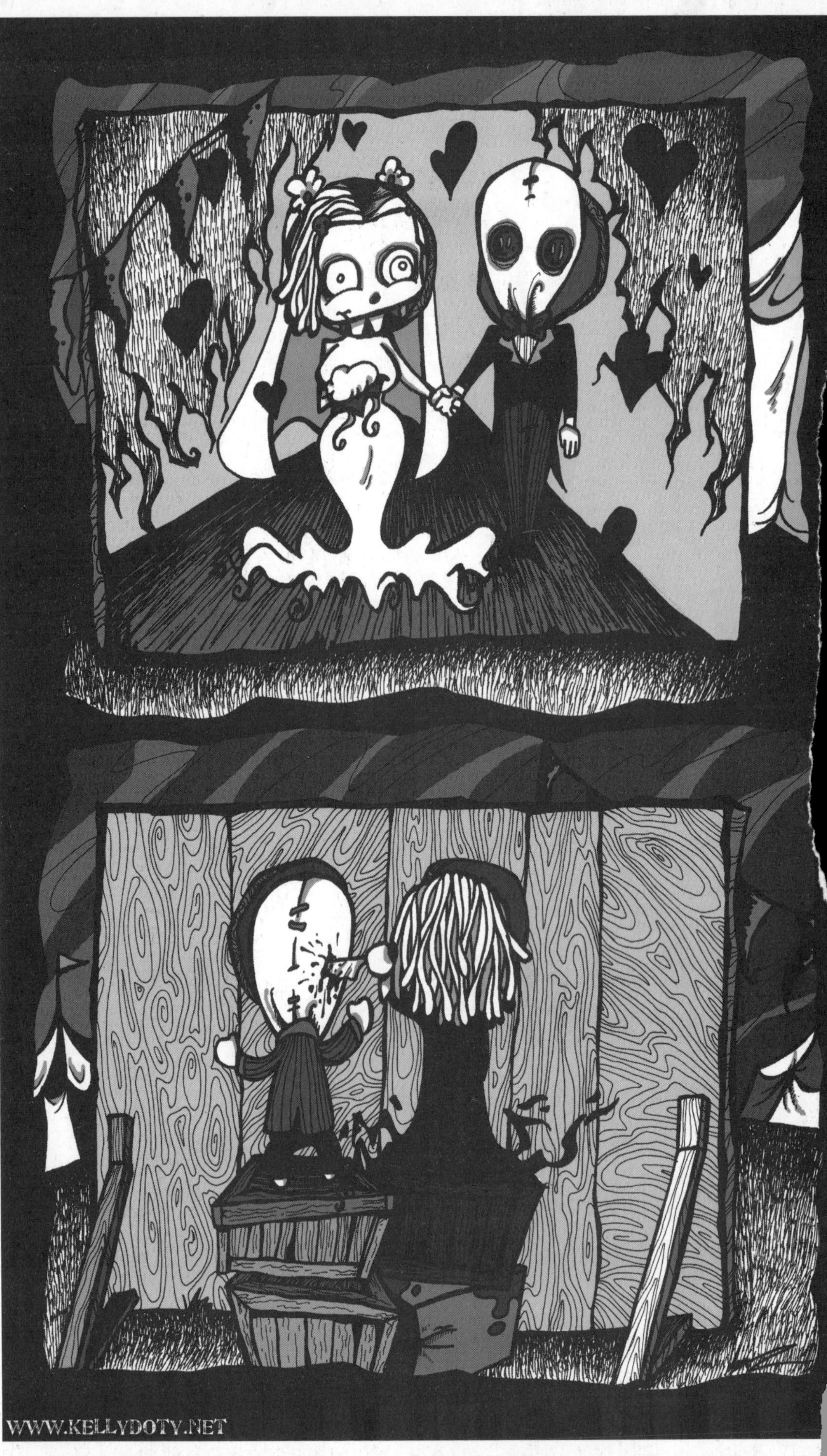
WWW.KELLYDOTY.NET